ABOVE THE
DIN OF WAR

AFGHANS SPEAK ABOUT THEIR LIVES, THEIR COUNTRY, AND THEIR FUTURE— AND WHY AMERICA SHOULD LISTEN

PETER EICHSTAEDT

Lawrence Hill Books
Chicago

Copyright © 2013 by Peter Eichstaedt
All rights reserved
Published by Lawrence Hill Books
An imprint of Chicago Review Press, Incorporated
814 North Franklin Street
Chicago, Illinois 60610
ISBN 978-1-61374-515-1

Library of Congress Cataloging-in-Publication Data
Eichstaedt, Peter H., 1947–
    Above the din of war : Afghans speak about their lives, their country, and their future—and why America should listen / Peter Eichstaedt.
        pages cm
    Includes index.
    ISBN 978-1-61374-515-1
    1. Postwar reconstruction—Afghanistan—Public opinion. 2. Afghanistan—Politics and government—2001—Public opinion. 3. Afghanistan—Social conditions—21st century—Public opinion. 4. Public opinion—Afghanistan.
I. Title.
    DS371.4.E37 2013
    958.104'71—dc23
                            2012045820

Interior design: Jonathan Hahn
Map design: Chris Erichsen
Photos: © Peter Eichstaedt

Printed in the United States of America
5 4 3 2 1

What is life, but to drink of the blood of the heart?
What is death, but a wall of wishes falling upon us?
—FROM "WHAT IS LIFE?" BY AHMED ZAHIR, AFGHAN SINGER

CONTENTS

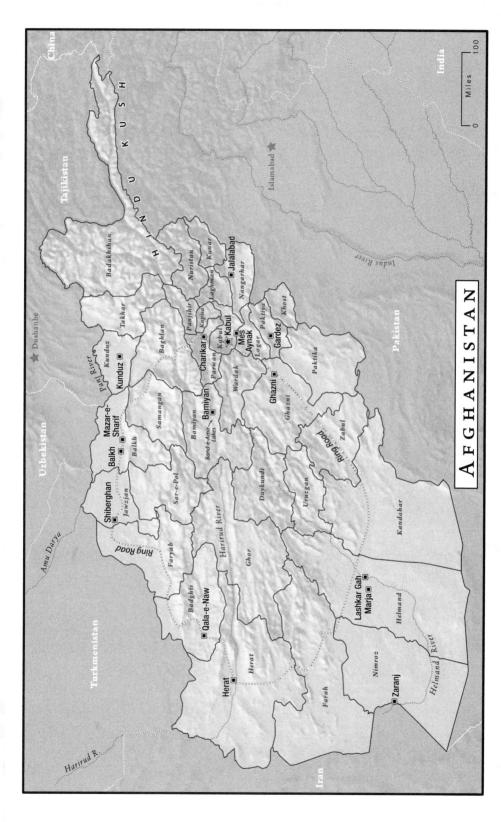

PROLOGUE

AFTER A SIX-YEAR ABSENCE, I was back in Kabul, Afghanistan. The streets were crowded and chaotic as ever, and the dust
lay like fog, obscuring the barren mountains at city's edge. Concrete
barriers channeled traffic through intersections manned by police
who casually checked cars. It was the "ring of steel," which served as
scant protection against occasional suicide bombers. You could still
find a drink in the restaurants, but only after negotiating the gauntlet
of armed guards and sandbagged entrances. Helicopters pounded the
air, reminders of the war that sporadically exploded in the city, shred-
ding Kabul's illusory calm.

I had spent most of 2004 in Afghanistan working for a British-
based nonprofit, the Institute for War and Peace Reporting, and had
helped build an independent news agency, the country's first. I was in
Kabul again with the same organization, once more helping Afghan
journalists tell their countrymen's stories, helping them document
their tortured history, shattered lives, and collective struggles to create
a future.

The Kabul I found in 2010 was largely cleaned up and crisscrossed by many newly paved boulevards, but the Afghan psyche had
faded since 2004. The heady optimism of a liberated capital had been
replaced by wary looks, sideways glances, and the unnerving knowl-

1

edge that insurgents could strike at will and often did. On any given day, violence exploded. A fuel truck would be attacked on the road between Kabul and Jalalabad, Afghanistan's big city near the Pakistan border, the vital supply route from the east. A car laden with explosives would ram a convoy of Scandinavian troops in the once-peaceful northern province of Balkh. Suicide bombers would assault United Nations offices in the western provincial capital of Herat. Motorcycle bombers would be gunned down in the streets of Kandahar.

None of these acts was decisive, and taken alone, each was meaningless. But collectively they were significant, indicative of the chaos that was creeping across a country that was crumbling at the edges and collapsing at its core. The chaos was cultivated by the Taliban masters known as the Quetta Shura, the Taliban council headed by the elusive one-eyed leader Mullah Mohammad Omar. Said to live in the Pakistan city of Quetta and in full view of the Pakistan intelligence agency, the Inter-Service Intelligence (ISI), Mullah Omar operated as a general in absentia, seemingly untouchable. Any Afghan would tell you that the ISI supported the Taliban—always had. Only reluctantly was this discussed openly by US policymakers, who had put billions of dollars into Pakistani pockets to buy their cooperation. It hadn't worked.

The growing insurgency was the reality of Afghanistan. The Taliban had a shadow government in each district and province in the country, including their own police, judiciary, governor, and department heads. As I traveled throughout Afghanistan over the course of the year, I would encounter this dark force at every turn. Afghans were turning to the Taliban out of necessity, not choice. The shadow Taliban leaders and commanders were the targets of routine night raids by US Special Forces, but like the mythological multiheaded Hydra, where one shadow commander was eliminated, more surfaced.

It was a war run amok. After the blitzkrieg defeat of the Afghan Taliban in late 2001, al-Qaeda leader Osama bin Laden, the target of post-9/11 American wrath, eluded US captors in the forbidding terrain of Afghanistan's eastern White Mountains and the caves of Tora Bora. So America's leaders turned to Iraq, claiming Saddam Hussein had weapons of mass destruction, which was an illusion at best and a venal deception at worst, and they launched a war that continued for eight years.

Meanwhile, Afghanistan festered.

In mid-October 2010, I sat on cushions in the front room of an old mud-brick house occupied by a soft-spoken mullah in the western city of Herat. Months before Afghanistan's parliamentary election in September 2010, he had declared himself a candidate. What followed was a tale of horror—his kidnapping and beating at the hands of Taliban militants, his enduring mock executions, and his eventual release in exchange for Taliban prisoners.

"Why did you stay?" I wondered aloud.

"Why not?" he said, lifting his eyes to heaven. "Inshallah [God willing], we should never submit to these animals."

Illusions can be more powerful than reality. Illusions help people sort through the fragments of reality that crackle like glass beneath their feet as they step into the darkness of a confused and uncertain future. Illusions drive people to drape themselves in explosives and crash their bomb-filled cars into convoys, obliterating themselves in a blinding, terrifying flash. Illusions convince people they are losing when they are winning and winning when they are losing. Like everything else, illusion and reality were at war in Afghanistan.

There was a hidden reality to Afghanistan that lay far beyond the headlines that told of troop surges and withdrawals, forward-operating bases, and special operations. It was a truth buried beneath the calculated quotes of generals, diplomats, presidents, and policymakers. It was a story of survival, tenacity, and inner strength that had allowed Afghans to carry on through three decades of calamity. I went to find this reality.

Following nearly ten years of inconclusive war in Afghanistan waged by American forces, and having surpassed Russia's bloody occupation of a decade earlier, President Barack Obama announced a three-year drawdown of the United States' nearly one hundred thousand soldiers. It would begin in July 2011. The rest of the world would follow. But the drawdown came as the Afghan Taliban insurgency was growing, not weakening. The pullout announcement had emboldened the Taliban and its allies, and Afghans were feeling the tide begin to change in late 2010 just as I arrived in the country. Afghans knew they would once again face choices most did not want to make: succumb to the Taliban or leave.

What would happen when international forces finally vacated Afghanistan? The answer was unknown, but if there was any hope for Afghanistan, it lay with the Afghan people. And that is what this book is about. It's about the people of Afghanistan and about how they have lived, and will continue to live, in a country that has been at war for as long as most people living there can remember. It is about people who have become extraordinary by the simple act of survival. It is about an ancient land called "the graveyard of empires," a rugged and often desolate terrain that most will never see and few can understand. It is a land of illusion and reality, hope and despair, love and hate. And if America is to salvage its dignity abroad and avoid yet another disaster such as occurred the last time it abandoned Afghanistan, then we must not forsake this country and its people.

1

PRISONER OF THE TALIBAN

THE RED SUN FLATTENED as it faded into the hazy horizon of western Afghanistan. Abdul Manan Nurzai, fifty-six, walked in the waning light through the streets of Shindand with his two youngest sons, heading to the neighborhood mosque. It was Ramadan, the high holy days, and his Muslim faith was strong. Prayer at the nearby mosque was mandatory, and he gladly complied. A motorcycle approached from behind. Gunshots crackled in calm evening air, bullets slamming into Nurzai's body. He crumpled to the ground as horror gripped the two young boys.

Nurzai's eldest son, Kaus Hashimi, heard the shots and ran up the street, his heart pounding. Nurzai had declared himself a candidate for parliament some months earlier and was confident he'd win. Few others in town were as popular or respected as Nurzai. The family had represented Shindand in the Kabul government before, and Nurzai was certain he could help his community prosper. It was his duty, he told Hashimi. It was his honor.

"When my father was shot, he was not far from our house," Hashimi said. "My younger brothers shouted for help. I took my father in my arms. He was still alive. He wanted to talk, but it was impossible."

Blood oozed from Nurzai's neck and chest, soaking his loose, white cotton clothes. Hashimi and his brothers found a car, lifted Nurzai into it, and soon pulled up to the hospital's doors. But there was little the poorly equipped and understaffed Shindand clinic could do except put a needle in Nurzai's arm and hook it to a bottle of plasma, Hashimi said. "We had no people to operate." The brothers drove their unconscious father to the hospital in Herat, nearly two hours to the north. On the long journey, their father died.

A gaggle of local reporters greeted the boys at the Herat hospital, asking questions, taking photos, filming it all. Hashimi wanted none of it. They kept Nurzai's body in the hospital overnight and then returned to Shindand the next day, intending to bury him as soon possible, as was the custom. The town turned out to share the family's grief. "Lots of people came to help. People were crying and shouting for him." In the late afternoon on the day after Nurzai had been murdered, Hashimi lowered his father's body into the ground.

Hashimi wore a black leather jacket when we met just a couple of months after his father's death. He sat stiffly, his feet flat on the floor, rubbing his palms on his knees as he talked. His dark eyes were fearful. He didn't know who had killed his father, and the police had done nothing to investigate. Not one officer had talked to him or his neighbors. It was as if the killing had never happened. The family stayed indoors and lived in fear. "We can't distinguish who are our enemies and who are our friends."

Stories published at the time quoted district chief Mohammad Omerzai as saying the local authorities had opened an investigation. When I asked Hashimi about that, he answered angrily. "It's entirely not true." He said he should know, because "I am the son of this man."

Nurzai's death typified the bloody mayhem that made the 2010 Afghan parliamentary election, especially in the provinces, a deadly undertaking. A declaration of candidacy could be a death wish. The killings and intimidation behind the election were routinely blamed on local Taliban insurgents who had been battling the government in most every corner of the country. Shindand District south of Herat was no exception, making it yet another treacherous corner of the Afghan mosaic. Though local officials attributed Nurzai's death to the Taliban, the local Taliban never claimed responsibility for it.

I asked Hashimi about that, suggesting that his father's death might have been part of a fight between factions wrestling for regional dominance. Hashimi insisted that his father was independent and not a pawn in someone else's game. "My father nominated himself." Nurzai ran because he felt that the community had been passed over as development money was being distributed in western Afghanistan. "My father was an active person," Hashimi said; his father had told his family and friends, "I can bring lots of facilities to my people." Nurzai was not a politician but according to his son was "confident he could become a good leader."

"Did your father have controversial backers, or were there others who didn't want him to run?" I asked.

Again, Hashimi said no. "Nobody supported him financially."

Nurzai's campaign had been a grassroots effort supported by friends and neighbors, many of whom survived on meager incomes—much like Hashimi, an auto mechanic who supplemented his income by selling used cars. He was involved in his father's campaign only because he felt it was the right thing to do. "I myself worked and supported my father. He got lots of supporters from our village" who hung his campaign posters around town. "People were ready to help," he said.

"Was your father worried about election violence?" I asked.

Hashimi shrugged and said violence was a part of Afghan life. "Shindand unfortunately has a lack of security." Other candidates traveled with armed bodyguards, but not his father. "My father was respected," and he refused to hire bodyguards, saying, "'I'm a popular person. I have support of my people.' Never did he think he would be in danger because never had he done anything wrong to his people."

"Who would want to kill him, then?" I asked.

Hashimi was reluctant to answer. "My idea is that my father expected to win. It was 100 percent certain that he could win." But there were others in the area who didn't want him in office because he was independent. So they had him killed. There was no evidence, Hashimi said, only a gut feeling. "Common people would not do this. It would be impossible for them." Nurzai's murder was never investigated, adding to suspicions that local authorities were involved. "No prosecutors or lawyers have come to our home."

"Why not?" I asked.

"If I was rich, I could ask for an investigation," Hashimi said. Substantial bribes were often required in Afghanistan to get governmental authorities to act. But it was more than money, Hashimi said. He didn't want to aggravate an already tense situation and did not want to irritate local officials, who he suspected were aware of those responsible for Nurzai's death. Asking too many questions was dangerous. "My mother is afraid. She won't leave the house," he said.

Hashimi tried to put his father's death behind him, because it had become his job to keep his family safe and alive. "Who should feed them?" he asked, if something should happen to him because of asking too many questions. The family wanted to leave Shindand, but that, too, had to wait for better times.

That Nurzai's death had gone uninvestigated was an indictment of the government that he had wished to join. His very public killing on a main street during the holiest time of the year spoke to the mayhem in Afghanistan. What dark forces were at play here? Why didn't the government respond? Didn't the government's lack of action only propel the swelling tide of support for the insurgency? The answers to these questions swirled as the Taliban, like a tornado, tore across the land.

Ambush Alley

"I'm not armed," proclaimed Abdul Hadi Jamshidi, a member of parliament from north of Herat. But he said nothing about the person with him, a chiseled man with a steel-gray turban and mirthless eyes who carefully monitored two cell phones arranged on the padded arm of his chair. Jamshidi had contacted me earlier that day and insisted that we meet later in a private room just off the lobby of a Herat hotel.

Jamshidi came from a political family, his father having been in the Afghan parliament in the early 1950s. He had been part of the

Loya Jirga, the 2002–2003 gathering of Afghans who had formed the country's current government and its constitution. It was a time of passion and positivism that had prompted Jamshidi to run for parliament. He was elected easily, served five years, and was running again. This time, things were different.

"From the first day, I was threatened [and told] not to run." The warnings didn't come from political rivals but from the Taliban, "because I would be one of their worst opponents. I would do something against them. They know I will fight them."

He was adamant that the Taliban be fought at every turn. "We should press against the Taliban" and the growing insurrection. "Let's solve this problem now. This is the time to remove these groups," Jamshidi said. While his hatred of the Taliban was deep, he knew that the Afghan government could never defeat the Taliban without international help. He was chagrined that the men, arms, and resources from around the world that had helped put Afghanistan on its feet during the past ten years were preparing to leave.

"Why has the Taliban rebounded?" I asked.

"Corruption has made people worried and frustrated," Jamshidi said. "People are disappointed. They've lost confidence in government." But the solutions were clear to him. "Give people a choice, better security. Pay attention to people. Don't let them be threatened. Get ideas from people."

I had to remind myself that I was talking to an elected official in the same government that was supposed to be doing what he said needed to be done. What had the government been doing for the past five years that Jamshidi had been in office? Was the reality that Afghanistan was a failed state for all practical purposes, except in the minds and pocketbooks of the army, police, and government officials who were propped up by international support? My suspicions deepened as Jamshidi talked.

Contributing to the growing insurgency in Herat Province was the annual turnover in the governor's post for the past six years. The revolving door in the governor's office had meant inconsistent programs and growth. The Taliban had capitalized on the situation. Jamshidi explained that some governors had blocked military operations that could have stopped the Taliban resurgence in its infancy, despite the dire consequences that inaction had and would continue to create. "It came true," he said of the Taliban rebound.

The extent of the Taliban resurgence was beyond what most people were willing to admit. Since 2004, Herat Province had been transformed from one of the safest into one of the most dangerous in Afghanistan. The Taliban's shadow government in the city and throughout the province meant most people considered them the true power. Jamshidi said without hesitation, "The Taliban government is stronger than the Afghan government."

Jamshidi regularly traveled between his office in Herat and his house in Taliban territory north of the city, relying on a cadre of bodyguards who were close friends and relatives to escort him. To travel safely required his own intelligence network that included area tribal elders. One evening in the midst of his campaign, Jamshidi called his brother, telling him he was about to head home. He asked if the road was safe. His brother said yes, there would be no problem that night. But the situation quickly changed once Jamshidi got under way. A few miles out of Herat, he received a call from an elder in his network saying that Taliban gunmen had set up an ambush.

"I called my brother and told him there were gunmen on the way," Jamshidi said. "My brother said he would go and check." His brother and a couple of cousins jumped on their motorcycles, planning to meet Jamshidi at the halfway point to escort him home. His brother sped into the darkness, the cousins following.

As Jamshidi's brother reached the crest of a hill, the cousins were far behind. The gunmen were already in place and opened fire, hitting Jamshidi's brother and knocking him off his motorcycle. Moments later, the cousins also rode into the ambush but managed to leap from their cycles and find cover. The Taliban emerged from hiding and found Jamshidi's brother lying by the side of the road, still alive. They shot him several more times.

The cousins called Jamshidi, telling him what had happened and warning him to turn back. Angered and vowing revenge, Jamshidi called his brother's phone, knowing that if he were alive, he would answer. The phone rang and rang. Jamshidi then called the local police commander, asking for help. The police chief said he would try to get there as soon as he could.

As Jamshidi approached the ambush scene with his bodyguards, he called the police commander again. The commander apologized, saying he was delayed. Realizing that no help was coming, Jamshidi and his guards barreled into the ambush, guns blazing. "We opened fire. We pushed them back."

As his bodyguards pursued the Taliban attackers, Jamshidi turned to his brother. "He was about to die." Jamshidi lifted his brother into the vehicle, found his two cousins, and took them all to the hospital in Herat. His brother died on the way, but his cousins survived, one requiring multiple surgeries.

As we lapsed into silence, Jamshidi looked at me stoically and explained that he had driven nearly two hours from the north to tell me his story.

"Why?" I asked.

No one had ever asked him about the details of the ambush and his brother's death, he said. Not the police, not the government, not the Afghan press. I was the first.

I asked how the government, his own countrymen, could not investigate an attack on an elected representative of parliament.

Jamshidi shrugged.

His story was sadly similar to what other candidates had also told me.

"Why didn't you quit?" I asked.

He shrugged again.

"Do you want revenge?" I asked.

"My house is in an insecure place. It was by chance that I lost my brother. I can tell you that 90 to 95 percent of the people support me. They are trying to stop me," he said of the Taliban. "Their target was me, not my brother. They were watching."

"Can there be peace with the Taliban?" I asked.

Jamshidi shook his head. "We never will be able to negotiate with the Taliban. Their policies are completely different. They don't share ideas. It's impossible."

I mentioned to him that NATO forces had reportedly given Taliban leaders safe passage to meet with President Karzai's peace commission.

"Karzai has offered 'safe passage' before, but [the Taliban] has rejected it," Jamshidi said.

"If it is impossible to negotiate with the Taliban, then what?" I asked.

"It's a complex issue," Jamshidi said. "When the people accept the government, then we will have a good country. But now, the government is not doing enough for the local people."

It was late when Jamshidi and I parted company. He thanked me for listening to his story, but I could not have been more dismayed. Here was an elected member of the government who could not find anyone to take action against the murder of his brother and the attack on his relatives. If this had been any other country, an attack on a national official would have prompted swift action. Jamshidi had said that if people accepted the government, they would have a good country. But what was there to accept? The existence of any government, any organized social system, demanded a functioning army, police, and courts. But in Afghanistan, candidates were killed in cold blood and their supporters kidnapped, bound, executed. No one lifted a finger.

Prisoner of the Taliban

Safiullah Mojaddedi lived in an ancient, mud-brick residence beside one of Herat's many mosques. In his midforties, he had a trimmed beard, a gentle demeanor, and the delicate hands of a respected Islamic scholar and mullah. It was a warm day when we met, and a cooling breeze billowed the curtains as he poured green tea.

Mojaddedi had been a candidate for parliament, but before entering the race, he had thought about it long and hard. "Three months before registering myself, I [sought] the advice of my family." They encouraged him to run and were confident he could win; a man of his intellect and respect in the community would do well. "I didn't feel it to be dangerous. I was a religious person. My family was not bad but rather was one of the most respected."

He considered hiring bodyguards but rejected the idea. The only reason one needed protection was if one had enemies. Mojaddedi had none. To be without bodyguards was to be respected by people, he said. Mojaddedi lived beside a mosque, and many of his supporters were former students. He felt perfectly safe and eagerly hit the campaign trail. Then reality descended.

"It was a Wednesday, one month ago. I was kidnapped."

The period for campaigning was drawing to a close, as was the fasting month of Ramadan. The campaign stop was to be routine—a meeting with village elders to hear their complaints and seek their advice. Another stop was planned for the following day, which was going to be the last of his campaign. The village was largely occupied by Kuchis, the traditionally nomadic people of Afghanistan. Mojaddedi didn't expect any trouble, despite seeing some armed men in the periphery of the village when he arrived. "I had been threatened many times," but none of the threats had been carried out. The sight of men with AK-47s caused him no concern.

Mojaddedi entered the elders' tent and sipped tea as the men conferred, but he noticed that as they talked, the tent was being surrounded. In the village was a man named Abdullah, the son of a local Taliban commander who had been killed by US forces. Mojaddedi had been advised to meet with Abdullah, whose family he had known for many years. Abdullah's father had been a friend, and Mojaddedi had taught Abdullah's brother and sister. He agreed to the meeting, not suspecting trouble. But Abdullah was nowhere to be found. Mojaddedi sent an aide to find Abdullah and invite him to the meeting. But Abdullah refused and sent the aide back. Moments later, Mojaddedi saw Abdullah leaving on a motorcycle. He asked his aide what was happening.

"Then, two armed men came to me and said they were sent by Abdullah." They wanted Mojaddedi to go to another village where villagers had asked him to settle a dispute between the families of a sixteen-year-old boy and a girl of fourteen years. Mojaddedi balked, saying he had to campaign. But Abdullah's men insisted. Mojaddedi finally agreed to go because he could earn votes in the village, making the trip worthwhile. "I didn't expect Abdullah was a Talib and would kidnap me," he said.

Mojaddedi drove his own car to the village, accompanied by several of his campaign staff and with two of Abdullah's armed guards sitting in the open trunk. Three other armed men rode motorcycles. Along the way, the group stopped to pray. After spreading their prayer rugs on the ground and making their offerings to God, the armed men left.

They were replaced by other men, who told Mojaddedi that he had to visit the man known as Sheikh, an associate of Abdullah. "I agreed to meet with him," he said. It was a decision that nearly cost him his life. "Unfortunately, old friends had changed into serious enemies."

When Mojaddedi and his colleagues were ordered out of their car when they arrived at the mouth of a small canyon, he sensed something was wrong. "The circumstances had changed." With guns at their backs, Mojaddedi and his companions were prodded into the canyon and up a mountainside.

After five hours, they arrived at a Taliban encampment in a cave, exhausted, hungry, and thirsty. There they found Sheikh, one of the region's most notorious Taliban commanders, who controlled three districts in the province. Despite obviously being a prisoner, Mojaddedi refused to accept his situation and challenged every order. "What kind of hospitality is this?" he asked.

Sheikh handed him a piece of paper, explaining that according to the rules of the Taliban's new Islamic republic, the Islamic Emirate of Afghanistan, anyone who was part of the Karzai government had to be killed. Since he was a candidate, Mojaddedi had to die. Sheikh told him to compose a farewell letter to his family.

Instead, Mojaddedi asked for time to pray. "I told them that even in Guantanamo, you can pray. What kind of Islamic government do you have that a person can't pray?"

Mojaddedi then tried to intimidate the Taliban fighters, banking on his status as an Islamic scholar. When his captors refused his request to pray, he made another. "Do you want to know about Islam?" he asked, reminding them, "You are not educated."

The fighters became defensive and told him to shut up. "Don't bother us with such garbage."

Mojaddedi then tried to distract the fighters from their threats to kill him.

"You have cheated us," he complained. "We went [to the village] to solve people's problems." He turned to Sheikh and asked, "I should be killed because I'm a friend of those people?"

Later, an older fighter named Faisal entered the cave. He was a rugged man with a beard dyed red, as was the custom among some of the elders. Faisal wanted Mojaddedi beheaded, saying that it had been too many days without a killing and he wanted to wash his hands in blood. Faisal hated foreigners and the government because he had lost several sons to attacks and raids by international forces, Mojaddedi explained. "He was a dangerous man." Mojaddedi knew that to anger Faisal unnecessarily meant certain death.

Then Faisal told Mojaddedi, "Since you're our friend, we haven't killed you for now."

But the generosity would not last. "We are under this [Islamic] government and should follow the orders. But I'm willing to change this order if you give us $200,000 in the morning," Sheikh said with a smile.

Mojaddedi swallowed hard. "I told him this was shameful" and stammered that he couldn't come up with that kind of money. Neither he nor his family had that much. Besides, it was still Ramadan and banks closed early. "It's impossible." Mojaddedi convinced the fighters to cut their demands in half, lowering the ransom to $100,000—still an impossible amount.

Mojaddedi could not arrange the money without making a phone call, he said, and there was no phone signal inside the cave. Sheikh called for two horses, and with two fighters, Mojaddedi rode to the top of a distant hill where he could get a weak phone signal. He had been warned, however, not to alert security forces. The only person to be contacted was his relative, Hazrat Sibghatullah Mojaddedi, head of the upper house of the Afghan parliament, known as the House of Elders. Mojaddedi contacted his relatives and told them of his capture and the ransom demand. They began collecting money.

Mojaddedi returned to the cave and spent a restless night under a thin wool blanket. The next morning he again was taken to the spot where he could get phone reception and learned that his relatives had been able to raise only $20,000. It was not enough, Sheikh said. The family had to come up with much more.

Over the next several days, Mojaddedi was repeatedly told that he was going to be beheaded. With his hands bound, he was taken to a place near the cave and forced to his knees. He pleaded for his life and those of his friends, saying that if someone had to die, it should be only him, not his friends. "I asked them to let my friends go and just kill me." He alternately berated his captors, chastising them for acting contrary to the Koran. He warned them to take care of their souls because they had deceived him and treated him like a prisoner rather than as a guest. He reminded them of the Afghan custom that once someone has "tasted their salt" by sharing a meal, the person was a guest and not brutalized.

Instead of answering, they would "put a gun to my head." During one such moment, Mojaddedi noticed that the gunman began to cry. He couldn't pull the trigger. Mojaddedi forgave the man, then lifted his eyes to heaven and offered a prayer. "I thanked God for changing their hearts."

As the days dragged on, Mojaddedi and his colleagues were moved several times, spending just a couple of nights in each of several Taliban camps. "The condition was getting serious," Mojaddedi said. They were forced to sit for hours on end, unable to move, even to relieve themselves. The fighters battered them with their rifle butts. "They started to torture us," he said, and kept Mojaddedi and his friends tied to one another so none could escape.

Then something changed. Mojaddedi and his companions were taken to a village, the same village that Mojaddedi had been asked to visit earlier to settle a dispute. He was given a room in a house that had fresh water and heat. Sheikh informed him that a negotiator had arrived from Quetta, Pakistan, to arrange his release. The negotiator was from the highest levels of the Taliban and was an emissary from the Quetta Shura, the Taliban ruling council.

Mojaddedi's elderly relative Sibghatullah Mojaddedi was not only leader of the Afghan upper house of parliament but was also chief negotiator between the Taliban and the Afghan government. The younger Mojaddedi was much more valuable alive than dead. The Quetta Shura had issued orders that Mojaddedi was not to be killed but would be ransomed by the Taliban, who would pay Abdullah and Sheikh for their successful capture of the man. Meanwhile eighteen Taliban prisoners were to be released by the Afghan government in exchange for Mojaddedi and his colleagues.

At first, Mojaddedi was reluctant to believe that he would be freed, fearing that the hope would be dashed. "I didn't believe them. They broke their oaths in the past." That evening, he was taken by motorcycle to another community, where he and his Taliban escorts pulled up to a large tent and stopped to pray. Prayers completed, his escorts dispersed. It was quiet as Mojaddedi looked around. "I took the opportunity to escape," he said, and walked some two hundred yards to a nearby house where he saw lights. Once inside, he called his family to tell them he was finally free.

Our pot of tea was empty. I sipped the last cold dregs from my cup. "What had it all meant?" I asked.

Abdullah and his men were not acting on their own, Mojaddedi was convinced, but were acting on orders from the top Taliban leaders to disrupt the Afghan elections as much as possible. The Taliban, in turn, were being supported and directed by Pakistan, he said.

"Even in western Afghanistan?" I asked, where Iran had great influence.

Yes, he said, explaining that Iran had its own economic and political reasons to keep Afghanistan in turmoil and therefore weak. Iran had the resources to manipulate the Taliban to achieve those ends. He noted that after his release, Abdullah and his brothers fled to Iran, where they remained.

"Will you return to politics after this ordeal?" I asked.

"Why not?" Mojaddedi said. "If God is willing. We should never submit to these animals. It would only increase their power. If we quit, we can't get revenge on these people."

Mojaddedi's mobile phone rang. It was the provincial governor asking him to come immediately. We rose and said good-bye as Mojaddedi climbed into an unmarked four-wheel-drive Toyota with two armed guards. As he disappeared around the corner, I felt somewhat better about the possibilities for Afghanistan. The conviction with which Mojaddedi had said the Taliban needed to be resisted was reason for hope.

But the optimism for Afghanistan's future that Mojaddedi had infused in me evaporated the next day. In one of the boldest moves ever in Herat, suicide bombers attacked the United Nations compound on the main road south of the city. At high noon a car filled with explosives and gunmen approached the compound's rear entrance. Shots were fired and guards were wounded. A firefight ensued, but the attackers were unable to breach the gate. The driver then detonated the vehicle, blowing open the gate and killing himself in the process. Three other fighters armed with RPGs and AK-47s and wearing bomb-laden vests rushed into the compound, where they encountered heavy fire from the UN guards. The fighters were killed either by gunfire or from detonating their bombs.

Although the attackers did not succeed in killing UN personnel, they sent a message. The Taliban were not going away and would strike at will. How long would the international community hold out in the face of such fanaticism?

2

YOU HAVE THE WATCHES;
WE HAVE THE TIME

THE VOTING STATION was in a concrete room that opened to the street and was part of a Kabul neighborhood post office. It was one of six-thousand-plus polling places in Afghanistan's 2010 parliamentary election. Next door was a bakery, a carpenter's stall, and a pharmacy. Across the street was a wood lot surrounded by a high chain-link fence, where several men split and stacked dense, dark firewood for the coming winter. The open dirt area fronting the voting station was marked with yellow plastic tape, the kind used at a crime scene. It was prophetic.

After receiving a cursory once-over from the police, two Afghan journalists and I stepped inside the tape boundary to join a dozen or so Afghans shouldering the hot sun as they waited in the dust and grit to vote. Women had a separate voting room, but this didn't stop my colleague, Zabihullah Noori, from marching to the front of the women's line and demanding to be let inside. He was denied, but he convinced a couple of young women to step out of line for an interview.

As Noori disappeared into a quiet corner to talk with the women, I turned toward the sound of shouting behind me, where half-a-dozen men had grabbed a teenage boy dressed in blousy black clothes. He had just voted and held up the tip of his ink-stained finger to prove it, glowering as sweat trickled down his temple. He was seventeen years old and took his voting card from his pocket, explaining that he had gotten it two years earlier when he was fifteen. The boy shrugged when told that the legal voting age was eighteen. He said the card had come from a legitimate election office.

Standing nearby was Saeed Niazi, a candidate in this parliamentary election. Niazi looked at me in disgust, grumbling that the situation was ludicrous. "I found him," he said, pointing to the boy in the black shirt. "A child voted." Why would officials here let a young boy vote, he asked, when he looked like he was just fourteen? Niazi gestured to men squatting nearby in the dirt. "They arrested six persons," each suspected of having fake voting cards, but the local police commander "doesn't know what to do with them."

The other Afghan journalist I was with, Habiburahman Ibrahimi, turned to the beleaguered police commander and asked what he was going to do about the teenager who had just voted and the six others accused of fraud. The commander explained that he was waiting for the voting-station supervisor to tell him what to do with the detainees. Ibrahimi then grabbed the voting supervisor by his shirtsleeve and asked what he was going to do with detainees. The supervisor said it was up to the police to make arrests, not him, and that the detainees were the responsibility of the police now. Ibrahimi turned to me and shrugged, knowing that he was going to get little else out of the officials.

Ibrahimi, a barrel-chested man who sported a long beard, traditional clothes, and a flat Afghan wool cap called a *pakule*, was imposing. We had teased him about being a member of the Taliban, since he came from Wardak Province, just southwest of Kabul, a notorious Taliban stronghold at Kabul's back door. Earlier, Ibrahimi had been on the phone with his friends in Wardak, where the Taliban had warned people to stay home on election day. Anyone stepping out of their houses, no matter the reason, would be shot. No one expected much of a voter turnout in Wardak.

Noori, meanwhile, had finished interviewing the young girls. He told me that they were both seventeen years old. They thought that voting would be a fun thing to do since it got them out of the stifling confines of their homes.

"There are a lot of women who brought fake cards," Niazi remarked, adding that, "These people should be arrested."

We turned to the six arrested men who still squatted in the dust. They were starting to sweat. One of them handed Noori his voter card, claiming it was legitimate and that he had gotten it a couple of years earlier from an election registration office. It had been punched, proving that he had voted in the 2009 presidential election that had put incumbent president Hamid Karzai back in office until 2014. The owner of the card told Noori that if he had known he would have this much trouble voting, he would never have come. Now he probably would never vote again.

A flood of fake voting cards was one of several problems that plagued the 2010 parliamentary election. Afghan and international television had shown video of Pakistani printing-shop owners with fat bundles of the cards, claiming that hundreds of thousands had been printed and shipped to Afghanistan. Officials with the Afghan Independent Election Commission downplayed the problem, saying that election workers were trained to spot the illegal cards. When I asked Ibrahimi about that, he showed me a fake card and one that was not. There was no discernible difference.

Candidate Niazi, meanwhile, ceased berating the police commander and the voting-station supervisor and told me that the two men "don't want [me] to complain" because it made them look bad. Niazi grumbled that "they're not educated" in the election procedures and didn't know what to do about the suspected cards or the people who were carrying them. Niazi said that earlier in the day he had witnessed a van containing about ten men who had arrived to vote. One had gotten out while the others waited. When the lone voter was turned away due to a suspected fake card, he climbed back in the van, which sped away, presumably to another voting station where they might pass scrutiny and vote.

The six men waiting in the dust were eventually taken by the police to a large detention center in Kabul, where they were likely questioned and released. The men were among more than a thousand in Kabul who were detained on election day and accused of holding fake cards. I asked Niazi how this rampant voter fraud could be stopped. He shrugged. "They need training," he said of the election workers, "and they need honesty."

Noori and I walked over to the neighboring bread shop, where several men watched the voting with mild amusement. The aroma of freshly baked naan, the hearty flat bread that is a staple of the Afghan diet, filled the air. One of the men watching the voting was Haji Mohammad Rahim, a businessman. "It's our responsibility" to vote, he said, despite the growing opposition to the government. It was late morning, and I asked if he'd already voted. He said no, but he would vote later.

When I gave him a doubtful look, he smiled sheepishly and confessed that if he voted, the indelible ink used to stain his finger to show that he'd voted would make him a marked man. He traveled around the country a lot, and this meant he moved through Taliban towns and territory. With an inked finger, he risked losing it or even his life, since the Taliban routinely sliced off fingers of those they found who had voted. If he voted, Rahim said, he couldn't travel until the ink stain was gone, and no travel meant no business or income.

The irony of the ink stain was that the Afghan election commission, backed by UN officials, just days earlier had announced that it had "high-quality" ink that couldn't be washed off easily. This ink was to prevent multiple voting. Ibrahimi's friends in Wardak said they probably would not vote due to the Taliban's threats. The indelible ink, meant to be a solution to voter fraud, made lower participation in the election a certainty.

In yet another irony, the government's claims about the high-quality ink were doubtful. Reports from around Afghanistan surfaced as the day wore on that the election ink could, in fact, be washed off easily. The problem was so bad in the western city of Herat that polling stations closed while election workers scrambled to find indelible ink.

Beside the bread shop was a carpentry stall, where a couple of men sawed laminated boards for a bookshelf. It was tedious work since they used handsaws, manual drills, hammers, and chisels. The carpenter told me he was going to vote later in the day, just like everyone else in his family.

"Is your family backing a certain candidate?" I asked.

"Everyone has their own mind and their own choice," he said.

Next door to the carpenter was a small pharmacy owned by Gulam Hussein, a portly man wearing a popular lambskin cap called a *karakul*. It was cool and quiet inside, and he gestured to the many plastic vials and boxes that filled the shelves behind him and below his glass countertop. He, too, said he was going to vote later because at the moment, far too many "people are coming and going." Then he asked, "Do you want something?"

I said no and waved good-bye.

As I monitored the election results during the following days, it was obvious that the problems I'd witnessed were relatively mild. Elsewhere, election workers were shot and killed—some fourteen people died—and many stations never opened due to threats and intimidation by the Taliban. In some locales, regional warlords and their militias stuffed premarked ballots into boxes as terrified and often complicit election workers looked on, knowing that to object meant certain death.

Such rampant abuse had turned the election of the Wolesi Jirga, the lower house of the Afghan parliament, into a circus of corruption. International election monitors grumbled and complained, of course, about the savaging of the process. But the real heroes of the day were ordinary Afghans who had risked their lives to vote—3.6 million out of about 10 million eligible voters.

In the days and weeks that followed, the extent of the electoral fraud was broadcast almost daily by citizen journalists who sent their clandestine telephone videos to Afghan television stations. Grainy videos depicted ten- and eleven-year-old boys waving voting cards and inked fingers, much like the seventeen-year-old I'd seen. Others showed people ticking off piles of blank ballots and stuffing them into ballot boxes, all while polling-station officials looked on and laughed. It was no wonder that Afghans had become cynical, detached, and downright hostile to the government.

Eventually, Afghanistan's electoral bodies threw out about 25 percent of the votes cast and disqualified more than twenty elected candidates for fraud—nearly 10 percent of the presumed winners. But the controversy didn't end, as the disqualified candidates protested their elimination. Many of those who did not vote in the election due to the Taliban's intimidation belonged to Afghanistan's largest ethnic group, the Pashtuns. This allowed smaller ethnic groups such as the Hazara, who voted in substantial numbers, to capture an inordinate share of the seats in parliament. Realizing that they would be grossly underrepresented, the Pashtuns turned to President Karzai, who forced the creation of a special court to review the election results with the idea that it could restore the balance by a court order.

After months of review, the special court announced that it found even more widespread fraud and abuse in the election than the Afghan election commission had discovered. The court declared that not just twenty, but sixty-two members of parliament had committed fraud and should be replaced. This nearly sparked a civil war, with some parliament members arming themselves and vowing to fight to the death. Meanwhile, the Afghan attorney general added fuel to the fire by filing criminal charges against some members of the election commission, citing apparent links to the election fraud.

The emotionally charged ethnic standoff was defused when Karzai finally succumbed to international pressure and backed down, agreeing that the initial election commission findings were valid. Ultimately, however, only nine of the original twenty or so candidates were banned from taking their seats in parliament. Of course, these nine vowed to fight.

While the election was "troubled," as international observers liked to say, it ultimately received their blessing mostly because it actually happened. But was it a legitimate election? The Taliban had used the election as an excuse to wage yet another campaign against the government. They succeeded in keeping two out of every three voters at home, which skewed the results. Meanwhile, local warlords had used it to carve a niche for themselves in Afghanistan's shaky halls of power.

The election was financed, organized, and overseen by the international community. It was a political exercise imposed on a largely terrified, reluctant, and skeptical populace. As events unfolded in the election's aftermath, it seemed that the election had been carried out more for the satisfaction of the international community than for the Afghan people. It justified the presence of foreign armies and was a declaration that Western civilization was there to save the day in Afghanistan. But Afghans knew better.

The Hills of Wardak

A couple of weeks after the election, I talked with Najeeb, a diminutive man who had worked as a house guard for me during 2004, the first year I had come to Afghanistan. He had since married and was now the father of two girls and a boy. His wife and children lived in a village in nearby Wardak Province. The government controlled less than 30 percent of the province, a situation that typified much of the country, he said. The figure was hard to verify, and the government undoubtedly would vehemently deny it. Even so, it was the general consensus.

His wife rarely ventured outside of their house.

"Not even for food?" I asked.

Najeeb explained that he brought supplies from Kabul, enough to last the family for a week, while he stayed in Kabul working and attending school. He had already earned a two-year degree in business and wanted to earn a four-year diploma, knowing that he needed it to get a job that would possibly help him and his family leave the country.

"Isn't it a miserable life for your wife?" I asked.

He shook his head and said that millions of Afghan women lived like that, rarely seeing the light of day due to the strict rules for women that were imposed and enforced by the Taliban.

Najeeb's life was touched by the Taliban in other ways. A good friend of his had been killed by the Taliban just the week before. The man was helping build roads in the province for the Provincial Reconstruction Team. The PRTs, as they're known, were military units that did contracting work. They epitomized how the US Army had struggled to win the hearts and minds of the people: work with us, and we'll give you money and build things. But the influence of PRTs was dwindling in the face of the growing Taliban threat. Najeeb's friend had been driving in the hilly backcountry of Wardak when he was stopped by a Taliban roadblock. He was taken from his car and told he was being held for ransom. Najeeb's friend refused to go along peacefully. The Taliban shot him dead, left him by the side of the road, and then took his car.

"People know who murdered him, then," I said. "They would know by who's driving his car."

"Yes," Najeeb said, "but there is nothing the people can do."

Just two years earlier in 2008, there were only eight or ten Taliban members in the hills near his village, he said. Now there were about two hundred in his valley, and more were joining every day. "They are in the center of town," he said, and were no longer hiding. As they had in the past, the Taliban avoided direct battles, preferring to wage their war from the shadows. The Taliban didn't need to fight, Najeeb said, because they knew the US and international armies were leaving. He, his friends, and his neighbors were forced to deal with the Taliban because of their growing presence. It was a matter of survival. "They say, just wait," he said of the local Taliban. "They [the international forces] will be gone." The Taliban were now telling the international community, "You have the watches; we have the time."

As Najeeb talked, it was obvious that the grip that the Karzai government and the international community, primarily based in Kabul, claimed to have on the country was an illusion. The general calm that hovered over the national capital was deceptive. During the seven-day period before and after the September 2011 parliamentary election, about five hundred "incidents" took place, according to the Afghan

NGO Security Office, a nonprofit group that provides security information for international aid agencies. These widespread incidents were generally small Taliban attacks, not just the big attacks reported by new media, and collectively provided a realistic picture of what was happening in Afghanistan. They included assaults on police and army posts, roadside bombings, and suicide attacks on national and international army convoys. The violence had become so scattered and diverse that it could no longer be attributed to "the Taliban" but to "armed opposition groups," some linked to armed supporters of local warlords bent on ensuring their election to the lower house of the Afghan parliament, the Wolesi Jirga. Here's a sampling of some incidents from around the country during the weeks before and after the election:

- Former police officer abducted and taken to village.
- Local council leader who was also a secondary school principal shot and killed.
- Son of a village chief abducted. Village elders negotiated release of the abductee in exchange for the father, who was wanted because he helped with the election. The father was released for a ransom.
- Grenade thrown inside a jail, injuring a prisoner, who escaped after he was taken to the hospital.
- About 150 residents and 80 candidates demonstrated over the lack of transparency in the election, demanding a second round of voting.
- Police arrested two men thought to be robbers, found with AK-47 rifles, thirty mobile phones, and 70,000 Afghanis ($3,500).
- Rockets fired at a police post, no injuries.
- International forces killed four opposition members, including a local commander, as the four planted a roadside bomb.
- Police arrested a man planting a roadside bomb and seized ten AK-47s, two RPG launchers, three remote-control devices,

twenty Motorola handheld radios, and three motorcycles—
typical equipment used in Taliban attacks.

- Police arrested a local opposition commander.
- A remote-controlled bomb hit a private security vehicle, killing a guard.
- Police post attacked with small arms (AK-47s) for thirty minutes, attackers retreated.
- Driver killed when a roadside bomb exploded near a supply convoy.
- Afghan agriculture department employee killed.
- National police defused multiple roadside bombs.
- Woman abducted under mysterious circumstances.
- Mortars fired at military base, causing no damage.
- International troops killed four opposition fighters in an air strike, destroying ammunitions.
- Police water truck attacked.
- Police patrol attacked.
- Police post attacked, one policeman killed.
- Afghan army convoy hit with roadside bomb.
- Guards for road-construction company attacked.
- Air strike killed opposition fighter and destroyed about twenty-five motorbikes.
- Man beheaded, accused of spying for international forces and Afghan government.
- District administrator abducted from his residence.
- Police vehicle ambushed, one officer killed and another injured.
- Convoy attacked on main Wardak-Ghazni road, killing two civilians in the crossfire.
- Police attacked with heavy weapons and small arms for forty-five minutes. Two police injured.
- A pro-government militia attacked. Fought opposition forces with Afghan army for twelve hours.
- Police patrol attacked, four attackers killed, three wounded.

It was a relentless pounding on the national psyche, but did it mean the Taliban were winning? It depended on who you asked. Even if you assumed that the Afghan national army, the Afghan police and security forces, and the nearly 140,000 US and NATO troops fighting in Afghanistan controlled the country, they were losing the psychological war. This became jarringly apparent when the Open Society Foundations, a George Soros–sponsored organization, released an October 7, 2010, study titled *The Trust Deficit: The Impact of Local Perceptions on Policy in Afghanistan*, which looked at Afghan attitudes toward US and NATO forces fighting the Taliban.

"Despite the outpourings of billions of dollars and hundreds of thousands of troops over the last eight years, many Afghans are angry and resentful at the international presence in Afghanistan," the report stated. "This reflects a growing divide between the perceptions of the Western public and policymakers and those of Afghan citizens about the intentions and accomplishments of international forces in Afghanistan. For the Western public, the international community is in Afghanistan to stabilize the government and stop the spread of terrorism. Western policymakers tend to act on the assumptions that the Taliban, Al Qaeda, and other insurgents bear the greatest responsibility for civilian casualties; and that international forces are in Afghanistan to improve the situation."

But Afghans had a completely different view, the study said, and the reasons were clear. "Incidents of civilian casualties, night raids, wrongful or abusive detentions, deteriorating security, and the perceived impunity of international forces have generated negative stereotypes of international forces as violent, abusive, and sometimes, deliberately malevolent in their conduct and nature."

The statistics, of course, were on the side of the US and international forces. A United Nations report said that about 80 percent of Afghan civilian deaths were due to the reckless attacks by the Taliban fighters and suicide bombers, and just 20 percent were by mistakes made by coalition forces. One example was a suicide bomber's attack west of the northern city of Mazar-e-Sharif just a couple of days before the election that killed a child and injured twenty-eight people. The wounded had been on their way to a wedding party, and their bus happened to be passing an international army convoy just as a suicide bomber detonated his car filled with explosives. Another took place on October 8, 2010, when a bomb destroyed a mosque, killing the governor of the northern province of Kunduz, along with sixteen others who were praying there. More than a hundred others were injured, according to initial reports.

Despite these deaths that could be directly attributed to the Taliban or "armed opposition," increasing numbers of Afghans blamed the events on the presence of international forces. Afghans felt that if the foreign forces were gone, their chances of dying as collateral damage during the Taliban attacks would also be gone. It was a simplistic logic that did not account for the brutal reality of Taliban tactics.

But an even more damaging and dangerous misconception was revealed by the report. After ten years of war, many Afghans had grave doubts about the commitment of the international community to defeat the Taliban and bring peace to the country. Many had come to believe that the United States and the coalition were keeping the Taliban alive to justify the war and their continued presence. "Many [Afghans] were even suspicious that international forces were directly or indirectly supporting insurgents," the Open Society report said. "These suspicions, in turn, have fed into broader shifts toward framing international forces as occupiers, rather than as a benefit to Afghanistan. Today, each incident of abuse, whether caused by international forces or insurgents, reinforces these negative perceptions and further undermines any remaining Afghan trust."

In short, Afghans could not understand why the Taliban couldn't be defeated. The United States had the world's most powerful military, with thousands of highly trained Special Forces soldiers and an elaborate, well-equipped intelligence apparatus. It was working with tens of thousands of NATO troops. These forces had been fighting the Taliban for ten years.

The Taliban, meanwhile, were a conglomeration of rag-tag fighters running around the countryside in sandals and carrying old weapons. They had no armored vehicles, no tanks, and no air force. After ten years of war, the Taliban were stronger than ever. Afghans were no better off now than when the Americans invaded in 2001. Afghans continued to die, at the hands of either the Taliban or the international forces. Most Afghans felt life was more dangerous than ever, not safer. It didn't matter who pulled the trigger or detonated the bomb. If the international forces would leave, the Taliban would stop fighting and peace might return. Or so many thought.

Corruption at the Core

If the fraudulent parliamentary election had been more of a stand-alone event, it might have been more digestible to the Afghan public. But it followed a discredited election just a year earlier when President Karzai was reelected to his second five-year term. Karzai took office only after his main challenger, Abdullah Abdullah, his former foreign minister and a former close associate of the late Northern Alliance commander Ahmad Shah Massoud, withdrew from an election runoff.

Once the US-led international community accepted the Karzai reelection, his administration was hit with one controversy after another. These scandals regularly surfaced in the US press, often via the *New York Times* bureau in Kabul, and revealed details involving Karzai's extended family. One concerned Karzai's brother, Mahmoud Karzai, who was among a wide circle of family and friends in the Karzai administration and had obtained huge loans from Kabul Bank. Contrary to bank rules, some members of the group used bank loans to buy pricey real estate in Dubai, the capital of the freewheeling United Arab Emirates. When the value of Dubai real estate plummeted, many of the loans went into default and Kabul Bank faced collapse. Afghans made a run on the bank's cash. The Afghan Central Bank took control of Kabul Bank and told Afghans not to worry. But they did worry, not so much about Karzai but for themselves and their future.

It was just the tip of the iceberg. In late October 2010, the *New York Times* reported that Karzai's other brother, Ahmad Wali Karzai, may have been on the payroll of the US Central Intelligence Agency. For the previous half-dozen years, Karzai's brother had been widely reported to be an opium kingpin. As head of the Kandahar provincial council, Wali Karzai had been in a good position to be in the drug trade because he wielded considerable power in the heart of opium country. His extensive business enterprises reputedly included some private security firms, the same companies that contracted with the US military to protect fuel and supply convoys and construction projects. Kandahar was the heartland of the Taliban and the nexus of intense fighting by US forces.

That Wali Karzai was on the CIA dole begged the question: was the United States indirectly supporting the opium trade by propping up Wali Karzai? Opium was a major source of income for the Taliban, allowing them to buy weapons and supplies to kill American troops. If Karzai was involved in the opium trade, then it was likely that he had been dealing with Taliban sympathizers. But more troubling was that various agencies of the US government were working at cross purposes; how could Karzai or anyone else in Afghanistan take the United States seriously if on the one hand it demanded an end to corruption while on the other it was secretly paying the Karzai brothers hundreds of thousands of dollars, effectively buying the support of the Karzai family and their friends?

The scandals continued. President Karzai then admitted that he had accepted "bags" of cash from Iran via his chief of staff, Umar Daudzai. Karzai justified this by claiming that he also accepted off-the-books payments from the United States, quipping that "patriotism has its price."

Such statements disgusted many Afghans, who began to think about Taliban promises to stamp out the plague of corruption that permeated government.

The Past as Prologue

Every day I ate lunch with the staff in my office. Among them was Hafizullah Gardesh, the senior editor of IWPR's Afghan Recovery Report, who was also an accomplished Afghan singer and recording artist. He had been conscripted by the Russian army and forced to fight against his own people, yet he survived the bloody Soviet occupation. He dreaded the 2014 withdrawal of US and NATO forces and what he and many others expected would be the inevitable collapse of the Karzai government. As events during 2010 and 2011 evolved, Gardesh found parallels to the withdrawal of Soviet forces from Afghanistan some twenty years earlier.

Much like the international community had done with Karzai in 2004, the Russians had orchestrated the election of Mohammad Najibullah, former head of the secret police in Afghanistan under the Soviets, as Afghanistan's president in November 1986. As had been done under the Karzai administration, Najibullah's regime adopted a new constitution that guaranteed a multiparty political system, freedom of expression, and an Islamic legal system presided over by an independent judiciary.

Najibullah enjoyed extensive financial support from the Soviets, and Afghanistan stabilized enough for the Russians to announce a withdrawal in July 1987 that would not be completed until nearly two years later in early 1989. Similarly, the Karzai government had enjoyed billions of dollars in support from the United States and the international community that provided a semblance of stability, enough so that the United States and the coalition could in 2011 announce a withdrawal from Afghanistan by July 2014.

Following the Soviet withdrawal, the late Najibullah slowly lost control as Afghanistan descended into an ethnic-based civil war. War raged during 1990 and 1991 as tens of thousands of former mujahideen fighters and their leaders grappled for control of Afghanistan, ultimately forcing Najibullah to resign in 1992. Najibullah took refuge in the UN compound in Kabul.

Similarly, fighting with the Taliban flared on a daily basis across Afghanistan during 2010 and 2011 as President Karzai spent most of his time holed up in the highly protected and fortified confines of the presidential palace.

From 1992 to 1996, under the presidency of a former mujahideen commander, Burhanuddin Rabbani, Afghanistan slipped deeper into civil war as regional warlords such as the Tajik commander Ahmad Shah Massoud, Uzbek general Abdul Rashid Dostum, and Hazara commander Mohammad Mohaqiq fought over Kabul, destroying it in the process. This chaos gave rise to the Taliban in Kandahar Province, who quickly grew in strength and eventually rolled into Kabul in the fall of 1996.

There were still more parallels between now and when the Taliban first came to power, Gardesh explained. Before the Taliban took over in 1996, Gardesh recalled that peace overtures had been made to the growing Taliban forces by then-president Rabbani. Then as now, the Taliban were having nothing to do with it.

Karzai had named a High Peace Council in 2010, ironically with former president Rabbani as the head and with the same purpose: to negotiate a peace with the Taliban. Then as now, the Taliban didn't need to negotiate, knowing that time and momentum were on their side. As if to underscore their position, on September 20, 2011, Rabbani would be killed in his Kabul home by a Taliban emissary who had come with a bomb hidden in his turban.

When the Taliban took control of Kabul in 1996, Rabbani and the other mujahideen commanders fled the city. Only Najibullah remained, despite offers by many to help him escape. Najibullah was captured by the Taliban and, along with his brother, killed. Their dead bodies were hung from one of the Soviet-style traffic towers in downtown Kabul and then dragged through the streets.

According to a *New York Times* article dated October 1, 1996, all but three United Nations staff members had left Kabul. Taliban fighters set up checkpoints all over the capital, ensuring that women wore burkas, men grew their beards long, girls did not attend school, and boys did not fly kites. Taliban leader Mullah Mohammad Omar issued a statement at the time that a "complete Islamic system will be enforced."

As we talked, Gardesh looked at me with fearful eyes. He wondered if the same scenario would play out once again in the wake of the withdrawal of international troops. I thought about the brutal way that Najibullah was killed and dragged through the streets of Kabul and wondered who else might meet that awful fate if the Taliban returned to power. I thought about Rabbani, Afghanistan's elder statesman, former president, and leader of the Northern Alliance, whose ignominious death at the hands of the Taliban was still months away. Gardesh's gaze told me he was not worried about Karzai or Rabbani, but for himself, his family and friends, and his country. "It's a big problem for us," he said of the withdrawal of US and international forces.

How many others had such a dire view of Afghan's future? I turned to some of Afghanistan's most astute and outspoken people: Afghan women both in and out of government. Gardesh's fears were far from being just his own. Afghans again were gazing into the abyss.

3

THE FEARLESS

I HAD LAST SEEN MASOUDA JALAL six years earlier when she ran for president of Afghanistan. It was an audacious move, to be sure, to run for the nation's highest office just three years after the fall of the Taliban. Their regime thrived on fanaticism, brutality against women, and destruction. The Taliban had been captured on film dragging a burka-covered woman to the city's football stadium and executing her near the goal line to the chants of thousands of bearded, turban-headed men. It was a savage display of misogynistic madness, the frightening reality of religious zealotry gone badly awry. Violence was Taliban sport.

Jalal had lived through that era and emerged alive and well but angry and ready to stick a finger in the eye of the Taliban's medieval idea of Islam. I had followed her for a day in the fall of 2004 as she campaigned in a village just outside of Kabul, where she had helped a group of women launch and operate a bakery as part of a World Food Program project. It was cramped, dark, and hot, but it gave the women, all widows with families, a way to keep body, soul, and family together. Loaves of naan flew from the bakery's wood-fired ovens.

Jalal was the only woman in a field of eighteen candidates that included designated president Hamid Karzai and a host of former mujahideen commanders who had led the Northern Alliance defeat of the Taliban in 2001. Jalal had little chance to win, but that wasn't the point.

After meeting with some women inside the bakery, Jalal had stepped outside to a small dirt courtyard cut by a trickling flow of wastewater. She spoke quietly to the women, explaining that they didn't need to be afraid to enter a voting station. It was their right, no matter what men said. As she talked, women shrouded in bright blue burkas and trailed by children gathered around her. "You will be in a room, alone," Jalal explained. Each could vote in private and for the candidate of her choosing. She asked the women to contact all of their friends and relatives and to ask them to vote for her, promising, "When I am president, I will be at your service." Women ululated as Jalal hugged them and their children.

Later, Jalal explained to me that her activism had begun shortly after she graduated from Kabul University's medical school. Her patients were suffering from health problems that she attributed to Afghanistan's abysmal social and economic conditions—problems she could not solve as a doctor. Her family had been aghast that she wanted to enter the political arena, not only because it went against Afghan taboos and traditions but because it was dangerous. "They were worried," Jalal told me at the time. "They were annoyed that I did not have a party or money or military support."

Jalal didn't win, of course, but she made a statement.

Shortly after my return to Afghanistan, I contacted Jalal. On the day of our interview, streets in Kabul's core, an area known as Shahr-e-Naw, were all but shut down. Word had spread that the area would be targeted that morning by suicide bombers, who likely would be driving two vehicles laden with explosives, specifically in the vicinity of the Ministry of the Interior building. The threat was further narrowed to the hours when I was to meet Jalal. Before I could ask for a postponement of our meeting, Jalal told me she was on her way.

Since I'd last seen her, Jalal had become internationally known for giving voice to the plight of Afghanistan's women. She headed her own organization, the Jalal Foundation, which was dedicated to improving the lives of Afghan women. In the preceding months, she had spoken in Switzerland, Canada, Germany, and Sri Lanka.

Our conversation quickly diverted from her travels to the Taliban, and I asked about the sixty-eight-member High Peace Council that President Karzai had appointed to negotiate a peace deal with the Taliban. Jalal said that she had been jailed twice by the Taliban for working to help women during the Taliban regime. Peace and reconciliation with the Taliban were impossible.

"How can I agree to have them as leaders of the country?" Jalal asked. If the Taliban were to come back to power, she said, "I will be hanged and dragged around the city as an example to all women."

Jalal had been employed by the UN when she was jailed by the Taliban for refusing to quit working and stay at home. She was arrested on direct orders from Taliban leader Mullah Omar, she said. "It was like a kidnapping." Men jumped in front of her car and held a gun to the driver's head while others yanked her from the car and forced her into a bus full of women whom she said were being shipped out of the country, apparently to work as slaves in Saudi Arabia. "I couldn't breathe because the bus was so full."

The UN intervened, and Jalal was released under an order from the Taliban's minister of justice, but only after she signed a letter acknowledging that her work had amounted to sin. "The edict of the Taliban is that women should stay at home and work. You are a *kafir*, a non-Muslim," the Taliban told her.

For a couple of years, she was forced to take a lower profile, and the UN wanted to evacuate her from the country, but she refused. When the Taliban fled from Kabul in late 2001 in the face of the US-backed Northern Alliance attack, the city collectively sighed in relief. "The day the Taliban left, I went back to the office," Jalal said. She tried to pick up where she left off.

Now, nearly ten years later, the idea that the Taliban might share the power in Afghanistan made her angry. "Now they want to make peace?" she asked. "To me, they are animals and should be arrested."

"A deal with the Taliban might be the only way to end war in Afghanistan," I said. If so, that meant they would share power.

It was not the Taliban who would be sharing power in the Afghan government, but Pakistan, Jalal said. The Taliban were not an independent entity but were controlled and supported by Pakistan. "If the Taliban come to power, Pakistan can control them. Iran also has a hand here. Whatever their ideology is," she said of the Taliban, "they belong to Pakistan."

I asked why Pakistan was so interested in Afghanistan that it would spend time and money supporting the Taliban and fighting the Karzai government.

Pakistan feared that India might someday control Afghanistan and then threaten Pakistan on both its western and eastern borders, she explained.

Pakistan's paranoia of India is hard for Westerners to grasp, I said. Afghanistan is hardly a threat to Pakistan, so Pakistan has no apparent need to control it.

Pakistan lives in mortal fear of India, Jalal explained. It is desperate to protect its backside by preventing Afghanistan from falling under the control of forces aligned with India, specifically the United States and Britain, each with strong historical and economic ties to India. As Jalal described this dynamic, I recalled the number of times that the Indian embassy in Kabul had been attacked, as well as guesthouses in the city that catered to Indian businessmen.

"All they want is power," Jalal said of the Taliban. And if they were to get it again, "what happens to women?" Afghan women would have two choices, she said, "leave or stay and risk being killed." For Jalal, the choice was clear: "We need to stay and struggle." If she were to die, she said, "I can have a clean conscience knowing that I did what I could."

Jalal helped craft provisions in the Afghan constitution that guaranteed women 25 percent of the seats in the Wolesi Jirga, the lower house of parliament. She also helped ensure that women held positions in the government and served as the former minister of women's affairs in President Karzai's first term.

If the Taliban were given key positions in government, they would repeal laws that helped women, she said, and possibly resurrect the infamous Ministry of Vice and Virtue, which enforced byzantine social rules. This included armed men patrolling the streets, grabbing women who were unaccompanied and accusing them of prostitution, throwing them in jail, and ultimately executing some of them. The rule enforcers took men into barber shops, ordered their heads shaved, and told them to grow beards. They pulled men into mosques to pray, stopped kite-flying, music-playing, and video-watching, and halted the lavish weddings that Afghans loved.

If Afghanistan conceded any power or control to the Talban, it would be a death knell for women, Jalal said. "Women are slaves. Men are benefitting because they are given women as slaves. Children are slaves. Even the lowest man will benefit."

Jalal had struggled to work as a doctor under the Taliban. The mullah who ran the hospital where she practiced believed that women should not be doctors. He eventually chased her and most of the other doctors out. When she complained that women and children were dying in the hospital due to the lack of care, the mullah just shrugged and said that it was God's will. He frequently checked the female doctors' offices, expecting to find men hiding there, she said, hoping that he could arrest the female medical staff for immorality.

Jalal had little confidence in the Karzai government, saying that Afghanistan's problems started at the top. "Who is the enemy of the country? Who is the friend? Karzai doesn't know. He doesn't know that extremism is destroying Afghanistan." Karzai's public statements and behavior of the recent months made her despair. These included his rants against the US and NATO forces, the corruption scandals, and tearful appeals for the Taliban to stop fighting. "He doesn't look to be normal. His prestige is completely gone. How can an administration work under him?" she asked.

The government had been made worse by the 2010 parliamentary election. "The parliament is the mafia network," Jalal said. "It's all the drug players. You don't need to look for the drug lords anywhere except in parliament." Afghanistan lacked leadership and needed to be rallied against the Taliban, Jalal said. "Call them criminals," she urged, and announce that "any act of violence will not be allowed. Talk to Pakistan, and tell them to stop [supporting the Taliban]." Pakistan posed a regional and global threat if its support for the Taliban and al-Qaeda–styled groups was not stopped. The danger posed by the Taliban and radical fundamentalists in Pakistan, a nuclear power, was grave. "If they get access to a bomb, they will destroy the world. They believe that they will go to heaven and the rest will go to hell."

The relationship between these groups and Pakistan is murky at best, but the dangers they present are very real. The difficulty of monitoring and curtailing such groups is due to their relative independence and loose alliances. Each operates with its own leaders and agendas, but they are united in their hatred of the United States, NATO countries, and their friends. The support these anti-Western entities draw from Pakistan is covert and emanates from deep within the Pakistani power structure. It is far from official and therefore unpredictable and unmanageable, which makes it such an unknown threat.

Afghanistan could be changed from within, Jalal was convinced, and this could only be done by women, not by men or the military. "Women can work from the bottom of the hole," she said. But women needed help from the international community, direct financial support that would help them improve women's roles in society.

Islam in Afghanistan and other Muslim countries had been hijacked by fanatics, Jalal said. Great religions teach people to be good, but this message was lost when extremists took control. "Extremism leads to power, and [religion] becomes political. When power comes to any religion or philosophy, it creates hatred. Islam teaches love and peace. But [Islam is] used for power. That brings war."

"What can be done to stop that?" I asked.

"The United States cannot defeat extremism, which is why women can do it. If they can become leaders, they can defeat extremism. You have to make the inside better. Women are part of the body of Islam. We can make it better from within. Thousands of women will say,

'We don't want the Taliban.' But [now], women have no voice. The Taliban is afraid of women leaders. They know that is how they can be defeated. That is why they fear us. Women are not involved in the extremism process. Let them fight. Give them the strength to fight."

An infusion of resources to help women in Afghanistan was needed, she said, otherwise, "How can we do it with empty hands?" As long as regional powers exert control and influence in Afghanistan, it will never have peace, Jalal said. "I hope for the international community to remain here so Afghanistan can have peace. Afghanistan is the home for [many] problems because it is unstable. Yet, it is strategic. If [the international community] goes, they lose this strategic location and opportunity. They just lose. Iran is a danger. If they gain access to a bomb . . . then there is no world."

Fauzia Gailani

Masouda Jalal was no longer on the jagged frontline of Afghan society and politics, but many other women were, despite the risk to their lives and the lives of their family and friends. Fauzia Gailani was running for reelection to parliament from the western province of Herat in late summer 2010, after serving one term. She was convinced that her reputation as a businesswoman and activist would easily get her reelected. In late August 2010, five of her supporters were found dead, each with their hands tied and a bullet wound to the head.

I met with Gailani in her apartment in Kabul, several months after her campaign had ended. She had fled Herat, fearing for her life. She welcomed me and a translator into her graciously appointed home, where she lived under armed protection.

"It was one of the worst memories I have," she said of the loss of her family and friends. "I don't know where to start."

Gailani joined the race for parliament just twenty days before the final day of campaigning. She was confident that didn't matter, since she was so well known in the area for her prior five years of work with local youth and the business community. She organized two teams of campaign workers, each with ten people. One of the teams was captured by the Taliban. Although five team members escaped, five others were held and killed. She had no doubt who did it, because "the Taliban called me the same day," she said. "They threatened me. I didn't believe it would come to this end."

The Taliban told her to arrange for the release of five jailed Taliban fighters if she wanted her campaign team to live. The man on the telephone then accused her of being an infidel, of having abandoned Islam and converted to Christianity, and of diluting her children by sending them to foreign countries and foreign schools. In hopes of saving the lives of her supporters, she agreed to stop her campaign. Gailani asked for twenty-four hours and immediately began making calls. "I agreed to it all. I tried my best to release [the Taliban fighters]."

She did not knowingly send her supporters into harm's way. "The area is safe. I'd been there before." But when she looked into the events that led up to the kidnapping and murders, the outline of a plot emerged. The supporters had been escorted in the community by a mullah, who said that it was safe. "We found out that the mullah encouraged the group to go to a village and there they were kidnapped."

Gailani was convinced that the kidnapping and murders went beyond local politics and involved Iranians who manipulated the local Taliban for their own ends. The threatening calls she received were made by people who had Iranian accents and who used Iranian phrases. "They didn't want a woman like me to be active. They have very closed minds."

Her candidacy was opposed by Iranian officials and powerbrokers who wanted to ensure that Iranian businesses dominated the economy in western Afghanistan. Gailani had actively supported the development of local production. "Iran does not want us to become [economically] independent." Iran had prevented Herat businesses and manufacturers from getting off the ground because they would compete with the import of Iranian products. "Iran wanted to import [goods] tax free," she said, "and didn't want Afghanistan to export tax free. These activities came back to hurt me. I wanted to do something as a woman and be responsive to my people."

Gailani had taken her cause to President Karzai, asking for his help. "Iranians are buying land. I told Karzai that. He didn't say anything. He was quiet."

When I noted that Karzai had admitted to accepting cash from the Iranian government, she nodded.

"There is a political hand behind all of this," Gailani said. That political hand had been deadly for her campaign. Those who arranged the killings "are definitely being supported by Iranians. I couldn't continue my campaign. The election was a disaster."

After Gailani dropped her campaign, she was called by Umar Daudzai, Karzai's former chief of staff who had been named as the bagman for Iranian cash funneled to Karzai's office. They discussed a possible appointment for Gailani to the upper house of parliament. Gailani was reluctant. "I hate this government. Look at my situation. I feel unsafe. They don't provide any security. I need two bodyguards. How can I go back to Herat to continue my work?"

As she pondered her future, Gailani offered little hope for Afghanistan. "I see the future of Afghanistan as very dark. I'm afraid for it. This is a disorganized system. I'm a small politician who wants to do something." She paused and nervously cracked her knuckles. "The US wants to bring us human rights, equality. How is that possible when the neighbors [Iran and Pakistan] are controlling the country?"

Iranians also owned news media outlets. "The people who accuse me have a voice in the media. There was a very big plan against me. I tried to push back. My votes were lost." Gailani had been elected to parliament in 2005 with eighteen thousand votes. "This election, I didn't have any."

Gailani was not hopeful about a brokered peace with the Taliban. "No. It doesn't work. Karzai does not have a strategy. He has no clear knowledge of the enemies of this country. People can't trust Karzai and his cabinet anymore. He says things but takes no action." Most Afghans trust the international forces fighting the Taliban much more than Karzai, she said. "I don't trust [the government], so how can ordinary people trust them?"

Rather than rally the Afghan people, listening to their needs and involving them in their government, Karzai remained aloof and disconnected. "The people should be involved. It is essential, but we miss that," Gailani said. Not only do the Afghan people distrust the government, they have become wary of international forces because the war has gone on for ten years and little has changed or improved. "This is a very dangerous [situation]. It keeps these people from their government. It's true and it's very dangerous."

"Was there an investigation into the killing of your campaign workers?" I asked.

Gailani's face went blank and her eyes darkened. "Please don't ask that question. My heart will explode."

But she did discuss it.

"I met with everyone I could," she said. Rather than help her find the killers, the local authorities blamed Gailani for the death of her campaign workers. "I was accused of killing these five people. Everything was against me. They investigated me. This was really strange. What can I do?"

The police had turned Gailani into a suspect rather than a victim, which alleviated them from pursing the real killers, whom they quite possibly knew and who may have threatened the police. That the tables had been turned on Gailani raised an ugly reality that local law enforcement and perhaps higher levels of government may have been aware of the killers. She had to flee the city.

Gailani feared her flight was not over. "They want me to go from Kabul," she said.

"But to where?" I asked.

"That place is under the earth," she said dejectedly.

Stung by the brutal and tragic events of her aborted campaign, Gailani cynically suggested that the international community was naïve about the Afghan reality. She hoped that when people heard the truth about her experiences they might "want to talk about human rights and women's rights. I hope I will be a lesson to other Afghan women."

"Will you stay in politics?" I asked.

She nodded. "I will continue. I was born once. I will die only once."

Gailani was not the only parliamentary candidate who was traumatized during the election. There were other women candidates who were elected and who carried on the struggle for women and progress in Afghanistan.

Never Give Up

It takes a certain kind of woman to storm the bastille of male domination that permeates life in Afghanistan, from the dark interiors of the dried mud homes in which most Afghans live to public life on the street, where women must be covered. Women are largely unseen and anonymous. That anonymity extends to the mosques, where women are banished to the back rows, and to parliament, where women have 25 percent of the seats but only because of international pressure.

I caught up with Shukoria Barekzai in a section of town dedicated to the Afghan parliament. Her office was in a single-story building in the parliamentary office complex behind a series of barricades manned by Afghan police. It was an hour past our appointed time and her staff apologized, explaining that a committee meeting had run overtime. Barekzai arrived in a flurry and, proclaiming she was famished, ushered me into an adjoining room where she could eat while we talked.

Barekzai was first elected to parliament in 2004. A Pashtun woman, she was eager to join the battle. Her background as a journalist had made her especially dangerous in the eyes of some. "I love to work with the truth," she said.

She became the first female speaker of the Wolesi Jirga, and it was immediately apparent what she was up against. "When I started to talk, [the men] would start making noise." She held her ground and yelled, "I am not afraid of you" as she banged the gavel and demanded order.

She organized a women's caucus that had taken difficult if not dangerous positions. "We stand against the amnesty bill," she explained. The legislation protected the warlords and militia commanders in parliament—many of whom were said to be responsible for widespread war crimes and crimes against humanity—from prosecution. This was a particularly controversial position and made Barekzai and her female colleagues the target of animosity and threats. The amnesty law was ultimately approved by the parliament.

The caucus didn't stop there. "We tried for all kinds of reforms." Aware of the highly conservative nature of Afghan society, they hoped for baby steps rather than big strides. "We try to be just pure Afghan." But pushing for progress within the Afghan context didn't always work, Barekzai confessed.

After five years in the parliament, Barekzai said she was exhausted by the demands of her job. She felt trapped in the daily ordeal of chipping away at the calcified consciousness in her country. She longed to escape the pressures of public office and find another, less stressful lifestyle, because the realities of Afghan political life had changed. Although ethnic armies weren't fighting in the streets of Kabul, they were waging costly propaganda wars in the Afghan media. Many ethnic leaders had launched television stations to promote specific views. To survive, one needed the deep pockets of warlords and drug lords or businessmen and banks.

"Elections in Afghanistan have become very costly," Barekzai said. But at the last minute, she had jumped back in, believing that even if she remained a voice in the wilderness, she could promote progressive ideas. "I started my campaign very late," she said, admitting that she was "disabled because of my constituency," which was not wealthy. She watched as other candidates rented buses, hosted lavish lunches and dinners, rented billboards, and plastered their posters all over the city. "There were millions and millions of dollars [spent]."

With a limited budget, Barekzai rented ten billboards and selected an image carefully: a single flower. This decision intentionally did not confront the social taboo of women showing their faces in public. It was just enough. "Luckily I survived." Her victory "didn't come from money or from any ethnic group," and neither did it come from "dirty money," she said proudly. "People went to the polling stations and voted."

While her election may have been a flower in the midst of a weed patch, it was much less costly than that of her former colleague, Fauzia Gailani. Barekzai nodded gravely about that reality, noting that overall, the 2010 parliamentary election "was costly not just in money," it was also "costly for women." Foreign countries exerted political influence by pouring money into some campaigns. "Money was not the only factor. Ethnicity was one factor. [Each group] voted for their own ethnic candidate," she said.

The tone of the parliamentary election had been set a year earlier in the presidential election. "What a mess they made," she said. "It's like another business, and I hate it. The international community interfered badly with the presidential election," justifying its presence by saying it was there to help. The result was that people no longer went to the polls to exercise their rights, and instead, "people now think that voting means receiving money."

With a parliament packed with militia commanders, ethnic warlords, and others now in office due to foreign funds, I wanted to know what kind of elective body she thought it would be. Would and could the parliament hold together? Could the parliament counter the corruption of the Karzai regime?

Barekzai offered a dismissive shrug. "We have to wait and watch."

"Is peace possible with the Taliban?" I asked.

"As a woman, I have sympathy for women living under Taliban control," Barekzai said. "I can't see going into negotiations from a weak position. It's not good for the government."

Afghanistan had lost control of much of the country, and without a substantial presence of international forces, it was doubtful that the Karzai government would continue to exist. Turning the tide of war had to begin on the ground and with the Afghan people, Barekzai said. "If the peace process starts by the people, there is a chance. We have to get the hearts and minds of the people. We have to build trust."

Barekzai had touched on the essential problem in Afghanistan. There was no popular uprising against the Taliban. Led by the United States, the coalition forces had been fighting the Taliban for ten years. The Afghan army and police, bolstered with billions of dollars in training and arms, were just beginning to do their part. But without the support of the Afghan people, the fight was useless. Most Afghans had taken a passive position, admitting only quietly that the Taliban were a deadly nuisance. The international forces were fighting the Taliban, so maybe they would defeat them. If not, the Afghans knew they would have to live with them.

"Are you optimistic about the future?" I asked.

"I don't have a choice," Barekzai said. "We have to have hope. If I don't have a solution, shall I say more war? For how many years? Another generation?" She paused and looked at me. "We never give up going forward."

4

TALKING WITH THE TALIBAN

SOME MONTHS AFTER I MET with Islamic scholar and former parliamentary candidate Safiullah Mojaddedi, I was back in Herat, talking with a couple of the Afghan journalists at our media center. One of Herat's best reporters, Shahpoor Saber, a lean and lanky man in his early thirties, told me about a recent story involving the Taliban insurgency. Saber had access to one of the region's local Taliban commanders, due in part to the Taliban's campaign to improve its image by making itself accessible to the news media to provide a counterbalance to the one-sided stories the Afghan government pushed.

"If he is that accessible, can I meet with him?" I asked.

Saber grinned. "It is possible to meet with the man, but it is not a wise thing to do."

"What are my chances of meeting with him in person and getting away?"

He shrugged. "Maybe sixty-forty," he said. "Probably fifty-fifty."

"Who is this guy, anyway?" I asked.

When he explained that this was the notorious Sheikh, the man who had engineered the kidnapping of Mojaddedi, I was even more curious. Sheikh had demanded a hefty ransom, and I was not about to get caught in the same situation. Still, I wanted to talk with him. "What about a phone interview?"

"Of course," Saber said. "Why not?"

An interview was arranged for later in the day, and I prepared questions.

The interview, which was conducted by Saber in Dari and recorded, then transcribed into English, began with the standard formalities.

"Please, first tell me what can I call you," Saber asked Sheikh on my behalf. "What title can I give you?"

"I'm one of the commanders in the Islamic Emirate of Afghanistan's mujahideen, in the areas of Pashtun Zarghun, Injil, and Guzara," he said. "I am known by the name of Sheikh."

His short answer illustrated the increasingly sophisticated public relations of the Taliban. Sheikh consistently referred to the Taliban fighters as *mujahideen*, capitalizing on the near-mythical status of the freedom fighters who, with US funding and weaponry, had driven the forces of the former Soviet Union from their land. By adopting this moniker, which literally means "those who wage jihad," the Taliban had cloaked themselves with a patriotic mantle aimed at attracting popular support for their antiforeigner cause.

The Taliban had been phenomenally resurgent in the past few years. I asked Sheikh's thoughts about that.

"The mujahideen of the Islamic Emirate of Afghanistan are fighting the colonized government of Afghanistan and foreign forces," Sheikh said. "Gradually, and if God is willing, the mujahideen are getting stronger. Jihad is [coming from] the people and people are cooperating with the mujahideen. They are giving [shelter] to the mujahideen. They guide the mujahideen and they help the mujahideen financially. People are joining the mujahideen, and jihad is getting stronger day by day in Afghanistan as [in the] past."

While Afghan cooperation with the Taliban may not have been as voluntary as he suggested, Sheikh portrayed the Taliban resurgence as a popular movement, which it had to be if it were to succeed. Yet many people I spoke with admitted that they cooperated with the Taliban out of necessity. Sheikh and the Taliban clearly hoped to capitalize on the failure of the US and coalition forces to capture the so-called hearts and minds of the Afghan people.

Sheikh had not explained *why* people were supporting the Taliban, so I pressed him for an answer.

"From the [beginning until] the end of Taliban's government [in 1996], due to propaganda of the West and Western media that said 'the Taliban are not good people, they are not Muslim, they are not Afghans, they are terrorists,' people really thought we were bad. But now, after the coming of America to Afghanistan, [it] is clear to all our people that [this] was propaganda of Western media, and our people know the reality now."

Sheikh's answer reflected a curious Taliban sensitivity to what he called the propaganda of the Western media, which portrayed the Taliban as bad people. It was true that the Taliban had been demonized by the Western press, and deservedly so. The Taliban's archaic concept of crime and punishment was abhorrent and barbaric. Harsh judgments were swiftly issued by community elders, none of whom were women, for transgressions from petty thefts to murder. Infidelity and alleged immorality were assumed to be the sole fault of women, as if men never originated such acts, resulting in women being partially buried and stoned to death.

This form of justice was medieval, of course, often justified by references to the Koran, the Muslims' holy book written fourteen hundred years ago. The Taliban adherence to their misogynistic notions denied that society had changed in fourteen centuries or that Islam itself had grown and changed. It supposed that knowledge, wisdom, and thinking about how humans can best manage their affairs was no different now than when Islam was conceived in the Arabian desert many dusty centuries ago. The Taliban, the plural form of the word *talib*, or "student of Islam," considered themselves protectors of Islamic faith, the true believers who had been born into a sea of immorality and evil. They saw only a world that had spun out of control and lacked both a moral compass and clarity of purpose. The Taliban answer to the kaleidoscope of modern life was to punish or kill those who did not agree.

As alien as such thinking was to the West, it was not that long ago that Western society behaved in much the same way. Joan of Arc was burned as a witch by the British in the early 1400s after she inspired the French in the Hundred Years War. Some three hundred years later, in the American colonies, the Salem witch trials of 1692 took place in four Massachusetts towns, resulting in fourteen women and five men being hung. Other accused witches died in prison. The trials were blamed on panic and fear among an isolated and extremist religious sect, the Puritans, who considered the practices of the Protestant Church of England too close to those of the Catholic Church.

The Puritans of yesteryear, as well as America's fundamentalist Christian evangelicals, have an ironic parallel to the Taliban's thinking of themselves as protectors and purveyors of a "pure" religious doctrine. Like the Puritans, the Taliban have operated in relative isolation among Afghanistan's rural population, the nearly 75 percent of the country who have limited access to various social amenities such as education, the international news media, or the Internet. Mobile telephones have changed that somewhat, but even so, the Taliban have been able to control telephone access in certain provinces.

The underlying reasons for the Taliban's strength across Afghanistan have little to do with the Taliban per se. The country ranks second in the world in its death rate for the general population and for infant mortality. Average life expectancy in Afghanistan is a mere forty-five years. One main reason for this is that Afghanistan has been in a state of war since the invasion of the Soviet Union forces in 1979, a span of more than thirty years. But there is also limited access to health care. If an Afghan becomes seriously ill or injured, he or she expects to die.

Given the bloodshed and primitive living conditions, it is no wonder that the majority of the people—those in the rural areas and who are the least educated—cling tenaciously to their religion. In the midst of swirling winds of war and the uncertainly of life, hard and fast rules of behavior provide pillars for social interaction and reassurance that there is a better life after this one. The same answers to life's questions that were available fourteen centuries ago are still valid, or so the Taliban contends.

For most of the Afghan population, coalition forces have failed to bring about the hoped-for transformation of the world's tenth-poorest country. The United States has devolved in the minds of most Afghans, becoming just the latest invader in Afghanistan's long and troubled history. Rather than the saviors that the internationals thought themselves to be, they have become a convenient target as the prospects for peace and prosperity dim and corruption among Kabul's ruling elite dominates the news. Scandal and corruption play perfectly into the Taliban agenda, fanning the flames of anti-Western sentiment by proclaiming that American-led forces installed an evil and corrupt regime. The Taliban sounded a rallying cry and appealed to the Afghans' faltering sense of nationalism, as leaders such as Sheikh argued that the Taliban's cause was both patriotic and morally correct.

"We fight against the Afghan government and the Americans," Sheikh said, "and the reason we are fighting . . . is that the administration is colonized by Americans and foreign forces. As you know, 99 percent of Afghanistan's people are Muslim, and it is [stated] in Islam that whenever someone attacks the religion and our culture, we should stand against them and fight against them. [The] Afghan people have proven themselves in fighting against Britain and Russia and they will fight against the West the same."

There was a perplexing if not contradictory basis to the support that the Taliban found among many Afghans. Statistics showed that the Taliban attacks, especially their suicide bombers, killed many more civilians than the errant civilian deaths attributed to US or coalition forces. Taliban attacks included the beheading and killing of those suspected of supporting or working for the Afghan government or international forces, companies, and nonprofit groups. The Taliban's violent tactics against their own people logically should have turned the Afghans against the Taliban, but they did not.

Was the Taliban not worried about turning people against them? I wondered. "What about kidnapping, harming, and killing of people by Taliban in different areas of Afghanistan?"

"What do you mean by kidnapping?" Sheikh responded.

"For example, [taking] hostages."

"The people who we are taking as hostages are those who are against the Taliban, working for [the Afghan] government, or they are spying. This word 'kidnapping' [used] by you is mistaken. Why don't you ask the same question of the Americans? Why do they go to people's houses, take innocent people away, and kill whoever they want? Why don't you ask them these questions?"

I pressed Sheikh a bit further. "Afghan troops and foreign troops claim to be helping the Afghan people," but the Taliban says they are not. "So, how does the Taliban help the people of Afghanistan?"

"The help that we can [provide for] our people is good security. In the areas under Taliban's control, there is no robbery, insecurity, and kidnapping. There is no one to ask for bribes in these areas, and people live under a secure environment," Sheikh said.

The claim was largely true, especially in areas where the Taliban were the most active, but there were exceptions. In these regions, US Special Forces conducted extensive night raids, descending on villages, blasting down doors of suspected militants, and killing and capturing Taliban at all levels. I'd been told in mid-2011 by an embassy official that the average life expectancy of a newly appointed Taliban commander had been reduced to thirty days in some areas. It was one of the bits of information one collects in a war zone like Afghanistan that was completely unverifiable. Even if remotely true, it was a testament to the effectiveness of the shifting emphasis to targeted killings and tightly focused operations meant to plunge a blade into the heart of the Taliban insurgency. But that blade was beginning to be withdrawn.

"What does the departure of foreign troops from Afghanistan mean?" I asked.

"Americans don't have the ability to resist and fight against the Taliban and the mujahideen anymore," Sheikh replied. "This is why they are saying that they'll leave Afghanistan in 2014. At first they didn't want to leave Afghanistan. Now I'm sure they'll leave even before 2014. These days look the same as those days when the Russians were leaving Afghanistan."

For Sheikh and the rest of the Taliban, the war already had been won. As with all other Afghan invaders in past millennia, the Taliban were claiming that the Americans and their allies had been defeated and were being driven from the land, proving that Allah was on the side of the Taliban.

In late June 2011, President Barack Obama announced that the thirty-three thousand additional US forces he had ordered to Afghanistan in December 2009 would be home within fifteen months. Of the surge force, ten thousand troops were to return by the end of 2011 and another twenty-three thousand would leave Afghanistan by September 2012. The rest would be back in America by the end of 2014. As Obama's words reverberated across Afghanistan, the Taliban breathed a sigh of relief, danced with delight, and made plans for their eventual return to power.

The parallels to the withdrawal from Afghanistan by the Soviet forces in 1989 were haunting, as Sheikh had said. But as Sheikh gloated over those parallels, it raised the specter of another bloody Afghan civil war. Lacking a common enemy upon the Soviet exit, the Afghans had turned on each other and launched one of the most vicious civil wars in modern history, replete with brutal summary executions and the near-total destruction of Kabul. The appalling nature of the civil war paved the way for the Taliban. If history was repeating itself, then what was Afghanistan's chance of peace?

"What do you think about the peace program?" I asked Sheikh. "Is it possible for you [and the Taliban] to join this [government]?"

"The people who are really mujahideen and want to fight in the way of God, they will never surrender and will never join the Americans' peace program. The people who are joining the peace programs or reconciliation commission were never part of the mujahideen. They were the people who couldn't live among us anymore, so they joined these programs."

Sheikh's answer carried an ominous warning. Afghans who were not fighting with the Taliban were traitors and sellouts, even if the truth was that they may have been sick of war and wanted peace. The

Taliban had no interest in peace, except for the kind of peace they would impose. Why would the Taliban negotiate when it didn't need to? Why would the Taliban talk with a government that controlled less than 30 percent of the country? Why negotiate with a government that was despised and corrupt and whose very existence helped the Taliban base grow every day, every week, and every month?

So who were those people reportedly negotiating "peace" with the government that Sheikh and the Taliban despised? In one particularly telling event in November 2010, British intelligence found a Pakistani man it thought was a high-ranking Taliban commander. After being paid a couple hundred thousand dollars for his cooperation, the man was flown to secret high-level meetings with NATO and Afghan representatives before he was unmasked. The man turned out to be a shopkeeper from Quetta, Pakistan.

The story died a quiet death like most of the others that didn't fit the coalition's spin on the war in Afghanistan. To be sure, it provided the Taliban with some laughs. The United States and its allies were so convinced that they were "winning" and were driving the Taliban to the bargaining table that they had been taken in by Taliban trickery. They fell victim to their own propaganda. It was a conceit of astronomical proportions that the United States and its NATO allies thought that all of its military force and sophisticated weaponry would carry the day in Afghanistan. It couldn't. The coalition was killing a lot of the Taliban, so that meant the coalition was winning and the Taliban wanted to negotiate a peace deal, right? The Taliban weren't buying it. Never had.

The Taliban tactic was to conserve people, money, and resources for the moment that the coalition would be gone. In the meantime, they would conduct dramatic, purposeful attacks, the kind of events that made virtually no difference in the broader military battle but grabbed headlines and gave them strings of victories in the psychological war.

In an attempt to find consensus among a broad cross-section of Afghanistan, President Karzai had packed his sixty-eight-member

High Peace Council with many former mujahideen fighters and community leaders from across the country. These men may have opposed the government publically but were weary of war. "What's the difference between you and these people?" I asked Sheikh. "They were against the Afghan government but are joining the peace programs."

"We don't actually have such people amongst our mujahideen [who will] join the reconciliation commission," Sheikh said. "They were only fighting because of money. As I mentioned before, they are those people who cannot live in our areas anymore, so they join these programs."

The insinuation that those joining the peace process supported the government only for financial gain could have been made about the Taliban as well. It was well known that the Taliban drew its fighters from impoverished rural areas and the fighters were paid. This meant that the Taliban were receiving money from both internal and external sources who took advantage of Afghanistan's poverty to wage war for their cause.

"The group that you are part of, or you are the commander of, will need a big financial support," I said. "So who or which countries are supporting your groups?"

"As it's clear that all the world is against the Taliban, there is no support from any country except support of our own people. As I mentioned before . . . some of our people . . . are supporting us financially," he said.

Sheikh's answer contradicted volumes of reports and statements that Pakistan, through its intelligence service; Iran; and fundamentalist elements from within Saudi Arabia provided money and support to the Taliban. Without it, the Taliban would cease to exist.

"Which country is helping you with all the weapons you are using?" I asked.

"No one is helping us with the weapons," he insisted. "All these weapons are those old weapons from the Russian time. You can come here and see them."

"What about Islamic countries?" I asked again. "What kind of help do they give to you?"

"There is no help from any Islamic country. Pakistan is a good example. A while ago, they arrested one of [our] mujahideen commanders and sold him for a few million dollars to the Americans."

"What [do you think] about the leaving of foreign troops in three years and turning over the security to Afghan troops?" I asked.

"When the [foreign forces] leave, the Afghan troops will not be able to stand against us. Karzai's administration is full of corruption, and as soon as the [departure] of foreign troops starts, Karzai's government will fall, [just] like Najibullah's government after the departure of the Russians," Sheikh said.

Without the presence of some 140,000 coalition forces, the collapse of the Karzai government was a certainty on the minds of most Afghans. As I learned during the ensuing months, Afghans were weighing their options, wondering if it was better to stay and take their chances with the Taliban or prepare to leave for a new life far beyond Afghanistan's borders.

Finding Saleh

It was March 2011, and the cold, gray skies of winter hovered over Kabul. The rhetoric from Sheikh was informative, but I wanted to dig deeper into the Taliban resurgence. I needed to go further afield and talk to people who lived with the Taliban and who could tell me of their frustrations and motivations to fight the government, even if it meant they joined the Taliban.

I first met Mohammad Saleh (not his real name) during one of my visits to the northern Afghan town of Mazar-e-Sharif. I was working with one of the town's most energetic reporters, Enayat Najafizada, a twenty-two-year-old freelancer who frequently assisted international reporters working in northern Afghanistan, helping them make the contacts they needed for stories. Our meeting with Saleh would be the first of several over the coming months. Najafizada and I picked up

Saleh one early morning in Mazar-e-Sharif and drove to the nearby town of Balkh, where we parked on the town's plaza under towering trees.

One of the major settlements in the eastern reaches of the Greek empire created by Alexander the Great around 325 BC, Balkh is one of Afghanistan's many historic locales. The ancient city's massive mud-brick ramparts melted back into the earth after more than two millennia, but their mounded outlines are still visible. Balkh is also the fabled birth city of the mystic poet Jalaluddin Rumi. History hangs in the air.

Saleh had agreed to find a couple of men for me who had turned to the Taliban to find the justice they could not obtain from the government courts. As we waited for them to arrive, I asked Saleh about the situation in Afghanistan. His opinion was more than the random thoughts of someone on the street. When the Taliban had control of much of the north, Saleh was a deputy to the Taliban governor of Balkh Province. The depth and breadth of his information about the region was impressive. He was part of the war against the Northern Alliance and part of the massive surrender of an estimated five thousand or so Taliban fighters in the neighboring Kunduz Province in late 2001, shortly after the US Special Forces swept through the north. He literally knew where the bones of his comrades were buried in the north and eventually would take me to an undiscovered mass grave near Mazar-e-Sharif where Taliban fighters had been executed.

Saleh was an ethnic Pashtun and linked with the many Pashtun communities scattered across northern Afghanistan. These communities had been complaining for years about discrimination at the hands of the ethnic Tajiks who controlled the north, specifically the governor of Balkh Province, Atta Mohammad Noor, a former Northern Alliance commander.

"People hate the Americans more than the Russians," Saleh told me bluntly, looking over his shoulder from the front seat. He grinned, as if to say that he personally did not share that opinion, his white teeth flashing in the midst of his dark beard. He wore a dark turban and traditional clothes. "They hate the government. The Balkh governor took lands by force. He is against the Pashtuns. There is no Pashtun language [program] on TV. If I had a gun, I would kill the governor."

Governor Atta, as he was known, enjoyed vast support from the Americans due to his role in the rapid defeat of the Taliban in 2001. I'd met with Atta in 2004 for an extensive interview during which he waxed nearly poetic about the future of Afghanistan. At the time, he was grappling for control of the north with another former Northern Alliance commander, General Abdul Rashid Dostum, whose home turf was Jawzjan Province to the west. While Dostum's influence faded, Atta's rose. Atta claimed ownership to vast swaths of land in and around Mazar-e-Sharif and reportedly grew wealthy. But as his power grew, the security in the north deteriorated, and now Atta traveled under armed guard.

"He has palaces and villas," Saleh complained of Atta. "I live in a village." While Atta's son drove around town in a luxury SUV, "my son does not have shoes to go to school. Where the Tajiks live, the roads are good and they have schools there. I am saying these things because of these poor people."

Discrimination and oppression were long-standing complaints of the Pashtuns in the north. The seething dissatisfaction that Saleh described was why the northern provinces of Afghanistan had gone from being among the safest to the most dangerous, even as the US and coalition forces crowed about gains in the southern provinces of Kandahar and Helmand. The northern Pashtuns turned to radical groups such as the Haqqani network and Hezb-e-Islami, a group led by former mujahideen commander Gulbuddin Hekmatyar.

Saleh nodded when I asked if he or other Taliban sympathizers would agree to talk with the government about peace. "Given the chance, I will talk. But people want there should be no discrimination and [there should be] balance in government." This meant that Pashtuns should be appointed to government positions and have a chance to participate in the governing of their communities, he explained. This had been written into the Bonn Conference agreement that had been signed ten years earlier but had never been fully implemented.

Saleh complained that the Karzai government was dominated by the former Northern Alliance commanders. "I don't have a chance to be in government."

"Most other Taliban won't talk with the government, so why would you?" I asked.

"The Taliban are afraid that if they join the government, they'll be killed." An impediment to peace talks was Karzai's appointment of former Afghan president Burhanuddin Rabbani, an ethnic Tajik and leader of the Northern Alliance, as head of the High Peace Council. The Taliban would never work with Rabbani due to his history of fighting against the Taliban, who are largely ethnic Pashtuns. "They will never surrender to Rabbani," Saleh said. This antipathy against Rabbani would be a factor in his later assassination in September 2011 at the hands of a so-called Taliban peace emissary.

Ethnic hatred smoldered across the north, Saleh said, because none of the billions of dollars in foreign aid that had poured into Afghanistan had reached the Pashtun communities. "Millions of dollars in aid were all spent in Kabul, and the rest was stolen." Not only Pashtuns but most Afghans were left out of the rebuilding of Afghanistan. "We will not have peace until the US goes to all four corners of Afghanistan and asks what [people] want. Then they need to implement their ideas." But even if that were done, Saleh doubted that it would ease the situation, since few people trusted the government or the international community. "People know the US and the international community only support the Tajiks."

I suggested that there may be time for more equitable development if the international community stayed longer in Afghanistan than most people expected. The US was proposing to establish semi-permanent bases in Afghanistan that would operate through 2024.

"It is unacceptable to have permanent bases here," Saleh said. "We will never let them have permanent bases. [The United States] is supporting our enemies, and the enemies are in the government." Saleh was convinced of the existence of a much larger, long-range plan behind the idea of permanent US bases in Afghanistan. "I know the plan for the region. They want to bring the other countries under their control. But they need to gain the trust of the Afghan people first. The main problem is the Pashtuns. They should slowly bring [Pashtuns] into the government. That's natural." Since the Pashtuns had been excluded from government, according to Saleh, the Taliban had turned to Pakistan and the ISI.

Near the time when Saleh and I spoke, suicide bombers had attacked a bank in Jalalabad, killing more than thirty innocent people. "How could antigovernment forces expect to win over the population with such tactics?" I asked.

"If it is true that the [Afghan] people are angry, why didn't they demonstrate [against such killings]?" Saleh responded. In fact, there had been wholesale condemnations, public and private outrage, but no demonstrations against the killings.

People were afraid to protest publically, I argued. They'd be killed. If the extremists would casually shoot people in a bank at point-blank range, killing street demonstrators would be easier. "What was the point of suicide bombers?" I asked, since they kill many more Afghans than anyone else does.

Saleh shrugged, explaining that suicide bombing was a form of protest as much as suicide. "When I'm in trouble, I don't care about anyone else," he said, even if innocent people die along with the suicide bomber.

It was a protest against what, exactly? I wondered. The purpose and reasons behind suicide bombing puzzled me for much of my year in Afghanistan. Over time, an answer took shape. It was a protest against the West, against an invasion by its armies and its culture. Suicide bombing was a desperate protest against a foreign way of life rapidly being adopted by an entire generation and the loss of another way of life that was being killed, physically and literally, by war. It was an act of hatred and outrage, a protest against the inability of Afghans to control their destiny.

Saleh and I fell silent as people meandered the central square of Balkh. He sighed and asked why the United States had not stayed in

Afghanistan after the Soviet Union withdrew in 1989. After all, the United States had supplied the mujahideen fighters with money and weapons that ultimately forced the Russians to leave. "Why didn't the US then help Afghanistan?"

I had no answer, at least none that I wanted to share, because that decision had been one of the worst in a long history of shortsighted US foreign-policy decisions. The United States had abandoned Afghanistan at a critical turning point in its history, and that ultimately gave rise to the Taliban. In mid-1996, shortly before the Taliban cemented its control over Afghanistan, Osama bin Laden fled Sudan and returned to Afghanistan, where he and his followers had participated heavily in the mujahiddeen war against the Soviets. Over the next five years, he forged an uneasy relationship with Taliban leader Mullah Omar, who granted bin Laden a base in Kabul from which he and his al-Qaeda organization waged their global jihad against the West. The most notable event of this jihad was the simultaneous bombings in August 1998 of the US embassies in Kenya and Tanzania that took hundreds of lives. Bin Laden then used this base to plan the 9/11 attacks on the United States that brought the Americans storming back to Afghanistan to topple the Taliban.

Undoubtedly, the situation in Afghanistan would have been completely different if America had infused the country with aid and development that could have prevented the civil war and blunted the rise of the Taliban. An American presence in Afghanistan throughout the 1990s most certainly would have forced bin Laden and his al-Qaeda organization to set up shop elsewhere and perhaps would have made the 9/11 attacks more difficult, if not preventable.

The 2001 invasion of Afghanistan was not necessary, Saleh said with a steady gaze. "The US didn't need to attack the Taliban but only had to bring the mujahideen commanders into the [Taliban] government."

I was puzzled but gave it some thought. Given the hardliners in the Taliban, I doubted that the Taliban would have agreed to such inclusions, since they had spent so much time, money, and lives subduing and crushing the Northern Alliance and its leaders. It was clear to me that Saleh deeply resented that he and his former Taliban associates had lost control of the government and were now banished outsiders, objects of hatred. Just as the Taliban once drove the Northern Alliance from power, the Taliban in turn were pushed from power.

Now, after ten years of foreign domination, the Taliban and their sympathizers were trying to blast their way back via suicide bombers and roadside detonations. As the Taliban caused more and more trouble, Saleh mused that the Russians must be looking on with pleasure. "Now it's Russia's turn to watch."

There had been some very recent attacks on Pashtun communities that were less than thirty minutes from where we sat, night raids by foreign and Afghan special forces. They were successful, according to the military, quelling the random Taliban attacks on government outposts and their illegal checkpoints on some main roads. When I asked Saleh about them, he shrugged, dismissing the claims that the night raids had hurt the Taliban in the north. "It's wintertime. The Taliban have left but are slowly coming back to the area."

"Is there a new spring offensive coming?" I asked.

Saleh nodded. "They are working on the structure now, who will be in [the shadow] government. There will be new violence. They want to show how strong they are. Every year, they are getting stronger."

Two months later, Saleh's forecast proved true. At the end of April, the Taliban announced its new offensive for the year. Four months after the spring offensive began, August 2011 officially became the deadliest month ever for US forces in Afghanistan.

5

TALIBAN JUSTICE

HE TWITCHED NERVOUSLY, tugging at his head scarf, his eyes downcast. Amanullah was a Taliban judge from Ghazni Province, about one hundred miles south of Kabul. He wanted to keep his face hidden, fearing that he might be identified and arrested.

I had been in Ghazni six years earlier, traveling through the back regions of the province embedded with US army reservists from Oklahoma and Kansas. It was a wild and bumpy ride across the most harsh, sunbaked terrain I'd ever seen. We rode in armor-plated Humvees topped with machine guns and stopped in several mountain villages to ask about the Taliban. Yes, the villagers said, the Taliban were around but weren't doing much.

During the intervening years, the Taliban had grown, and they now controlled most of the province. Ghazni was where twenty-three South Korean missionaries—sixteen women and seven men—were captured by the Taliban in mid-July 2007 and held hostage for six weeks. Two Korean men were executed before a deal could be reached for their release. The kidnapping reportedly came after the Afghan bus driver for the Koreans let a couple of men on board. They fired their weapons and commandeered the bus. The hostages were divided into groups and moved frequently before finally being released on August

29 and 30, amid reports that the South Korean government had paid $20 million for their freedom.

While the Taliban resurgence was attributed to Afghans' disgust at the pervasive corruption of the Karzai government, one major target of criticism was the judicial system. It was extremely slow and outrageously costly, which put justice beyond the reach of most Afghans. The Taliban bragged that their brand of justice was not only swift and final, but free. As an added bonus, it was also holy, since Sharia law was derived from the Koran.

Judge Amanullah was willing to meet me in my office, but I declined, preferring that neither he nor his handler know where I worked and lived. I suggested that we meet in a public yet quiet place. We agreed on an Afghan restaurant. Although Amanullah and his translator insisted that they had no ulterior motive for the meeting, I wanted to minimize the risk of a setup. There had been too many incidents in which journalists were grabbed, despite claims that their safety was assured. It was a rumored practice for low-level Taliban or organized-crime networks to take a hostage, most often a wealthy Afghan, then sell them to other larger criminal groups for higher and higher prices.

I had come with a translator, which was why Amanullah was trying to hide his face. He complained that I was to have come alone, and since I had not, he was at risk of being identified by an Afghan who might also be a government spy. I agreed to have my translator sit in an adjoining room so that we could continue talking.

Amanullah said he was twenty-nine, but he looked a little older. He had studied in madrassas, or religious schools, in Afghanistan and Pakistan for eleven years, learning Sharia law. After an apprenticeship under other judges, he was assigned to a district in Ghazni Province where he worked as a circuit rider, much like judges of the old American West did, travelling from town to town to dispense justice.

"The reason people come to us is that there is too much corruption," Amanullah said, anxiously stroking his beard. "People are sick of [it]. Many have been to the government courts" and have had to wait one or two years for decisions to be handed out. "People say they've spent money on [the courts] and still they get nothing. They come to us and ask us to solve their problems."

"People in rural areas have little choice but to turn to the Taliban," I said, "since the Taliban controls most of the territory outside of the cities."

Even if the government courts wanted to pursue cases in the rural areas, which it normally didn't, it was nearly impossible, Amanullah conceded. "They can't [get] any witnesses" to appear in court, "but [the Taliban] can do it."

As Amanullah talked, it became clear that the Taliban had, in fact, established a widespread and organized shadow government across the country. While they might not operate effectively in the cities, they did so quietly and consistently throughout the countryside. It was a matter of supply and demand. Government services and police protection did not extend effectively beyond the outskirts of most towns and cities, where the Taliban were strong and operated with protection and impunity

One of Amanullah's recent cases involved a land dispute between two men from Ghazni. One had sold a parcel of land to another for $143,000. After accepting the money from the buyer, the seller had second thoughts, realizing that the land was worth more than the final sale price. With the help of a local official, whom Amanullah described as a "government commander"—which implied that the man was with the police or military—the original seller took the land back. The buyer was outraged. "The owner came to us. We investigated it." The Taliban arrested the seller, put him in their jail, and then confronted the man with the sales documents. The seller admitted to what he had done and agreed that the land belonged to the buyer.

The seller's partner, the government commander, "was very angry, but there was nothing he could do," Amanullah said proudly. The Taliban wanted to punish this commander as well but lacked the power to do so. "We still cannot take any action with this commander," Amanullah said, because he has the protection of the government.

Each month Amanullah's caseload fluctuated, depending on how active the Afghan or international forces were in his district. He averaged ten to fifteen cases per month. When international forces were active, the Taliban were forced into hiding, and his work stopped. But the situation for the Taliban was improving. Amanullah had started work about a year and a half earlier, and during this time, Taliban control over Ghazni Province solidified. "When I first came, I was not able to go everywhere. It was not safe for me. Now I can go anywhere."

"Why had the situation changed in such a short time?" I asked.

"There are many reasons we've gotten stronger," Amanullah said, but government corruption topped the list. "You have to pay bribes everywhere." In contrast, "we do not accept any gift from any side. For us, all the community is the same. That is why people support us. They realize that we work for their welfare," while the foreigners do not, he said.

The Taliban were growing stronger also because the coalition forces had been unable to establish peace. "Foreign troops came here to bring peace. But they failed. Security was better before. We know we have defeated them. They will withdraw."

Though Amanullah blamed government corruption as the cause of Taliban resurgence, he didn't blame President Karzai, which puzzled me. "Did the Taliban want to see Karzai removed from office?" I asked.

Amanullah said no. "We don't have any problem with [Karzai] if he accepts Sharia law."

"Is it really that simple?" I asked.

Amanullah nodded yes, saying that Sharia law worked well in Afghanistan. "Everyone is happy with it."

"So if Karzai instituted Sharia law," I said, a move that would essentially cede police and judicial powers to the Taliban, "the war would be over?"

"We will stop fighting," he said.

I looked at Amanullah skeptically.

He shrugged and continued. "In rural areas, many people support us. Otherwise, how can we get stronger? People realize that the government doesn't care about them." The Taliban power was derived from the Afghan people, not from some outside force, he said, and that power was from Allah. "People power is the power of God."

I recalled the beleaguered parliament members from Herat who said that the Afghan government needed to pay attention to the people, not serve just those at the top. But that wasn't happening. Amanullah explained how a local government commander in Ghazni had tried to use his position to enrich himself and his friend. It was not the way to inspire confidence in government, and the Taliban were moving quickly to exploit such cases.

"Do people truly support the harsh punishments handed out by the Taliban under Sharia law?" I asked. Women were stoned to death, hands and arms were chopped off, and suspected spies were beheaded, I noted.

Amanullah said that not all punishments were harsh and that as an outsider and non-Muslim, I didn't understand Sharia law. "[The punishment] depends on which kind of crime."

"For most of the world, chopping off heads and limbs and stoning women to death is considered barbaric," I said.

He shrugged. "We don't have a prison for them," he said of the accused, explaining that was why justice had to be swift and final.

There was a system, he said, and not all punishments involved chopping off body parts. Spies were beheaded, but "for that we have to have evidence and a confession." When someone was accused of spying, "our response is to collect information. We have another commission above us. They advise us what to do." If someone was accused of being a spy, but no one had died because of the spying, then the supposed spy was allowed to live. "But if people have died, then he is beheaded or severely lashed."

Amanullah recounted a murder case that involved a man named Mohammad who had killed a man in his village. "He ran away for a while," so the Taliban arrested Mohammad's brother and held him until Mohammad returned and confessed. To show that the Taliban could be fair and impartial, Amanullah explained that "it was not our responsibility to kill him." Instead, the Taliban asked the victim's family what the punishment should be, so that the family could either forgive the murderer or seek a punishment. "We asked his wife what to do with [Mohammad]." The widow didn't want to kill Mohammad herself but wanted an appropriate punishment.

"We hanged him at night," Amanullah said. "We informed the family [of the murderer] to come take the body." When the Taliban told the murdered man's widow of the hanging, "She was very happy." Even the murderer's family accepted the punishment, and the murderer's wife agreed, he claimed, saying, "It was what he deserved. Thank God that he has been punished." The case had few, if any, lingering resentments. "We still have a good relationship with the murderer's family."

Like all systems of justice, the Taliban punishment fits the crime, he said. "In Sharia law, for every robbery, there is a different punishment." The more valuable the object, the more severe the punishment. Something worth the equivalent of 180 grams of gold, about $8,000, called for the lopping off of a hand. Something more valuable demanded the loss of an arm at the elbow. Theft of an even more valuable item could mean the loss of both arms.

To carry out the sentences, the Taliban hired local butchers. "Every judge should have two or three butchers working with him in court," Amanullah said. "It is not a big deal. Anyone can do it," he said of severing limbs. "But with head cutting, it takes someone with some training."

Following the prescribed punishments, "the judge will show the butcher where to cut," be it at a knuckle, wrist or elbow. "People inform the family, and they can bring a doctor" when the punishment is carried out. "They can then go to the hospital," he said of the convicted criminal, after the limb is cut off. "Then they are free to go. They are no longer a criminal."

My stomach turned at the thought of these gruesome punishments. "Why did you agree to talk with me?" I asked.

"It is good to inform people about what is Sharia law. Maybe they will convert."

"Why did you become a judge?" I asked.

Amanullah had family in Gardez, the capital of neighboring Paktiya Province. American forces had killed two of his cousins, he said, and wounded his aunt. "They were innocent," he said, and this pushed him to join the Taliban. While his friends "do military operations" for the Taliban, he preferred other ways to help his people.

"Are you angry about the death of your relatives?" I asked.

"It makes not only me angry, it makes the whole nation angry," he said. US forces had bombed a village where family and friends lived, killing thirteen people even though the Taliban had abandoned the place. Taking advantage of the growing resentment against foreign forces "is how the Taliban is taking back the country."

More Afghans were dying at the hands of the Taliban than at the hands of foreign forces, I said. "So why are people not angry at the Taliban?" I asked.

"We are fighting for Islam," he said, as if it justified the Taliban killing of hundreds of innocent Afghans. "We don't care about the power. We want Sharia law. We don't want foreigners to kill innocent people. If they are killed, we will retaliate."

The Taliban didn't want power? I balked at that remark, because Amanullah was suggesting that the Taliban had given up its quest to retake control of the government.

"Is that the truth?" I asked.

"We don't want any ministries or care if Mullah Omar or Karzai is in power. We want peace and Sharia law. We don't want power. It is not our aim. Step by step, we will put in Sharia law," he said.

Rumors had spread in recent weeks that rifts had opened among the Taliban ranks and that local and regional commanders were rejecting the leadership of Taliban commander Mullah Omar in Quetta, Pakistan. This dissention, some suggested, was due to the toll that US Special Forces operations were taking on the Taliban with their night raids on suspected Taliban villages. The night raids had become the cornerstone of US military tactics and targeted the Taliban command structure.

"The reason we are suffering a lot," Amanullah admitted, "is because we don't have any place to stay," suggesting that the Taliban were frequently on the run.

I asked Amanullah if our meeting was part of a Taliban information offensive to seek peace instead of war.

"I came here myself. It was my own decision," he said.

"But why?" I asked.

"The way of fighting is not a good way to convert people to Islam," he said. It was not good "jihad." Amanullah was saying that the word *jihad* had been widely misused and properly meant that one could fight for Islam by living well and doing good, not just by waging war. In meeting with me, "I am committing jihad," he explained. "Guns and swords and force are for when people attack us."

"I have a message for the international community," he continued. "People in power are not [working] for the benefit of the country. They are filling their own pockets." The Afghan warlords who committed mass killings during the civil war were still in power. "There should be justice even for them in Sharia courts." Amanullah added a message for foreign forces: "Please do not kill more innocent people. They are not fighters."

Because the international community supported the current government, it was responsible for the abuses committed by the government, he said. "It is the responsibility of the international community to fix this. They put those people in power. We don't want power. We want justice. Then we will have a secure Afghanistan. Where there is justice, there is peace and security."

It was both surprising and heartening to hear this from Amanullah, and it echoed a call for justice that had been made often by human rights and civil-society activists working in Afghanistan. But was he serious? Rather than seeking a peaceful resolution to the situation in Afghanistan, the Taliban waged war. "The Taliban is making life more dangerous, not more safe, with its suicide attacks," I said.

"Why is there no security?" he asked. "[The government] has made everyone their enemy."

"Is there hope for peace in Afghanistan?" I asked.

"We are optimistic for the future," he said. "That is why we are suffering. [It is] our sacrifice for Islam."

Taliban Courts

Amanullah's assurance that average Afghans supported Taliban justice was not mere propaganda. The faltering Afghan judiciary was lambasted in a scathing report dated November 17, 2010, produced by the International Crisis Group. Titled *Reforming Afghanistan's Broken Judiciary*, the report presented the pathetic situation that gave Afghans little choice but to turn to the Taliban:

> Afghanistan's justice system is in a catastrophic state of disrepair. Despite repeated pledges over the last nine years, the majority of Afghans still have little or no access to judicial institutions. Lack of justice has destabilized the country and judicial institutions have withered to near non-existence. Many courts are inoperable and those that do function are understaffed. Insecurity, lack of proper training and low salaries have driven many judges and prosecutors from their jobs. Those who remain are highly susceptible to corruption. Indeed, there is very little that is systematic about the legal system, and there is little evidence that the Afghan government has the resources or political will to tackle the challenge. The public, consequently, has no confidence in the formal justice sector amid an atmosphere of impunity. A growing majority of Afghans have been forced to accept the rough justice of Taliban and criminal powerbrokers in areas of the country that lie beyond government control.

With this in mind, I wanted to hear from the people who had turned to the Taliban for justice. I had that opportunity during my earlier visit to the ancient city of Balkh, just about twenty miles west of Mazar-e-Sharif, when I was with Taliban sympathizer Saleh and the Afghan journalist Enayat Najafizada. Saleh had arranged for me to meet two of his friends, both of whom had recently turned to the local Taliban for justice.

We wheeled off the main road and drove down Balkh's main street, a paved road lined with shops and teahouses that lead to the town plaza, where we parked. As Saleh ran off to find his friends, we waited and watched the slow pace of life in rural Afghanistan. An occasional car passed, followed by a heavily laden donkey or two, trotting stiff-legged under their burdens. Vegetable vendors sat amid their pro-duce—bright-red tomatoes, dirt-brown potatoes, fresh radishes, white cauliflowers, and fat, long turnips—sipping tea and hailing friends. Shopkeepers sat beside their wares: teapots, brooms, and shovels. There were few buyers. I wondered how long it would be safe to wait.

Saleh suddenly reappeared, opened the door, and took my seat in the passenger side as I climbed into the backseat. The two men were nearby, he said, but were waiting and watching for any sign of trouble. I wondered why these two men would be worried, since Balkh was a Pashtun town. Such meetings were typically fraught with tension, however, as they feared repercussions from talking with a "Westerner."

Eventually one of Saleh's friends arrived, a man named Dad Mohammad. Visibly nervous, he climbed into the backseat beside me. He was thirty-three, had six children, and had turned to the Taliban to solve a land dispute with another man in his village. Dad Mohammad and his family had left his village in nearby Chimtal District more than twenty years prior and had spent sixteen years in Quetta, Pakistan. He returned two years after the Taliban regime collapsed.

"I was happy there was a new government in my country," he said, and he had hoped that he and his family could make a new start in his home village. He was quickly disappointed. His family's land, about fifty acres, now belonged to someone else. The new occupant, Alalam, had built a house on the land and was making money by farming it, quite possibly by growing poppies. "They had become rich," he said, even though "it was my land."

Dad Mohammad went to the local Balkh court. "I followed my claim to the end"—a process that took two years. Resolving the claim would cost him about $10,000 in legal fees and other costs, he was told. Since he could raise only $500, the court dismissed his claim. Dad Mohammad was convinced that the court was against him and claimed that the land occupant "had a link with people in the government." Dad Mohammad asked for a review of the case with the regional appeals court, but that court came back with the same decision. "They decided against me. It was the same with the appeals court."

With nowhere else to turn, "I then complained to the Taliban and went to the elders," Dad Mohammad said. "They had a gathering and the elders decided in favor of me." The elders prepared and signed a document that gave the land back to Dad Mohammad. Alalam and his family fled, fearing for their lives despite the backing of the Afghan courts.

Dad Mohammad felt vindicated. "Everyone is agreed. Everyone prefers the Taliban court because no one is taking a bribe and [they are] doing the right thing."

"But what about Alalam?" I asked. "He was tossed off his land."

Dad Mohammad shrugged, saying that now thirty members of his extended family lived on the land, including his six brothers and their wives and children. They raised goats and sheep.

"What else do you like about Taliban justice?" I asked.

The Taliban had stopped "all kinds of crimes," he said, including "illegal relations between men and women."

"Do you approve of cutting off limbs and stoning women to death?" I asked.

"I haven't seen such things," he said dismissively. "There is Taliban and it is secure. They control the area" and had done so for the past two years. The result was "no robbery and no crimes."

"Can't the government do the same thing?" I asked.

Dad Mohammad said no. "The people become Taliban . . . because the government is corrupt. The Taliban are in power because there is discrimination [against the Pashtuns]. I can show you that where

Pashtuns are living, there are no facilities. I can take you to those places and they don't have anything."

Saleh had raised that same complaint earlier, saying that the government was not addressing community needs on an equal basis. This inequity had alienated people like Dad Mohammad. He had returned from Pakistan years earlier, hoping to be part of what he thought would be a major turnaround for the country. It didn't happen. While he did not join the Taliban, he was deeply frustrated and turned to them for help.

"Why are so many people angry at the government?" I asked.

Rather than returning to a new and improved Afghanistan, "the situation was worse," Dad Mohammad complained. "Those who were in power before the Taliban are in power again." The former power structure, which was based on regional warlords and their ethnic-based militias, had become institutionalized. There was no equanimity. "Everything they have is for themselves, and that is not good for the people." The government officials were "looting, beating, and using their force and power."

Dad Mohammad fell silent, then asked if I had any more questions. I didn't and thanked him for his willingness to meet with me. We shook hands, and he quickly climbed out of the car. Saleh went off to find his other friend, a man named Namatullah.

Both Dad Mohammad and Saleh had complained bitterly about the Tajik administrators and commanders who were using their positions to punish the Pashtun communities in the north. Their complaints reinforced the frequent reports of Pashtun villagers who had been killed after being accused of siding with the Taliban and being enemies of the government. It was a situation that I suspected would not change soon and that only strengthened the Taliban, who routinely set up temporary roadblocks and randomly attacked the Afghan army, police, and international forces. These attacks in turn prompted retaliatory operations by Afghan and international forces, spurring violence that was spiraling out of control across the north.

Saleh soon returned and introduced his friend Namatullah, explaining that he was from a village in the explosive Char Bolak District, the site of frequent hit-and run Taliban attacks and roadblocks. When someone stole thirty-five of Namatullah's livestock, ten goats and twenty-five sheep, he first went to the local police. The theft had been at night, he said, some three months prior. The animals were grazing in desert lands in northern Char Bolak, tended by his cousin and a couple of guard dogs. Four men attacked his cousin, "then tied his hands and took the animals." His cousin was found later by other shepherds, who helped him home.

The police in Char Bolak District told Namatullah to find the thieves himself, he said, so he turned to the local Taliban. "The Taliban found [the thieves]," with the sheep and goats. The culprits were two Arab Afghans and two Pashtuns who confessed the crime to the Taliban.

"The thieves came to my house and begged me to forgive them." The Taliban and the community elders told Namatullah that the thieves had promised never to steal again and urged him to forgive them. After meeting with the thieves, Namatullah accepted their apologies.

"I was more than happy that I got my sheep back. I was happy that they were punished."

"The punishment seemed rather light," I said, "considering other punishments that the Taliban were known to give."

"I had to forgive them because I did not want to make an enemy for the future."

"Is the community safer under the Taliban control?" I asked.

"There are Taliban around. Security at night is difficult to guarantee," Namatullah said. The danger was not due to thieves but to the frequent clashes between the Taliban and Afghan forces backed by NATO troops. "The Taliban are coming out at night, and people are afraid of fights with police and government."

"Can Afghanistan ever find peace?" I asked.

"Inshallah," Namatullah said—if God is willing. "If government corruption continues, we won't have any peace. But if the government improves, then we will have peace. If there are changes in the government and the police, there will be peace." He hoped that "educated people" who aren't corrupt would take control of the government. If that happened, "then things will be fine. But now they are only making money."

Namatullah became increasingly anxious, saying he had business to finish in Balkh and wanted to return to his village. I thanked him, said good-bye, then watched as he quickly disappeared onto the Balkh streets.

As we headed back to Mazar-e-Sharif, we were stopped at a checkpoint not far outside of Balkh and directed to the side of the road. The stop was manned by local police and a half-dozen heavily armed men from the Afghan National Directorate of Security—the Afghan secret police. Directing the checkpoint was a young Afghan wearing an ivory sport coat and jeans. Saleh, who was returning with us, was dressed in traditional Afghan clothes and was clearly a Pashtun. We were ordered out of the car. It was searched thoroughly, inside and out. The checkpoint commander proceeded to rip a strip of window tinting from the inside of our car's windshield while a soldier patted me down. With his face just inches from mine, the soldier screamed, "What were you doing in Balkh? Don't you know the Taliban will tear you to pieces?"

"I'll be more careful next time," I mumbled.

The Government Judge

I later arranged to meet with a well-known Afghan judge, Qazawatpah Ziaullaq Denarkhel, head of the Provincial Appeals Court based in Mazar-e-Sharif. This was the same court to which Dad Mohammad had appealed his land-claim case that had been turned down by the lower court.

Denarkhel led me into an empty court chamber where we could talk in quiet. The chamber reminded me of a typical community courtroom in any small town in America. It had seats for about a hundred people, two large tables, one each for the defense and prosecuting attorneys, and three black leather chairs behind the judges' bench.

With graying hair and a deliberate manner, Denarkhel was calm and knowledgeable. He had practiced law in Afghanistan for forty-four years, much of that time behind the bench, beginning under the rule of former Afghan king Zahir Shah. Denarkhel fled the country during the communist regime but returned to private practice in Kabul during the mujahideen and Taliban times.

Because Denarkhel had graduated from Kabul University law school then worked in the governmental courts, the Taliban didn't trust him. The Taliban only wanted judges and jurists who followed the dictates of Sharia law. "When I was in Kabul, I was in contact with the Taliban courts," he said, but he was prevented from being a judge. So he was a defense attorney in the Taliban courts. "We were victims of the Taliban system," he said of his fellow judges. "They pushed me out of my office."

As a defense attorney, he was often frustrated. "The Taliban did not allow anyone to make a defense. They were not respecting the law and those who had the documents" to back their claims. "They would just sentence someone to hang."

When Karzai was named president, Denarkhel returned to the bench as head of the appeals court in Balkh Province, where he presided over appeal cases from five northern provinces. "Our judicial system is from Islamic Sharia law and is in accord with international law," Denarkhel explained. "When people come to us, we ask them to bring us a complaint letter" that outlines the details of their case. The accused have a month to respond; otherwise the case is set aside. Defendants then have up to one and a half years to respond to a complaint, and anytime during that period, the case could be reactivated, if the delay could be reasonably explained.

Most of the appeals court cases involved land disputes similar to Dad Mohammad's case, Denarkhel said. The Afghan courts wanted witnesses who were "neutral" and were community experts and officials, not family members on either side of an issue, who became emotional. As he explained the procedures that were followed, it all seemed quite familiar and typical of Western courts.

"So, why is Taliban justice making a comeback?" I asked.

"We can't say that Taliban justice is a system," Denarkhel replied. "They are used to making quick decisions." Most Afghans are uneducated and "want a decision quickly. That's why they like it." Taliban justice is preferred by people who are disgruntled with the civilian courts, who do not want to be bothered with collecting documents and witnesses, or who cannot afford to hire a lawyer. Quick decisions create lingering resentments, however, and are commonly reversed as soon as a new government or group of judges is in power. "They're not thinking of the future," Denarkhel said of the Taliban courts, only local popularity. Snap decisions provide "no guarantees for the future," since such decisions are not based on evidence or documents.

"The Taliban system is injustice," Denarkhel complained. "We don't allow stoning of someone. Taliban justice is cruel. Their judicial system is according to Sharia law. The difference is, we will find out what their case is about" before rendering a decision.

Denarkhel fell silent and looked at me, seemingly lost in thought. He had been dispensing justice for more than four decades. His somber gaze told me he was not one to agonize over the miscarriages of justice that were happening across the country on a daily basis. He provided an alternative to brutal Taliban justice, and if people wanted his alternative, it was available. Denarkhel's eyes refocused, and he asked if I had any more questions. I didn't. We rose and said our goodbyes, then I watched him shuffle across the courtyard in the waning light of the late afternoon.

The Afghan judicial system's justice did seem agonizingly slow. Taliban justice was brutal yet swift. Little did I know that there were other more immediate dangers than miscarriages of justice, some just around the corner from where I lived. When the mullah of a mosque not far from my house was arrested for hiding packages of highly dangerous explosives, I went there.

6

THE MULLAH IS A TERRORIST

THE BOMBS WERE WRAPPED in plastic and scrawled with Arabic words that spelled death for anyone who might be near the explosions.

"It means, 'This will send people to hell,'" said Lutfullah Mashal, the loquacious spokesman for the Afghan National Directorate of Security. It was late March 2011, and we sat in Mashal's office discussing the twenty-four packages of explosives found in a small mosque in the sprawling, mud-walled District 4 neighborhood in Kabul. The discovery sent shockwaves through the community, leaving local elders aghast and outraged that they had unwittingly been part of a terrorist network.

The bombs had been found in a large tin box, buried under the carpet-covered dirt floor in the one-room domicile of a young mullah who managed the nondescript Omar Farooq Mosque. Mullah Abdul Rahman was in his twenties and had been guiding the daily prayers and the study of the Koran and teaching local children to read and write. He was arrested in an evening raid.

"It was a network," Mashal continued. "The mullah was not a suicide bomber" but provided a safe house for the explosives, which were part of an underground system in which bombs and suicide bombers were moved into the city separately. When the orders came, explosives

were collected from secret locations, sewn into vests, then put on suicide bombers—sometimes young people convinced by their handlers
that they were ridding the world of a terrible evil while guaranteeing
themselves a place in heaven.

In the past, terrorist networks had used private houses of sympathizers to hide their bombs and the people who carried them. But "we
have an eye on all real estate businesses now," Mashal said, "and we
know which houses belong to whom. The Taliban has changed tactics.
Instead of using houses, they now use mosques. This was the first time
we saw they had used a mosque."

The arrest led Afghan security agents to another mosque, the al-
Haji Algul Mosque in the Pul-e-Charkhi neighborhood, an impoverished area on the far eastern side of Kabul known for Afghanistan's
sprawling prison complex, industrial warehouses, and military posts.
The al-Haji Algul Mosque "was used to keep suicide attackers," Mashal
said, while the "bombs were kept close to sites that would be attacked.
They'd bring suicide attackers into the city." Mullah Rahman downplayed his role in the network, insisting that "he was only responsible
for keeping the bombs." On occasion, Mashal said, Rahman would get
a call and then ride his bicycle to the al-Haji Algul Mosque, where he
would apparently contact the terrorist network's operatives.

Security officials were convinced that the terrorist underground
was devised by the infamous Haqqani network, a particularly ruthless and radical militia aligned with the Taliban and headed by the
famed mujahideen commander Maulvi Jalaluddin Haqqani and of late
by his son Sirajuddin Haqqani. The organization was said to be based
in North Waziristan, Pakistan, with links to other terrorist groups and
Pakistan's intelligence agency. Haqqani had been heavily supported by
the CIA against the Russian occupation of the 1980s.

The Haqqani network's signature was exceptionally vicious attacks
that grabbed global attention due to their appallingly high civilian
casualties. Events attributed to Haqqani included the January 14,
2008, assault on the luxury Serena Hotel in Kabul; repeated assassination attempts on the life of President Karzai; a devastating July 7, 2008,

bombing of the Indian embassy in Kabul; the November 10, 2008, kidnapping of *New York Times* reporter David Rhode, who escaped after a year of captivity; the December 30, 2009, attack on Camp Chapman in which CIA agents were killed; and the February 19, 2011, attack on the Kabul Bank in Jalalabad.

Due to Jalaluddin Haqqani's reported ill health, his son Sirajuddin was thought to be making the major decisions. He was considered more radical than his father. "It was his idea to use the mosques" to hide their explosives, Mashal said of Sirajuddin. "The son is the real person [behind the network] and is the son of [Jalaluddin's] Arab wife." Sirajuddin's Arab ties have provided links to terrorist networks in the Middle East, Mashal said. As much as 80 percent of all antigovernment attacks in Afghanistan may have involved the Haqqani network.

From North Waziristan, the Haqqani network had reportedly moved across northern Afghanistan and established ties with the north's patchwork of angry ethnic Pashtun communities, providing weapons, fighters, and suicide bombers for operations. The network was blamed for an attack in northern Kunduz Province that had killed the notorious Afghan police officer General Daud Daud, who once controlled the dangerous Spin Boldak border region between southern Kandahar Province and Pakistan.

"We [learned of] him through sources on the [Pakistan] border areas," Mashal confided about Mullah Rahman, where Afghan security personnel had followed the influx of weapons, materiel, and terrorists into the country. The discovery of these bombs in the modest mud-brick neighborhood of Kabul gave security agents hope that a network had been disrupted.

That Rahman was a mullah presented problems. Because three out of four Afghans were illiterate, a mullah's ability to read and write and then recite and interpret the Koran made him a key member of the community. The arrest of mullahs suspected of antigovernment activity had sparked violent protests in other communities, so this time security agents quietly informed the community leader, or *wakil*, about the pending arrest. "When we make an arrest, we do not inform the police, because [we fear] a leak," Mashal said. This case was an exception. "We informed the community because the [suspect] was a mullah." The *wakil* then contacted the neighborhood elders and asked them to be present when the mullah was confronted. They agreed, yet were incredulous that their young, unassuming Hazara mullah could be a terrorist.

When security agents and the elders knocked on Rahman's door, he was surprised at who confronted him. The accusations were made, and he was shown a picture of the van that had delivered the bombs to the door of his mosque. "In this mosque he had a room," Mashal said. "He had dug a big hole under the carpet, [where] he had all of these explosives. In front of the elders, he pulled back the carpet and . . . there were explosives. When the elders saw this, they started to beat him and shouted, 'Our children came to you! You are not to do this!'"

Once in custody, Rahman led agents to the al-Haji Algul Mosque east of Kabul, the safe house for young suicide bombers. As agents entered the front door of the mosque, three escaped out the back, but one was captured. Under interrogation, the boy revealed how the Haqqani network and the Taliban took uneducated boys from rural regions, indoctrinated them, and turned them into suicide bombers.

"These young boys are deceived, misled. It is not the Islam way," Mashal said.

Words of the *Wakil*

At the age of fifty-eight, Abdul Manan was a lean man with a neatly trimmed white beard. A former police commander, he had retired nearly eighteen years earlier. He was coping with wounds that he suffered in the line of duty. With the use of just one hand, he operated a neighborhood real estate office in addition to his work as the community leader. As the *wakil*, Manan led the delegation of elders at the neighborhood mosque where Mullah Rahman was arrested with his stockpile of explosives.

"This guy was a student in another mosque," Manan said as we talked in the cool darkness of his dingy office one sunny afternoon in late March, several weeks after Rahman was arrested. Manan recalled that the young mullah had asked for a chance to teach at the local mosque and to lead prayers. Since Rahman seemed quite calm and studious, the local elders agreed. In retrospect, Manan said, he should have been more suspicious, since Rahman came from Gorband District in Parwan Province, which was just north of Kabul and known for fierce antigovernment and pro-Taliban activity. Only after Rahman's arrest did Manan learn that Rahman's father had been a Taliban member. He also suspected that Rahman was much older than the twenty-three years he had claimed to be.

During the five years that Rahman was at the mosque, he sparked no suspicions that he was radical. "He was not talking about politics," Manan said. "He was a quiet guy" and usually retired to his room after he finished leading the community prayers five times a day. Many evenings he would travel to the Haji Yaqoob Mosque in downtown Kabul, where he attended a well-known madrassa to deepen his knowledge of Islam. The city mosque was not known to harbor radicals. "His behavior was good with people," Manan said. "He was young and not thinking like an older person. He was teaching little kids using basic religious books. He taught the Arabic alphabet."

One afternoon in early March, security agents had come to Manan's office, asking him to join them in a security truck. They showed him a list of names. One was Abdul Rahman. Manan nodded that yes, he knew the man, explaining that Rahman was the mullah at one of the neighborhood's six small mosques. "Someone is saying he has bombs," the police said, then pointed to a man sitting in the backseat of the truck who was hooded and handcuffed. Manan and the agents then went to the mosque, hoping to find Rahman, but he was gone. The police agreed to return after evening prayers.

Prayers finished about 6 PM. Manan asked the elders, about twenty in all, to stay in the mosque afterward. Moments later, security agents entered the compound with the informant. The group confronted

Mullah Rahman and pulled the hood off the informant. He identified Rahman. "When Mullah Rahman saw [the man], he admitted what he had done, that he had bombs. The elders would have killed him if the [agents] were not there," Manan said, with a shake of his head. "All were very angry. Some were crying. They trusted him for five years. [The bombs] would kill innocent people."

Manan still struggled with the realization that Rahman was not the quiet, unassuming character that he had presented to the world. He learned later that Rahman had a hand in an earlier suicide bombing in Kabul that had killed Manan's cousin. "If I had known that, I would have killed him myself," he said.

Manan was exasperated about the frequency of the suicide bombings in Kabul and across Afghanistan that were tearing the society apart. Now such a bombing could have happened in his own neighborhood. "Nobody likes these attacks," he said. "They are killing the people of this country." Manan leaned back in his chair and stared out at the busy boulevard that fronted his small office. His biggest fear was that the government would go easy on Rahman and let him out of prison. "If [Rahman] gets out, then [other] mullahs are going to be doing this. People think that if these other suicide bombers are not punished . . . this will happen again. People in Islamic countries trust their mullahs more than anyone. All people will trust him, so [the Taliban] use it. It's very bad. It's against Islam. [A mosque] is the Prophet's place. It's for prayer and religion, not for bombs and explosions," Manan said.

Finding Mullah Rahman

The Pul-e-Charkhi federal prison sat on an expanse of parched earth east of Kabul. Dust swirled under a relentless sun as my translator, Noorullah, and I trekked from the distant parking place toward the looming prison. We passed through several checkpoints, one that required us to empty our pockets of money and cell phones and another that guarded a gaping, gravel trench that encircled the sprawling prison. At one checkpoint, a gray-uniformed guard informed me in English that this was not a prison but a guesthouse. He grinned and shrugged, implying that prisoners here were treated far too well. This was our second attempt to find Mullah Rahman, our first having ended when prison officials couldn't decide which of the 124 men named Abdul Rahman who were incarcerated was the prisoner we wanted to meet.

Rahman was being held in a section of the prison known as Block 4, a relatively new structure of painted concrete walls, blue metal doors, and thick steel bars. As we waited for Rahman to be retrieved from his cell, Noorullah explained the manifesto painted on the wall that proclaimed prisoners' rights.

When Rahman arrived, I was not at all surprised to find that he was the mild, unassuming character that Manan had described. He wore a white cap and neatly pressed light-blue *shalwar-chamise*, the traditional flowing Afghan clothes. He gently shook my hand and nodded as we sat on a couch in the block commander's office. With the distinctly oriental appearance of his Hazara ethnicity and a wispy beard that he stroked as he talked, Rahman was not the figure of a terrorist.

Rahman confirmed that he was from Gorband District and said he had attended school there until the ninth grade, when he moved to Kabul to attend a high school, hoping that later he could attend an engineering institute. But when his father fell ill just three months into the school year, he dropped out and returned home. As the eldest son, he had an obligation to take care of his family. He had always been devout and liked religious studies, so his neighbors urged him to take over duties at the local mosque. Needing a job, he had readily accepted the position. He soon relished the routine and respect the position garnered in the community. Rahman said he later learned that a neighborhood in Kabul needed a mullah. He took the position because it afforded him the opportunity to continue both of his passions: his studies and his religious duties.

"Was the madrassa in Kabul where you became radicalized?" I asked.

"I was not in a class with radicals," he said, with a shake of his head.

Rahman admitted that he had kept the explosives in his room at the mosque, but his story of how they got there and were discovered differed widely from what Mashal had told me. Rahman said he didn't really know what was in the heavy sack that had been dropped off at the mosque by a friend from the madrassa. His friend told him it was a sack of books. Rahman was busy doing something else when the "books" were delivered. "I was too tired to look at the sack." But later when his friend was long gone and Rahman moved the sack, "it was heavier than fourteen books." He looked inside and saw the plastic-wrapped packages of explosives but didn't know what to do. "If I [had known] they were bombs and not books, I would have reported them. People know how good I was there. You can ask the people in the neighborhood what they thought of me."

"Didn't you suspect something was very wrong?" I asked.

Rahman nodded, saying that he "knew that it was something dangerous," and claimed he kept the sack outside of his room, not in it, and left it hidden until the day of his arrest.

"If you knew the packages were dangerous," I asked, "why didn't you call your friend who dropped off the sack?"

Rahman shrugged, saying that the man's name was Fazal Malik and he did call him, but Malik's phone was always turned off. "I was intentionally set up." Rahman had kept with his story throughout his extensive interrogation by national security agents, whom he accused of torture. "They kept asking me who the guy was. I said, 'No, I was not involved.'" Rahman eventually signed a confession but now recanted it. "I didn't know what I was signing. They made me sign things that I had not said. When they read these things in court, I had not said them."

Although Rahman's version of events was doubtful, his insistence that he was innocent was not surprising, despite the fact that he had been caught with enough explosives to have demolished much of his neighborhood and everyone who lived there. During my years as a newspaper reporter, I'd had occasional conversations with prison inmates, all of whom insisted on their innocence. They claimed they were framed, were at the wrong place at the wrong time, or were victims of zealous prosecutors who put them behind bars on trumped-up charges. Rahman was no different.

The day of his arrest was much like many previous days at the mosque, Rahman explained. He had conducted his daily classes in Islam for the neighborhood children, about eighty boys in the morning and more than a hundred girls at midday.

"It was late afternoon," he recalled, when he was first visited by Afghan government agents, who had said they wanted to talk to him about the city's plans to spread gravel on the narrow dirt lanes that defined the neighborhood. Rahman asked them to come back later, since it was time for the evening prayers. When the agents suddenly asked him what he was hiding in the mosque, "I was shocked. I figured something was wrong."

Rahman said he dutifully conducted the evening prayers and waited for the agents to return. When they did, he was arrested. The fact that he didn't run proved his innocence, he said. "If I knew I was a suspect, I would have escaped. But I didn't know anything about [the explosives]."

But he had checked the sack, I reminded Rahman, and he had suspicions, and then had called Malik about it.

"If I knew [Malik] was a radical," he said, "I would have checked the bag" when it was first delivered.

"Were you or your family threatened by Malik or anyone else and forced to take the bag?" I asked.

Rahman said no. "On one hand, I thought [the packages] would not be dangerous. Why would my friend bring them? I didn't call the police because I thought it was not dangerous. I was just waiting for my friend to come back," to collect the sack.

Malik never returned, and instead, Afghan security agents showed up. Now Rahman was serving a twelve-year sentence. "Are you bitter now that you're in jail?" I asked.

"Maybe God wants this. Maybe God is punishing me."

"Why would God do that?" I asked.

"Because I lost my mind. . . . I didn't check the bag [of explosives] and do something about it."

"If you could relive the past, would you do anything differently?" I asked.

"I would have checked those things at first, given them back [to Malik], and asked, 'Why are you giving me these things?'"

"What about your future?" I asked.

"I am sad," he said, because he was unable to take care of his family. "I'm always worried about my family. I am the eldest. Who is feeding them?" He also missed his fiancée, whom he still intended to marry once he was released.

Rahman said that life in prison was "hard," not because it was dangerous, but because he was confined. "It's like being in a cage." He then told me a story about a boy who asked his father why a bird in a cage would sing. The boy's father explained that the bird was not singing but rather was crying for its freedom. "I hope every day that I'll be free," Rahman said. His family had hired a lawyer and his case was being appealed. "It has given me some hope."

I reminded Rahman that the members of the terrorist network that had given him the explosives and the suicide bombers that would carry them were still prepared to kill again. "Does that bother you?" I asked.

He nodded. "It worries me, of course. It brings insecurity and war."

"Do you support suicide bombings?" I asked.

Rahman sighed and said that he had "no higher knowledge" of the goodness or evil of such acts but personally believed that "it is not a good way to kill some people. Who are they killing? They are killing the people of our own nation."

Religion and Suicide Bombers

Religion, I had been taught, was supposed to be a civilizing influence on society. It was meant to check worldly thoughts, passions, and desires, redirecting the mind and spirit toward something higher, more noble, fine, and holy, perhaps even closer to God. Yet here was Mullah Rahman, a humble, soft-spoken and modest man, stroking his wispy beard and proclaiming his innocence even as he was arrested with twenty-four packets of highly potent explosives. He had claimed he was a bystander waiting for the packages to be taken from his humble mosque and used in missions that could take hundreds of lives in grotesque and bloody explosions.

My Afghan friends and acquaintances were disgusted as suicide bombers conducted frequent attacks in all corners of the country. This was not Islam, they said. The people of Afghanistan often seemed more horrified than the outside world as to what was happening to them and around them. Yet here was Rahman, a man deeply embedded into the social fabric of Afghanistan, who had been a part of the terrorist underground, the Taliban, and their ilk. Because Rahman had been an integral member of Afghan society, I began to sense that perhaps the Taliban and their tactics were not as alien as was so often suggested by officials and the news media, but was a part of the Afghan psyche.

Religion was the fabric that held together Afghan society as the gale force winds of war had swept across Afghanistan for a millennium, toppling governments like tumbleweeds. Over the centuries, tradition based on tribe and clan merged with religious devotion and gave order to a senseless world. Mullahs were the knots that tied society and religion together and, as a result, had become a perfect weapon in a deadly war waged by extremists against the Western "occupiers" and their supporters. Religion had become a mechanism of destruction.

One of the most shocking examples of religion turned riotous took place in the northern Afghan city of Mazar-e-Sharif on Friday, April 1, 2011. Rage had roiled across the Muslim world in the wake of the burning of a Koran by the Gainesville, Florida, pastor Terry Jones, who had conducted what he called a "mock trial" of Islam. He held a match to a Koran as some thirty church members looked on. Ten days later, three angry mullahs in Mazar's majestic Blue Mosque delivered impassioned diatribes against Jones, the West, and Afghanistan's foreign invaders. They urged the crowd of young devotees to avenge the desecration of Islam's holy book. Hundreds of men streamed out of the mosque, some carrying signs that read DOWN WITH AMERICA and DEATH TO OBAMA.

The mob first went to newly built US consulate offices. Realizing that the building was unoccupied, the horde reversed direction, stormed across town, and attacked the United Nations compound. It was a drawn-out assault, and online video shows frightened and overwhelmed Afghan police firing aimlessly into the air, hoping to chase the protesters away. Their shots had no effect on the protestors, who overpowered the UN's armed Nepalese guards, who were reportedly under orders not to shoot to kill. The mob killed the UN guards with their own weapons, then spread throughout the compound, where they found a handful of UN workers in their offices. In the end, at least twelve people were dead, including five Afghans and seven United Nations workers—four Nepalese guards and three Europeans, one each from Romania, Sweden, and Norway. At least one victim had her throat cut.

Balkh provincial governor Atta Mohammad Noor said the Taliban had infiltrated the mob, provoking the violence and distributing weapons. In the days following the attack, twenty-seven suspects were arrested, some of whom were said to be from Kandahar and other provinces under Taliban control. While the anti-American protest against Koran burning may have been hijacked by extremists, rumors of government complicity with the religious leaders who had instigated the ordeal swirled in the wake of the killings.

In mid-August 2011, I traveled back to Mazar-e-Sharif. Months had passed since the killings at the United Nations compound, but the connection between the mosque and the vicious deaths had left a tangible fear in the air of this once-peaceful city. For many of the locals and for the international community, Mazar-e-Sharif had changed forever.

The religious community in Mazar-e-Sharif was controlled by the local ulema council, the presiding body of mullahs. I took the opportunity to visit the home of Mawlawi Abdul Raouf Tawana, the secretary of the council. Tawana lived in one of the city's concrete-block apartment buildings that had been built by the Soviets. As in most Afghan cities, these sturdy but aging buildings housed the upper-middle- and professional-class families. The day was sunny and warm, and the apartment complex seemed nearly abandoned and void of life, as most of the men were away at work and children were at school.

We were greeted outside by Tawana's young son and slipped past rickety bicycles clustered in the bottom stairwell. The boy led us up two flights of dusty concrete stairs to the door of a spacious apartment. As was customary, we left our shoes in the hallway, and we were shown into a room crowded with couches covered with white linens. Tawana was tall, with a neatly trimmed beard and the gracious demeanor of a cleric. He apologized that he could not offer me tea and sweets since it was the middle of the holy month of Ramadan.

I thanked Tawana for meeting with me and told him truthfully that I'd had plenty of tea already that day. I explained that I wanted his thoughts on the tragic deaths of the UN workers of the months past, now that emotions had seemingly cooled. Specifically, I was curious about the role and responsibility that the mosque had in the events of that day as well as the deteriorating situation across northern Afghanistan.

"We were always saying that security would worsen, but no one was listening," Tawana said about the rising tide of violence across the north. He blamed the violence on the disinterest of the political powers in addressing people's problems. Growing frustration had devolved into anger, yet nothing was being done to alleviate it. "We're not looking at the root causes of these problems," he said. In such a situation, a small incident can spark a firestorm.

"Why did UN workers, who were only trying to help, have to die?" I asked.

The attack on the UN compound was due to instigators who "infiltrated into the demonstration," Tawana said. "We had hundreds of [protests] before, and without problems. We condemn the killing of people—not only us, but the religion. Even I am not happy about the killing of any animal, let alone a human being. If religions will condemn violence, then it will lessen. We are happy to contribute to peace."

If extremists had hijacked the protest, "Was that a metaphor for Islam as a whole?" I asked. "Had extremists taken over Islam?"

"Extremists are everywhere and in every religion," Tawana said. The purpose of the tragedy in Mazar-e-Sharif was to protest not only the burning of a Koran by an American pastor but also the fact that he was not punished. "If someone in our country insulted the holy book of the Christians, he would be sentenced to hang."

I doubted that an Afghan would ever be hung for insulting the Bible but understood that Tawana was expressing his and his countrymen's frustration that Pastor Jones had not been punished. In fact, Jones had been severely criticized by members of the American military establishment, who knew that Jones's behavior put the lives of American soldiers, as well as civilian aid workers, at risk by fanning the flames of anti-American sentiment. At the core, it was an issue of free speech and freedom of religion, but I didn't want to go into that. For most Afghans, like those living in many other Muslim countries, religion was part and parcel of public and governmental life. It was similar to arguments pushed by Christian conservatives in the United States that religion should be integral to public life and policy.

While Tawana wanted Jones punished, he professed religious tolerance and understanding. "I'm a Muslim and I'm aware of other religions," he said, and defended Islam against critics such as Jones, who said that Islam was a religion of violence, saying, "There has not been a good explanation of Islam." Tawana lamented that Islam and Christianity were at odds. "I'm very sad about the situation in the world. We all believe in one God. Now [we] have turned to killing each other."

"Was religious conflict due to extremists?" I asked.

"All religions need to fight extremists. The Muslims need to stand against the Muslims who present Islam as an extremist religion. If such disputes [between religions] continue, it means the end of the world.

We're not in favor of killing any Americans or Germans or anyone," Tawana said.

However, Afghans were frustrated and angry with the international community, Tawana conceded. "We would like them to leave this country. Living in [an occupied country] is like being in a prison." Afghanistan was suffering, Tawana said. When people asked what the problem was with Afghanistan, it was like a doctor asking a dying patient where the pain was. "It is better to ask where the pain is not," he said.

When the international forces first arrived, Tawana said, "People thought they'd get their freedom. People had the expectation that life would become better." Instead, they had less freedom, since political power was concentrated in the hands of the same few who controlled government before the Taliban. "The international community is supporting the warlords despite their violations of human rights. They have not introduced democracy in a real way to the people."

"It's all a lie," Tawana said of claims that Afghanistan had progressed. "Only certain people have a better life. The rest of the country is in bad condition. Nothing is being done to help people. Afghanistan is staying in a dark condition. Afghanistan needs a new system."

Democracy as it had been presented in Afghanistan might not be the best form of government there because the lives of most Afghans had not improved under it, Tawana said. Yet the international community supported former commanders even though they "don't know one word about democracy." These same power brokers "keep the international community in the dark. Democracy is good, but it needs to be done in a right way."

This situation had created pent-up anger against the international community. Events like the rampage in early April happened because "[People] can't get their voices heard." Despite the anger that erupted, people still harbored positive feelings for the United States. "They supported the mujahideen. We will never forget it."

Given the growing danger in the north and the deadly attack against the UN compound, those good feelings seemed like scant compensation, I thought.

Tawana apologized, saying he had to end the interview due to his bad back. He could sit no longer. It had been a rambling discussion. I had hoped Tawana would condemn terrorism and those who used it to kill innocent people, but he had given me a mild refutation, saying only that he and his fellow Muslims condemned killing. He explained that after the Taliban were flushed from the north, many Afghans tried to start over. But ten years on, the shouts of joy had faded to murmurs and outright anger. Afghans had wanted to believe but felt deceived. Extremists now built networks, and people like Mullah Rahman were helping. Afghans were again dying as suicide bombers detonated themselves with anti-infidel chants on their lips.

I decided to look for some of these suicide bombers. I did not have to go far.

7

CONFESSIONS OF A
SUICIDE BOMBER

———————

THE STORIES WERE DISTURBING and unimaginable. Children were brought by their fathers to mullahs in Afghanistan and Pakistan, desperate for their sons get an education, a chance at a life other than herding sheep and goats, hauling water from a nearby stream, and living life in the rugged foothills. Instead of getting an education, these boys would be convinced that strapping on a suicide vest was the surest way to salvation.

When I was talking with Lutfullah Mashal, the spokesman for the Afghan security directorate who told me of the capture of Mullah Rahman, he digressed at one point. He mentioned a boy who was captured in the same operation and then groomed to be a suicide bomber. The Taliban thought that young boys might easily slip past security guards while wearing vests loaded with the deadly explosives like those that Rahman had hidden. "This boy went to Peshawar [Pakistan] and sold five goats to raise the 4,000 rupees [$45] to spend so he could spend a year in a madrassa," Mashal said.

It all started after the boy, with the blessing of his father, entered a madrassa in North Waziristan, the lawless region in northwest Pakistan that borders Afghanistan and was in the grip of the Haqqani network and other radical elements. The boy was singled out by the mullahs for a special assignment. "[The mullahs] brainwash their targets," Mashal explained. Some of the boys who were targeted were either mentally slower than the rest or exceptionally gullible. "All suicide attackers are . . . naive people. They know only *kafirs* [nonbelievers] and Islam," he said.

The selected boys were paid the equivalent of about one dollar per month to attend a special madrassa. They read selected writings designed to convince them that all *kafirs* should be killed and were repeatedly told they had been chosen for special assignments. They were shown films in which young boys dressed as women were raped and brutalized by others dressed as US soldiers. "It's a bogus film," Mashal said. Some of the films also showed American soldiers kicking and stomping on the Koran. The boys were shown bombed-out buildings and told that these were mosques destroyed by American forces. The goal was simple: "to make the minds of the suicide [bombers] ready for this," Mashal said.

Some of these would-be suicide bombers had been captured before they could act and had provided security agents with details of their training. "They used to give us tablets," one boy told Mashal, indicating that they were drugged. "Then every word that came out of the teacher's mouth was good. It inspired us."

The boys were told that "Kabul has become a hell." The mullahs would ask for volunteers to stamp out the evil, saying, "Who will help us?" When everyone in the class stood, the mullah picked the targeted boy, who assumed he had been selected for the honor above all the others. The boy was told he was guaranteed a place in paradise.

During the training, the boys were told, "Just click it"—meaning the detonator. "You will turn into light and will not be torn to pieces." The boys also learned to use small arms, such as pistols and AK-47s.

The training complete, the young suicide bombers were sent to Quetta, home of the Taliban ruling council and Taliban leader Mullah Omar, Mashal said, where they were assigned suicide missions in Afghanistan. The young boy captured when Mullah Rahman led authorities to the al-Haji Algul Mosque had been brought to Kabul for such a mission, he said.

Some of the boys were so completely brainwashed that they didn't believe anyone outside of the Taliban were Muslims. This particular boy refused to speak until his Afghan interrogator convinced the boy that he was also a Muslim by taking him to the small mosque at the security directorate offices, where they both prayed. At that point, Mashal explained, the boy said, "Bring me a cup of tea" and proceeded to tell agents his story.

In Search of an Uncle

The Afghan juvenile prison was a complex of buildings on gently sloping land in a neighborhood on the north side of Kabul. High stone walls surrounded the prison. On a quiet Saturday in late spring 2011, I met inside the prison walls with three young boys who had been captured by Afghan security forces as they crossed the border from Pakistan into Afghanistan.

The boys were alone and acted lost, which is what drew the attention of the border police. They were immediately arrested, accused of being suicide bombers, and taken to this prison. As we spoke in the dim light and quiet confines of a counselor's office, the boys painted a portrait of the ruthless and depraved fanaticism that drove the Taliban, the Haqqani network, and others to use innocent children like cannon fodder in their terrorist war on the West.

Fazal Rahman was nine years old. He faced me as he sat on the edge of a bed. His head was shaved, giving him the look of a prisoner, and he wore a *shalwar-chamise* made of coarse brown cloth. As we talked, he distractedly looked around the room, picked at the cloth, and fidgeted like any nervous nine-year-old would. Yes, he said, he had been captured by security forces at the border, but he said he really didn't know why. He was not a suicide bomber, he said, and knew nothing about that. He had left a village called Khairabad in Pakistan and headed for his uncle's house in Kabul, traveling with three other boys his age.

The boys had been given a bus ticket that took them to the Afghan border crossing at Torkham, about fifty kilometers from the sprawling Pakistan city of Peshawar. When they climbed down from the bus and crossed into Afghanistan, they looked for the bus that would take them to Kabul. Instead of getting on that bus, the boys were taken into custody.

"We were told to confess that we were suicide bombers or we would be killed," Rahman said. "We were offered 10,000 Afghani [$200] to confess and were told we would be allowed to go home. I am not a suicide bomber."

I had been warned that it was common practice for the Taliban to instruct young boys and anyone else taken into police custody to deny any knowledge of or involvement with terrorist activities and to claim they had been beaten into giving confessions. The boy had done just that, saying, "We were beaten at the checkpoint, and my friends were cursed."

As we continued to talk, however, Rahman's answers revealed that he may have been part of an underground network such as Mashal had described, in which young boys, all potential suicide bombers, were funneled into Kabul. He supposedly was asked by an uncle, whose name he did not know, to work in a Kabul factory that made solar panels. Rahman said he hoped to make some money and that was the only reason he came. He was Afghan and explained that his family originally was from Logar Province, just south of Kabul. How he had gotten from Logar to Pakistan was unclear.

"Did you call this uncle so he could bail you out?" I asked.

Rahman fidgeted for a minute, glancing around the room. His eyes watered and tears dripped down his cheeks. I felt sorry for the kid, stuck in a prison in Kabul, far from what family and friends he may have had, with little hope of ever going back. "I want to go home," he sobbed.

Two of Rahman's companions, Mohammad Niaz, eight, and his friend Mohammad Yunise, nine, came into the counselor's office after Rahman left wiping his tears on his sleeve. Niaz explained that they all had lived in the same neighborhood back in Pakistan, and each was offered $200 to travel to Kabul to work at the mysterious uncle's factory.

"Who was this uncle that you were supposed to meet?" I asked.

It was the uncle of a friend, he said.

"Did you travel with your parents' permission?"

Niaz said no, that no one knew they had left. "The mullah told us he would inform our families," he said.

"The whole trip was arranged by a mullah?" I asked.

Niaz nodded and said that others from the village had made a similar trip, never to be heard from again. "I didn't understand [why] the mullah would lie, but [I] didn't know this uncle." They had been given some money and a telephone number that they were supposed to use to find the "uncle" when they arrived in Kabul.

Niaz's friend Yunise explained that he had a mother and a father who was much older than his mother. "He's going to die," Yunise said, which may have explained why he agreed to go on this trip, expecting to help provide for his mother. The mullah in their community selected them specifically for the trip, he said, saying that the boys were being given a good opportunity to work. "We thought we would get some money. The mullah said no one would arrest us. No one is going to do anything."

Yunise and his friends never expected to end up in a Kabul prison. Like Rahman, he and Niaz wanted to go home. "If they tell us we can go, we will go by foot," he said, all the way back to Pakistan.

"Have you been able to contact your mother?" I asked.

Yunise shook his head, no. "No one knows where we are," he said. "The mullah told us not to tell our families and that he would tell them. I didn't know anything would happen."

"Do you have contact information for the uncle?" I asked.

Mohammad nodded and recited two numbers. Neither number worked when they tried to call, he said.

"Were you betrayed?" I asked.

Yunise nodded again. "The mullah is now arrested by the village people," he said, along with another person from Logar Province who was said to be a member of the Taliban. Both were in prison, he said.

"Why did the villagers arrest the mullah?" I asked.

Girls and boys were being taught in the local mosque, Yunise explained. "The mullah was touching the girls."

"Do you want revenge on the mullah for what has happened to you?"

Again he nodded. "Once we go there [the villagers] will throw him off the hill."

While the boys' stories were rather cryptic, they shed light on a world in which fanatics felt justified in taking the lives of young and innocent people for their own warped ends. These boys were uneducated, except for a couple of years each had spent in grade school. They could barely read or write, let alone construct and explain a detailed chronology of their short lives. But what had emerged was the outline of the terrorist network.

The three boys were from Logar Province, a place under the sway of the Taliban and the Haqqani network, and the land of antigovernment violence. Boys who had lost one or both parents, or for other reasons largely lived on the streets, were gathered in the local mosques and then sent to madrassas in Pakistan that were run by radical mullahs. Oblivious to what was happening, these children were then fed into a pipeline that took them to mosques in the Kabul area for nefarious purposes. If they had not been apprehended, they would have spent some five more years separated from their families and under intense indoctrination, at which point these eight- and nine-year-old boys would be in their midteens and have become prime candidates to carry out suicide bombings. How many others were out there who had not been caught? I wondered.

Mohammad's Story

While the details of the three boys' lives were elusive, those of another would-be suicide bomber in the prison were crystal clear. Noor Mohammad was fourteen years old and had been born and raised in a village of Bata in Andar District, a dry and rocky region south of

Ghazni, the capital of Ghazni Province in south-central Afghanistan. He had completed the sixth grade, but his education abruptly ended at the age of twelve when the Taliban shuttered his school, saying that since it was funded by the government, it was evil.

Having lost his mother several years earlier, Mohammad stayed at home and read the Koran, the only piece of reading material to be had. He began visiting the local mosque, which was run by a mullah who was also an active member of the Taliban and carried a walkie-talkie and an AK-47. The mullah told Mohammad to make himself useful to the Taliban by hanging around the police station. He was to keep an eye on the police and report back to him. If the police questioned him, Mohammad was to explain that he couldn't study because the Taliban had closed the school. Mohammad complied, but soon found that he had become entangled in a web of lies and deceit that nearly cost him his life.

After loitering around the local police station, the police suspected Mohammad of trying to steal weapons from them and took him into custody. A day later, a group of Taliban went to Mohammad's father and told him that he had to get his son out of police custody and keep the boy at home. His father went to the police station with three local elders, who pleaded for the son's release. The police refused, saying that Mohammad had to spend another three nights in jail. Only then could his father take him, on the condition that Mohammad was sent back to school.

Mohammad's homecoming was short-lived. The Taliban showed up the next day and accused him of working for the government and being a spy—an accusation that was punishable by beheading. This reversal by the local Taliban raised suspicions that he had been set up, since it was not the first time the family had run afoul of the Taliban.

Mohammad's older brother was beheaded by the Taliban after he too was accused of being a spy. His brother had been involved in a bitter family feud, the full details of which Mohammad did not reveal, except to say that his older brother had gotten into an argument with his aunt. The aunt had turned to the local Taliban after accusing

Mohammad's older brother of being a government spy. His brother was taken by the Taliban, who told his father that they were only going to hold him for a couple of days. The next day Mohammad's older brother was found beheaded.

Faced with the same accusation as his dead brother, Mohammad was taken by the Taliban to a makeshift prison in a house near the village and kept for more than two weeks with several other prisoners. He was unsure at first as to where he was, since he had been blindfolded. When his eyes were uncovered, he was told to stay near the house and not go to the village bazaar. When his detention ended, Mohammad was allowed to return home.

Sometime afterward, a wedding was held in the neighborhood. Mohammad said he was hanging around the fringes of the party when he was grabbed by a guard and accused of stealing two telephones and some money. The footprints of the thief's shoes apparently matched Mohammad's, his accuser charged, although Mohammad denied that he had taken either the phones or the money. The tread pattern of the footprints, in fact, did not match his shoes, Mohammad said, only the size of his sandal. The host of the wedding party was furious, and soon several Taliban showed up. They listened to the accusations, then took Mohammad into custody.

"They beat me and that night took me to another village," Mohammad said. The wedding party host asked for an immediate Taliban judgment, which was readily granted. "They slapped me," Mohammad said, and shouted, "Do you know what is going to happen? You will lose a hand or leg." The Taliban let him think about it for a while, then made him an offer. "Will you do something for us if we ask you?"

Mohammad was quick to agree, thinking that anything was better than amputation. "It's OK, I can do it," he said, without asking what he would have to do.

The Taliban members warned him, "If you don't do this, we will arrest you again" and carry out the punishment. They then told him he was to attack the nearby camp of a US Army Provincial Reconstruction Team, military units that issued contracts for local road and building projects, as a suicide bomber. Mohammad's mind raced. Even loaded down with explosives, he figured he might still have a chance to escape a deadly fate.

"They trained me how to use a gun," he said, and how to detonate an explosives-laden vest. He was shown that all he had to do was to touch the red wire to the green wire. For days he trained with a vest loaded down with weights that simulated the weight of the explosives that he would carry. Mohammad was told to kill as many people as possible with his gun before detonating his suicide vest.

"I knew I would die," Mohammad said, "but I was afraid of losing a hand or leg. But even so, I knew I would not do it."

When the Taliban felt he was ready, they put the vest on Mohammad and he climbed onto the back of a motorcycle. He was taken to a village near the military camp and told to walk the rest of the way. Mohammad watched as the Taliban motorcyclist drove away, then went to the nearest tree and sat down in the shade. "I took off the vest and left it under the tree. I then walked to the PRT." He told the Afghans who guarded the gate that he had been captured by the Taliban but wanted to turn himself and his gun in.

The Afghan guards didn't know what to do with Mohammad, fearing it was some sort of Taliban trick. "The [guards] were afraid of me," he said, and they told him to sleep outside the gate of the PRT until the next morning. Mohammad climbed atop a truck and spent the night.

The next morning, US soldiers came out of the gate and questioned him. Mohammad told his story and soldiers listened. Deciding that Mohammad could be useful, they later took him on a night raid to guide them to the Taliban houses and prison in the nearby village. The soldiers searched homes, where they found weapons and improvised bombs. The raid erupted into a firefight that killed two Taliban and chased several others out of the village.

The dead Taliban were stripped of their papers, which provided the US soldiers with intelligence for future missions. The raid had been a success thanks to Mohammad, and he was praised for his work and cooperation. He was given a tent in which he could stay and told he could earn a salary of $200 per month if he wanted to keep working with the soldiers.

Several days later, however, Mohammad was taken to the Ghazni governor's office. Feeling sympathy for the fourteen-year-old and knowing that his life was in danger if he stayed in the province, the governor gave Mohammad some money and sent him to the juvenile prison in Kabul.

While Mohammad was grateful to be alive, he told me that he was puzzled as to why he was kept in the juvenile prison.

"I was not arrested, so why am I here? I surrendered," Mohammad said.

"Have you tried to contact your father or family?" I asked.

Mohammad said no. "I don't know what happened to my brothers and father," he said, adding that he felt abandoned. He did not want to stay in the prison but had nowhere else to go. "I cannot ever go back to Ghazni. Two Taliban were killed because of me. I don't know what I will do."

Terrorism and the Mullah

The mosque in the Wazir Akbar Khan neighborhood of Kabul sat along one of the city's main roads. It was surrounded by a stone and wrought-iron fence, and as worshippers passed through the gates, they encountered a handful of shoeshine boys and women crouched under blue burkas, hands outstretched and begging for baksheesh, or gifts. The mosque was one of many in the city, and in late August 2011, near the end of Ramadan, I sat on a bench outside it, under a sagging canvas tarp strung by ropes to provide shade from the relentless sun that had baked the city for the past couple of months.

There was a frenzy of activity as the late afternoon call to prayers was about to end. Worshippers scurried in, kicking off their shoes at the edge of a carpeted platform, then slipped into the mosque's darkened interior to join the ritual standing, bowing, and touching of the forehead to the ground. The voice of a mullah blared from loudspeakers, proclaiming *"Allah Akbar"*—God is great. At one corner of the carpeted porch, a legless man in a dingy white robe and turban sat alone, bowing as the others did, having removed his two prosthetic limbs and rested them against the platform just behind him.

I was there to see the mosque's top mullah, a man named Mohammad Ayaz Niazi, who doubled as a professor of Sharia law at Kabul University. He was one of Kabul's most outspoken critics of suicide bombers, and he railed during his Friday sermons against the tragic loss of life that these bombings had inflicted on Afghan society. Such acts were against Islam, he insisted, because they took the life not only of the bomber but also of many innocent people. Niazi was a voice in the wilderness, one of the few mullahs in Kabul, I had been told, who was willing to go public against this vicious tactic of the Taliban.

I waited until the short prayer service ended, and watched as dozens of men drifted out. Moments later Niazi appeared, trailed by a half-dozen others, each of whom had urgent questions, the answers to which he dispensed readily. He was of average height, wore a vest over his *shalwar-chamise*, sported a trimmed dark beard, and had a neatly tied turban on his head. He apologized for the short delay, saying that many people had questions. We settled into hastily arranged folding chairs in a small, dimly lighted, and sparsely furnished office with a tile floor that was adjacent to the mosque. As we spoke, Niazi's assistant busied himself at a nearby desk.

Suicide bombings had become a favorite tactic for the Taliban and other groups, I explained, but had become a major problem for many Afghans. Now young boys were being groomed to be suicide bombers, some of whom I had recently interviewed. "What can you tell me about suicide bombers and the practice of using young boys for that purpose?" I asked.

As my colleague Noorullah translated my words, Niazi's eyes grew wide at the mention of *intahari*, the Dari word for "suicide bomber." Niazi waved his hand and shook his head. "If it puts my security at risk, I don't want to talk about it."

I sat back, stunned, wondering what had happened. But it was obvious. He had been threatened. The Taliban had gotten to him, warning him to shut up about suicide bombers or he would be next. The threats had worked. I understood why. As I waited during the prayers, I had seen the flow of people in and out of the mosque from one of Kabul's busiest streets. Anyone could walk in off the street, loaded down with explosives under their loose, blousy clothes, and no one would notice until it was too late. There had been police attending the prayer service, but they were not there for security. They were traffic cops who stepped away from their posts on the street to pay their respects to God.

Afghan mosques had been attacked by suicide bombers to great effect. In October 2010, the governor of the northern Kunduz Province was killed in a mosque by a suicide bomber who took the lives of some fifteen people. In mid-July 2011, a suicide bomber struck at a mosque in Kandahar, killing four people, including a senior cleric, during a prayer service for Ahmad Wali Karzai, the murdered brother of President Karzai. The suicide bomber hid the explosives in his turban. Then in December 2011, a bomber struck a Shiite mosque in Kabul, killing nearly sixty people, including men, women, and children.

When I asked Niazi to explain why he would not talk about suicide bombers, he weakly offered that he wasn't interested in politics.

As another of the mosque's mullahs shouted prayers over the speakers, I tried to provoke Niazi into a response. "Do you agree, then, when people say that Islam was a religion of violence?" I asked.

Niazi grew animated, waving a finger in disagreement. "When someone says that Islam is the religion of violence . . . it is an unfair judgment. It should be investigated as to why [a Muslim] is violent. Islam is a religion of brotherhood. If someone is ready to kill himself, what is the reason?" he said.

Niazi's response was neither a condemnation of violence in the name of Islam nor an endorsement. Rather, it was an effort to deflect attention from the destruction caused by suicide bombers and the loose logic behind them and to focus on the apparent cause of the attacks. The reason people were driven to such drastic measures must first be understood, he said, before the virtue, or lack of it, surrounding the act could be discussed.

"Have you changed your mind about the violence that you once condemned?" I asked.

"All humans are brothers," Niazi replied. "They all came from one God. Our religion does not allow violence at all. People who come to violence, people should find out why."

"What was the justification for taking innocent lives?" I asked.

All people needed to be treated equally, Niazi explained, and all living creatures deserved respect. "Fairness in Islam is worldwide. If I do a bad thing to you, Islam will punish me," he said. "Fairness is [for] all living things, including animals. If you hurt an animal, you will be punished." Afghanistan and the Muslim world needed to be treated fairly by the rest of the world, Niazi complained. Inequality hurt everyone, not just the victims, he said. "We are all in the same ship. If there is a hole in the ship, we will all go down."

Islam, especially in Afghanistan, was not respected by the foreign community, Niazi implied—neither its people and sovereignty nor its religion and culture. A violent response to this lack of respect was then apparently justified.

"We should respect each other's culture," Niazi said. "It is not allowed for other religions to say bad things about Islam. We all trust Allah. Humans shouldn't worship other humans." The International Declaration of Human Rights "puts all humans on the same level. We should have the right to have a government according our culture. Democracy should not be imposed on all countries. I don't have the right to go to America and tell them their government is wrong."

"I want security in the world," Niazi continued. To reach that goal, "All the insurgents should be invited to a table and we should talk. Then we will see who is the source of tyranny. Everyone should stand against tyranny. If we do that, then all the world will live together as brothers."

The people Niazi suggested were the perpetrators of tyranny were the forty or so countries that had a presence in the country and had for a decade. Consequently, the blame for Afghanistan's condition, as well as continued violence and suicide bombings, fell on the international community. But the world was not at war with Afghanistan. It was at war with the Taliban and its supporters. The foreign community had propped up the Afghan government with all its faults and failings and trained and paid for its military and police to keep peace and order. That was tyranny? It certainly was not the kind of tyranny that had been described to me by the Afghans who were threatened and intimidated by the Taliban and who routinely murdered and maimed anyone they suspected of not supporting their cause.

We clearly had two different definitions of tyranny. Niazi's comments, however, made it painfully obvious that the work of the international community had failed if one of Afghanistan's leading clerics, one of its most outspoken critics of violence, and also one of the country's leading scholars of Islamic law was now calling the international community a bunch of tyrants.

"The world has misused the situation in Afghanistan," Niazi said.

"If Afghanistan does not have security or a stable government, how can it progress?" I asked.

"Bringing peace and security is easy, [if] one wants to find the cause of the war. We first need security, then we can have an economy. Those countries [in Afghanistan] only think of themselves and don't try to find the cause of violence."

There were two causes of violence in Afghanistan, Niazi explained, one being external and the other internal. The internal struggle was between the Afghan ethnic groups that largely pitted the Pashtun Taliban against the government, which was controlled by northern Tajiks, Hazaras, and Uzbeks. "The sides are not allowed to talk to each other," Niazi charged, the implication being that the foreign community was somehow preventing peace. As Niazi spoke, I recalled that the United States had frequently tried to initiate peace talks with the Taliban, yet was being resisted by the Afghans themselves. But I also wondered why the Taliban needed to negotiate at all. They could wait until the international community left.

The other cause of Afghan violence was external and due to meddling by its neighbors, Iran and Pakistan, and the presence of the international community, Niazi said. "They don't think about [what is good for] Afghanistan," Niazi said. "Afghans think that because there is no peace and security, they can't have a good education and a good economy." This caused deep resentment among Afghans, and they expressed that frustration with violence.

I left Niazi and his mosque empty-handed. He was the second ranking mullah I'd met who said killing was against Islam and that Islam was not the religion of violence. But neither would condemn the acts of suicide bombers in Afghanistan or those who used it as a tactic of terror. The reasons behind the act need to be understood, they said, but then what? While Afghans and internationals alike shuddered at the viciousness of such attacks, some Afghans seemed to harbor a morbid sympathy for the attackers. It was not sympathy for the Taliban itself but for their tenacious resistance to the foreign invaders.

But I suspected there was more to the bombings in Afghanistan than a deeply rooted antipathy for the "foreign invaders." There was an internal war going on that pitted Afghans against Afghans, and overtly it had little do with the Western world, although the Western world was being blamed. Evidence of this war erupted in the eastern Afghanistan city of Jalalabad, and I went there to look a little closer at its roots.

8

THE JALALABAD VIDEO WAR

I HUNKERED DOWN ON THE THIN, worn carpet of the Melat
Music shop in Jalalabad, Afghanistan's major city on the eastern
border with Pakistan, surrounded by shelves of audiocassettes and
digital videodiscs. Steam spiraled from a small glass of sugary green
tea poured by the shop's owner, Abdul Ghani. He waved his hands
and railed against the "motherfuckers" who were making the video-
shop business one of the most dangerous in eastern Afghanistan, akin
to war itself. Unknown men had been blowing up the video shops
in Jalalabad for the past eight months, and Ghani didn't know how
long he and the other shop owners could hold out. He'd been in the
business for nine years and was respected by his fellow shop owners,
enough so that they had elected him head of their association.

Ghani glanced at a piece of paper on which he'd scribbled copious
notes. Of the fifteen video shops that had been bombed, about half of
the owners had left the business completely. The rest had diversified
or sold other things, mostly cell phones and other small electronics.
Several had been injured and one child had been killed. The bombs
normally exploded under the cover of darkness, around 9 or 10 PM or
just before dawn at about 5 or 6 AM. A few bombs had been tossed into
the shops during the day, destroying everything and injuring everyone
nearby.

"I don't have any movies that are against our culture," Ghani said, exasperation contorting his face. He gestured to the glass-door cabinets that covered one wall where DVDs of Bollywood musical dramas, Hollywood action movies, and Pakistani films filled the shelves. "Afghani people like action," he explained, and as any shop owner would, he gave his customers what they wanted. The appeal of action movies was understandable. It was what most people lived. The profit margins were thin, he said, since he sold a DVD or music tape for as little as sixty cents. But business was brisk.

The videos were pirated, of course, and dubbed into the Pashto language, most having been made in the Pashtun regions of western Pakistan, a wide swath of territory that stretched from the city of Quetta in the south to Peshawar in the north and included the deadly northwest tribal areas. In addition, audiocassette tapes in brightly colored boxes were stacked to the ceiling all around me and were largely by Pashto singers. The cassettes shared similar origins outside of Afghanistan, having been recorded in Pakistan or as far away as the United States and Europe.

Ghani's family had fled Afghanistan during the civil war of the early 1990s, and he attended high school in Pakistan, where he picked up fluency in English. But he gave up his schooling when he returned to Jalalabad, where video shops were banned under the Taliban regime, so he had made bricks for a living. He had opened his video shop not long after the Taliban fell. "It is an easy business for me. The production is someone else's problem."

But the business had turned deadly. The bombings had everyone on edge. "Many people were injured. Those [shop owners] are scared. Most don't want to be in the [business]. Most people [are] scared to tell the truth" and won't go public about the threats they have received. But Ghani wasn't afraid to speak the truth. "I don't care. I don't care if I die because of this interview."

Despite his bravado, Ghani was clearly anxious. His shop, not far from the gnarled and chaotic core of Jalalabad, was among many narrow one-room shops that fronted a crowded road. Each night the shop owners rolled down their garage-like doors and padlocked them shut. The thin, corrugated metal, however, was scant protection against the explosives that ripped apart the shops and their contents, rattling shops nearby. The collateral damage put yet more pressure on video-shop owners, since neighboring shopkeepers didn't want to suffer due to video stores selling controversial products. Because of all of this, so as not to attract unwanted attention, we sat behind the counter, hidden from public view.

Not long after we'd begun to talk, we were joined by Khalil Rahman, thirty-three, a video-store shopkeeper whose shop had been bombed just two weeks earlier. He was still visibly shaken from the attack, which had demolished his shop. As he sat with us on the floor and a fresh cup of tea was poured, he gingerly touched his lower leg, which was still wrapped in gauze and covered with large, dark scabs.

Rahman had been in his shop in another part of town watching a small television and sipping tea when he heard a strange noise, a thump, as if something had fallen. He turned toward it, and then the bomb went off, knocking him from his stool. He was lacerated with flying glass, he said. Stunned and bleeding, he was taken to the hospital, where he spent three days and nights. He escaped serious injury but lost most everything in his shop.

"I was scared because I was hurt," he said with an ashen face. "I am scared now, even when I'm at my house."

He had no idea who had tossed the bomb, which made the attack all the more unnerving. It could have been a customer, or someone who had visited the shop earlier and planted the bomb while he was looking away. It meant that his shop had been watched, that someone had planned the event, plotted how to get the bomb in quickly and quietly, and how to detonate it. It was organized by people capable of making such bombs. It was terrorism, plain and simple.

There had been no prior threats. Rahman had heard of other video shopkeepers who had received notorious "night letters," but he had received none himself. These night letters were hand-scrawled warnings nailed at night to the doors of girls' schools, businesses, or other places of activity that the Taliban and their sympathizers thought went against their notions of Afghan culture and Islam.

In the aftermath, Rahman had begun to repair his shop, but he doubted that he would stay in the video- and music-sales business. It was just too dangerous, and he was not sure he would survive another blast. He offered a fearful shrug. "If I didn't have a family, I wouldn't be in this business," he said. He gazed at me, his eyes filled with fear. "Maybe I'll sell electronics."

"Did the Taliban do it?" I asked.

Ghani answered no, the Taliban had been contacted, and although the Taliban frequently took responsibility for such attacks, the Taliban spokesman had said they were not behind the bombings.

"Some religious people think that these movies will destroy the culture," he said, "but it is those people who are destroying the culture themselves. They give guns to children rather than pens."

"What do your customers say about these attacks?" I asked.

Ghani grinned. "They say that I am the only brave person here," he said. "People are angry and say they'll support me. But still, there is nothing they can do about it." The reality was that Afghans were being denied the right to enjoy entertainment that was neither evil nor diluted their culture, he said. "I like Michael Jackson and Jennifer Lopez. [Michael Jackson] was the best singer and dancer in the world. I know his songs by heart, and I first heard them eleven years ago. Music is something that everyone can enjoy."

If the attackers succeed in shuttering all of the video shops, the customers would still buy videos and music, he said. "They will bring [videos] here from Pakistan and Kabul." This made the bombings all the more absurd, he said, and the resulting death and destruction meaningless. The attempts to close the video and music shops reminded Ghani of life under the Taliban, when no video shops were allowed. It was a suffocating existence. "We couldn't get oxygen without permission from the Taliban."

Likewise, movies were not evil, Ghani argued, growing increasingly animated. The late US president Ronald Reagan was an actor, and action star Arnold Schwarzenegger was the governor of California. They were not evil people, he said. Movies expanded people's knowledge of the world, and that was important. "There is no life without education."

"What are the police doing about the bombings?" I asked.

Ghani had gone to the police, but they'd told him, "Be careful with your shop."

"That is not reassuring," I said.

Ghani said there were only twenty-two policemen for his section of the city, and they were too few in number to provide any protection, since the attacks were random and unpredictable. "It's not enough," he said of the police force, which itself had been attacked. "They cannot protect themselves, so how can they protect us? They can't control this area."

"Do the police know who is attacking the shops?" I asked.

Ghani started shouting. "I don't know who these people are. The Taliban say they're not doing it. So I cannot blame anyone. There are some foreign people who are interfering in Afghanistan," he said, suggesting that it could be members of Hezb-e-Islami, the fundamentalist militia lead by Gulbuddin Hekmatyar, who had been operating in the region for years and who seemed to be gathering strength. Hekmatyar had been linked to other antigovernment forces, including the Haqqani network, which reportedly had ties to al-Qaeda.

Ghani was willing to limit his inventory if someone would tell him what the attackers considered good and not good. "I'll bring [the movies] they want. Just tell me. I have to have movies that people demand," he said, so he could stay in business. He would never sell pornography, he said, because "everyone is against pornography."

The attacks on the video shops were another facet of Afghanistan's ongoing war, Ghani said, and he feared that the war would never end. "People are tired of war. But some people don't want it to end, because they are making money off of it."

Ghani paused, drained of words. Our tea had grown cold and our tiny teapots were empty. I stood and surveyed his shop. He too was converting his merchandise to mobile phones, desperate to stay in business since he had eleven family members to support. He followed me into the stark light of day and gave me a bear hug before I climbed into my car. It had been an emotional hour.

The Jalalabad Bank Massacre

We drove through the clogged heart of Jalalabad, our car lurching through the traffic as grizzled, turbaned men perched on the concrete median strip like birds of prey, gazing into our car, their faces close enough to touch. We approached the charred hulk of the Kabul Bank building, the scene of one of the most horrific attacks ever perpetrated by antigovernment forces.

It took place on Saturday, February 19, 2011, just before noon, when government workers, off-duty soldiers, and police filled the bank to collect their pay. Seven men wearing police garb had walked into the bank fifteen minutes before noon. Two explosions, one inside and one outside, launched the massacre. The first to fall were bank tellers and customers close at hand. Ten minutes later, two more bombs exploded inside the building, thought to have been hand grenades flung as the attackers ran throughout the bank, blasting anyone they saw. Word of the attack spread quickly, and soon Afghan police and international forces arrived at the scene, beginning what would be a long and intense firefight. Pinned inside the building and in the upper floors, the attackers were put on the defensive, allowing nearly twenty of the injured to be pulled from the bank's ground floor by rescuers.

The attack was captured quite clearly on the bank's color surveillance cameras and later was broadcast repeatedly on national television and posted on the Internet. One of the attackers, a man dressed in the drab gray of an Afghan police uniform, casually walked around the bank randomly shooting people at point-blank range with his AK-47. His victims crumpled and writhed on the floor, some dying immediately. The killer moved methodically as people cringed and cowered, women bunched in corners under blue burkas, with nowhere to hide from the shooter's bullets.

As emergency personnel treated the wounded, one of the suicide attackers was thought to have pulled on pieces of bloodied clothing and lay sprawled among the wounded. Rescuers dutifully carried the man to an ambulance, where he detonated his explosives-laden vest amidst the medics and soldiers, killing more than a dozen and injuring many more, including the provincial police chief and the head of the Nangarhar national police. Meanwhile, the shooting at the bank continued until nearly 5 PM as the attackers barricaded themselves in the upper floors.

According to reports, the final death toll included twelve police, four Afghan soldiers, two national security operatives, and seventeen civilians, many of whom were off-duty military. Five of the seven attackers were killed, and one was captured. The seventh was gone, apparently the one who blew himself up. A total of ninety-two people were injured.

After interrogation by the police, the sole remaining attacker confessed that he was from North Waziristan and was part of the Haqqani network. He had come to Jalalabad with the others, who were given a week's worth of training for the attack. They had been housed in the compound of an antigovernment clan in a nearby district and had been given guns and explosives. Afghan national security officers raided the compound the day after the attack, arresting the owner and confiscating the vehicle thought to have taken the attackers to the bank.

Clean Thoughts

The offices of the provincial department of information and culture were in another section of Jalalabad. It was there that I found Aurang Samim, head of the agency that was supposed to regulate the area's video stores. I had been told Samim was a deeply devout man. This was confirmed when just moments after we were seated in his spacious, couch-lined office, Samim rose from behind his desk and excused himself, saying he had to pray. He spread his rug on the floor nearby and went through his routine of bowing, kneeling, and touching his forehead to the ground.

This public display of devotion was no longer the jarring contrast to Western habits that it had once been for me. Religion played a very visible role in Afghan society, unlike the West's common practice of silent prayer and the acceptance that one's relationship with God, the cosmos, or whatever, was a mostly a personal matter. Prayer here was a public event, as was the display of one's commitment to Islam. Beards were grown full and long as a sign of this, as was the bruise one acquired from pressing the forehead to one's prayer rug.

Samim finished, folded his prayer rug, and quickly settled into his high-backed chair after adjusting his wool *pakule* cap. "I want to tell you the truth of this matter. I feel very badly about the shops because they distribute Afghan [songs and film]. We [need] them. But what should they sell to the people?"

I felt like answering that the shops should be able to sell whatever they want. But this was Afghanistan and he was not going to agree. I shrugged.

Samim smiled, nodded, and answered his own question. "The shops should work with the media and introduce Afghan culture to people, and international culture to Afghanistan." He made it seem so logical and benign, a reciprocal relationship between Afghanistan and the world. "But how?" he asked. "The person with these shops should be ensuring that people are having clean thoughts." But they were not, Samim indicated with a shake of his head. Instead, video shop owners "are making shops that are unlawful. CDs come from other countries illegally, especially Pakistan and Iran."

"What is in these movies that is so bad?" I asked.

"Movies are destroying the young generation's thoughts," he said. "They destroy our young generation. Insurgents are using this." By selling and promoting Western music and movies, video-shop owners were playing into the hands of insurgent forces who used them as examples of how corrupted the Afghan government had become since it was controlled by the decadent West, he said. The existence of video shops, the insurgents were saying, was yet another reason why the government, to say nothing of the Western world in general, needed to be destroyed. "Insurgents think [it] is the policy of the government to have the shops open. But the policy is not this."

For the video-shop violence to end, the shop owners needed to have their inventories approved by the government, which would weed out the bad influences. "They need to have the movies go through customs and pay taxes," he said. "These videos should come through the ministry so they don't destroy the young generation." Samim laced his fingers together and nodded again. "That is why they are destroying the shops." It was all part of a larger war against the government and the West, he said, and the war was killing and maiming more than just the video-shop owners. "They're just killing people with suicide bombings."

"So who are these people?" I asked.

"The insurgents are the Taliban," he said calmly, ". . . or whoever is against the government."

I shot him a puzzled look. "Are these people locals or outsiders who are bringing jihad to Afghanistan?" I asked.

Samim shrugged. "People who are in this society are against these movies. Our society is different. In our Afghan society, it is impossible to have these things."

"But what about satellite TV and radio?" I asked.

It was easy to find "objectionable things" via satellite, he agreed, but broadcasters were at least licensed by the government, unlike the proliferating video and music shops. "The best way is to sell only videos that aren't against Islam or the culture, things they're proud of. Then they'll be safe."

"It is just that simple?" I asked.

"The shopkeepers should have good and beautiful [movies and music] for people, or are they selling them only for money? Money is not important. They should have pride in their lives." Foreign movies and music were ruining Afghan culture and values, he explained, and the shop owners were immoral for selling these products. If the video-store owners wouldn't police themselves, they would face more of the wrath that they'd already tasted.

Samim offered himself and his agency to the video-store owners, saying he could help save their lives. "If they want to do this legally, I can help."

But what Samim offered was neither a solution nor protection. He wanted to step in and do what the bombers wanted the shop owners to do: get rid of Western and non-Islamic movies and music. Samim disliked Western culture as much as anyone but would never say that. In reality, there was little difference between those who bombed the shops and people like Samim who stood on the sidelines and watched, their arms crossed, brows furrowed.

"Do you think the shop owners would agree to censorship of their merchandise?" I asked.

Probably not, he said, and again smiled. "Behind these shops are the hands of some powerful people," he said, implying that the attacks may not have been ideological but spurred by business interests wanting to control the lucrative video trade. "No one can tell them anything," Samim said, but he refused to elaborate, which only roused my suspicions further.

"Can't the police do more to help?" I asked.

Samim was doubtful. "The police have their responsibilities. I haven't talked to them." But the police were trying to help, he said, and would "go to shops and explain to [shop owners] that they needed a license." But the shop owners routinely ignored such requests. This clearly was a major problem for Samim, who waved his hand and blurted, "Everything here is illegal. Even the media," then glared at me.

Frustrated at the chaos that surrounded him, he sat glumly clenching his jaw. Yes, sinister forces were bombing the video shops, waging a slow and deadly war against innocent shopkeepers who some believed were the enemies of Afghanistan. If Samim knew the truth, he wouldn't say. Most likely, he didn't know and didn't want to know. Regardless, he was unable to stop it. His was a country of chaos, a country at war for thirty-some years that was crumbling apart. For many people such as Samim, refuge could be found in the past, Afghanistan's ancient culture that had changed little in the past thousand years. They could cling to religion like a life buoy in a perfect storm. But the onslaught of modern culture was relentless, a tsunami of images and ideas washing over the country. The holy warriors fought back the only way they knew how, a bomb here, a bomb there. If innocent people died, it was a sacrifice for the betterment of society.

I stepped from the quiet darkness of Samim's office into thin sunlight filtering through high clouds. It was spring 2011, and the warmth in the air held the promise of a new year, something that would outlast all of this, all of us. I glanced overhead to the soft buzz of a small plane. It was a drone prowling the skies, one of America's airborne robots, mechanical agents of war. My stomach sank. Was I that close to the front? But in this war, there were no front lines. The fighting, the death, the destruction was random and it was everywhere. It was next door and it was far away. It was yesterday and it was today and would be tomorrow.

The Jalalabad video war was just another battle in a bigger war that had no foreseeable end. I stared at the mechanical raptor droning lazily overhead, looking for prey, guided by its strangely downturned tail and sniffing the air with its rounded nose. Would it suddenly spit out some howling piece of weaponry? The drone disappeared. I headed for my hotel.

Sugarcane and Gravestones

Early the next morning, I waved weakly at the uniformed guesthouse guards who squatted under a covering of corrugated tin and behind the low barrier of green woven plastic sandbags. They poured tea from a steaming kettle and sat in the same positions where I'd seen them the night before.

The paved road to Kabul held a stream of cars and the elaborately painted cargo trucks that rolled out of Pakistan carrying the materiel necessary for the international armies that fought in Afghanistan. The trucks groaned and swayed, fringed with decorative chains dangling and jingling as they prowled the long and winding road to Kabul.

Outside of Jalalabad, houses hugged the banks of the meandering Kabul River as it spread across a wide valley that was just now greening. The south-facing mud walls of the houses were plastered with drying cow dung that was peeled off, then put in large plastic bags and stacked along the road to be sold and burned for cooking fuel. It was a necessity for the Kuchi nomads, the largely ethnic Pashtuns who camped not far from the road in their low and sweeping tents spread on the rocky slopes that rose steadily to the distant White Mountains. These nomads lived as they had for centuries, if not thousands of years, following the seasons that greened then faded from the Afghan land. Only lately had the Kuchi nomads begun to give up their ways, reluctantly taking up residency in abandoned and crumbling structures of rock and dried mud that they roofed with thatch gleaned from the riverine swamps.

At the intersection of the road north to Laghman, Kunar, and Badakhshan Provinces, more shops lined the highway, each selling pink plastic bags bulging with peeled and cut sugarcane called *mai shaker*. We chewed the pulpy chunks of cane, savoring the sweet juices and spitting out the fiber as we rolled past tethered camels and donkey carts that hugged the shoulder, piled high with bundles of river reeds and ripe white cauliflower heads.

At a detour, we dropped off the road and around a bridge under repair, where burka-covered women crouched in the choking fine dust, holding babies as they reached with henna-decorated hands to passing cars and trucks, begging for baksheesh. We slowly plowed through the powdery ruts where a young girl with black hair dusted white and wearing a colorful dress that barely covered her bare feet held out her hand. I gave her an Afghani note, which she took and then turned away. In the distance, boys batted a volleyball over a nonexistent net.

The graveyards came often along the road and were marked with headstones of flat, jagged slate and green flags fluttering in the harsh wind, a proclamation that here lies a martyr. Pickup trucks loaded with heavily armed men sped past, their heads wrapped in black-and-white scarves and clutching their Kalashnikovs. Some were paramilitary and some were security details for privateers who plied the highways between Kabul and Peshawar. There were camouflaged and open Humvees provided by the US forces to the Afghan military, who mounted them with .50-caliber machine guns. They were parked sporadically along the road, barrels pointed to the steep granite hills of the narrow canyons that hid Taliban fighters.

We were waved aside at a checkpoint manned by a cluster of Afghan National Army soldiers and backed by some French troops, then told to pass since the soldiers were preoccupied with a car of Pashtun men, each with a dark turban and bushy beard. We rounded a sharp curve in the narrowing river canyon, stopping at yet another checkpoint, this one with soldiers in bright-green berets, waving new weapons. They questioned each car: Where are you going? Where are you from? I said I was a journalist. They nodded and waved us on.

As we drew near to the dam at Sorobi, the rocky canyon walls became impossibly steep, providing excellent cover for Taliban attackers who routinely blasted the fuel tankers that crawled up the rising roadway. Once hit, the tankers became fireballs, spewing blackened smoke and melting the asphalt, jamming traffic for miles. Charred and rusted hulks from past attacks lay at the roadside like rotting carcasses, reminders of the menacing presence in the rocks above.

At a curving tunnel, a boy stood in the middle of the road waving a flattened plastic bottle, signaling cars in both directions to be careful of the trucks that clogged and hogged the road. The dam at Sorobi was a harbinger of civilization. Behind the dam, the river was again wide and meandering through a desertscape interrupted by an occasional billboard showing grinning faces of ecstatic cell phone users.

We swerved around an accident where some twenty people had gathered in the middle of the highway, a small Corolla having collided head-on with a behemoth cargo truck. There was no blood and no bodies, only agony and dismay on their faces.

We followed a bus called Allah Motor Coach up the winding canyon and finally cruised into Kabul, where we were pulled aside yet again for a security check. Fifteen minutes later, after our car was searched, our backseat removed and replaced, we entered the city. A cluster of boys ran across the road, collecting soda cans from piles of garbage, their heads shaved and their clothes little more than rags. They were overseen by President Hamid Karzai, who stared down at them from a billboard, his head turbaned, his beard trimmed, and his eyes smiling.

The trip back to Kabul had put some distance between me and Jalalabad, but the words, sounds, and images of the quiet war there knotted my stomach. Ghani's fear and outrage were disturbing. The video of the bank massacre was as haunting as it had been horrifying to watch. Samim's attitude had been that the shopkeepers got what they deserved. Where would it all end? I wondered. But there was yet another war going on that made this one seem mild, and it was in the southern province of Helmand, the heartland of the poppy belt and one of the country's opium capitals. I headed there.

9

THE KILLING FIELDS
OF MARJA

IN LATE MARCH 2011, President Karzai announced that the city of Lashkar Gah, the capital of Helmand Province in Afghanistan's deadly south, would be among the first of all Afghan provincial capitals to be "secured" by the Afghan National Army and Afghan National Police. The move was meant to show that yes, indeed, the Afghan forces, trained and equipped largely by the United States, were prepared to keep their country safe and free of Taliban control. The Karzai statement preceded President Barack Obama's formal announcement that beginning in July 2011, US forces would begin a three-year withdrawal from Afghanistan, methodically handing control to the homegrown forces.

To many, the news came as a shock. Helmand was notorious as one of the most deadly provinces in all of Afghanistan for Americans. More than eight hundred US soldiers had died there, nearly half of all US fatalities. Helmand was poppy country and produced the lion's share of Afghan opium, the country's major export, accounting for an estimated 90 percent of the world's supply. This was where Afghans made their money, and it was where the Taliban fought hard to keep control, depending on opium and heroin sales to finance their war.

Helmand Province had been handed to the British forces in 2001 when Afghanistan was divided among the dozens of coalition countries that provided the soldiers who composed the International Security Assistance Force (ISAF). Besides battling the Taliban, the British were to eradicate poppy production, cutting off a key source of Taliban funding, and to convince farmers to grow wheat, a more laborious and much less lucrative crop. The effort failed miserably. The only successful drop in poppy production had come from nature, when a withering blight attacked the poppy plants during 2009 and 2010, cutting opium production in half and driving the price of heroin sky high. Helmand Province had been hard on Britain's 9,500 troops, which had suffered about 360 fatalities since 2001, with many more wounded. British forces had battled the Taliban to a stalemate.

In early February 2010, the first major operation for Obama's thirty-thousand-troop surge into Afghanistan sent a force of about seventy-five hundred coalition troops, largely US Marines, into the town of Marja, in central Helmand Province. The battle for Marja was critical for both military and political reasons. The marines, it was hoped, would turn the tide of the war before the July 2011 drawdown. The battle was an attack of overwhelming force, as each marine battalion was paired with an Afghan counterpart. The attack was widely telegraphed by then-ISAF commander US General Stanley McChrystal, who said the battle for Marja was a warm-up exercise to a much larger assault on neighboring Kandahar Province. The Kandahar attack never materialized. McChrystal would lose his command in late June 2010 following the publication of a story about him in *Rolling Stone* magazine in which he was critical of President Obama.

In mid-April 2011, I was in Lashkar Gah meeting with Helmand journalists with whom I had been working for the past six months. Marja was just thirty miles to the west of Lashkar Gah, and because few foreign journalists had set foot in Marja in the past year, I wanted to see how the surge had fared. Were Afghan forces prepared to take control of the capital city and ultimately the province?

Shortly after arriving, however, I encountered a major problem. The phones didn't work, except between the hours of 9 AM and 3 PM, just six hours every day. When I asked my Afghan colleagues at the Helmand press center about the phones, they answered with a shrug.

The Taliban apparently had destroyed a couple of telephone towers in the region, then told telephone companies to restrict phone service as they commanded or more towers would fall. The reason for the attacks was that the Taliban claimed that the telephone service was giving the coalition forces an advantage. The Taliban's nighttime telephone calls could be monitored and tracked, making them targets of night raids by Special Forces. The telephone companies readily complied with the Taliban demands, since each tower reportedly cost them $200,000.

"How long is this going to go on?" I asked.

Again my Afghan colleagues shrugged.

The implication was staggering. If the Taliban could order national telephone companies to shut down service, it meant they controlled the province. It also meant they were exerting enormous influence over the entire telecommunications network across Afghanistan.

Later that day, I sat on one of the plush couches in the spacious, air-conditioned offices of Daud Ahmadi, the spokesman for Helmand provincial governor Mohammad Mangal. I had met Mangal five months earlier during my first visit to Lashkar Gah and found him to be welcoming and friendly, which was perhaps why he was one of Karzai's most successful gubernatorial appointees. But this time Mangal was in Kabul, Ahmadi explained apologetically, trying to convince telephone companies to restore full service to the province.

"It's still unclear as to why all the telephone companies stopped their networks," Ahmadi said. "If they had a security problem, they should have told the government [here] and talked with the governor. They still haven't done it." Dressed in Western clothes and sporting a closely trimmed mustache, Ahmadi gauged me for a reaction.

"The situation is obvious," I said. "The Taliban are everywhere in the province and have threatened to blow up more relay towers."

Ahmadi disagreed. "There are rumors that the Taliban have threatened the telephone companies. They are [just] rumors." Threats had been made against telephone companies in several neighboring provinces but not in Helmand. The problem was somewhere else but not in Helmand, he said, and the telephone companies were running scared. "If it's right that the Taliban have said they will burn towers in [neighboring provinces], then it is not the responsibility of the Helmand government." If the companies had only turned to the government for help, there was no need to cut back service in Helmand, he said. That the companies had not done so spoke volumes, implying that they did not trust the government.

"If the Taliban can limit telephone service here to just six hours a day, and the government can't stop that, it means that the Taliban controls the province," I said.

"The most important thing is that the Taliban be removed from the area and that poppies be eradicated," Ahmadi said.

"That may be true," I said, "but the Taliban are still in control here."

Ahmadi became animated and accused the companies of "helping the Taliban. The government has stopped [Taliban] smuggling, yet, they're going to prove their presence. They want to show there is no peace in Helmand. The enemy is who wants to do these things."

"The fact is that the government has no control beyond the city limits," I said.

Ahmadi's eyes darted around the room and he shifted uncomfortably. "You can go to Marja now, without security," he said. "The governor can drive there himself. The Taliban is defeated in Helmand. If the telephone companies don't start their service again . . . the government is ready to turn their towers off." The telephone towers were erected on government land, he said, and under government authority. The government could shut them down. Yet "they are accepting the Taliban demands. The government is ready to cancel contracts and put them off the land and take everything down," he said. "It is unacceptable."

"Would the government really cancel telephone company contracts?" I asked.

"Governor Mangal went to Kabul to solve this issue. What if they did the same thing in Kabul?" Ahmadi asked. "The government is present in every district in Helmand. The government is going to solve their problems." The government had offered to post sentries at each of the towers, he explained, but the telephone companies refused, saying it would only attract more Taliban attacks, not prevent them.

"Why don't the telephone companies trust the government?" I asked.

Ahmadi shrugged and said that only one tower in the province had been attacked and that it was only damaged, not destroyed. Afghan police had responded quickly. A second tower had been attacked in Kandahar Province, not Helmand. "Helmand is a secure province. This is not acceptable. The Taliban can't cultivate their poppies and do their smuggling. They only want to prove the province is insecure."

Although I had been in Lashkar Gah only a short time, I knew that Ahmadi's assessment of the situation was way off-base. But I also knew that he was only doing his job. To prove his point, however, he agreed to make arrangements for me to visit Marja. In the meantime, I went to find out what others in town thought about the throttled phone service.

Talk Radio

Later that same day, I sat in the offices of Bost Radio, one of the few independent radio stations in Lashkar Gah, and talked with the station owner and manager, Abdul Salam Zahid. His station was being hit hard by the lack of phone service. The station's most popular programs were call-in shows, and the station broadcast them morning, noon, and night. These shows were popular among women, who used mobile phones to link with the outside world from their houses, where they were confined by their tradition-minded husbands. Without phone service, the radio talk shows had died and were replaced by music or religious programming.

"Today the telephone is very important for everybody. It is very important for radio," Zahid said. It was unclear as to the circumstances that resulted in the phone service cut. "Some say it was blocked because the Taliban are worried that the government is [using] information" from the companies against them. "It has not been clear about who is behind it."

Since the Taliban did not control the city of Lashkar Gah, Zahid wanted telephone companies to allow the towers in the capital city to provide service twenty-four hours a day. "If the Taliban are in Marja, they should close [service to] that area, but they should not close the city areas. The city is the responsibility of the governor. The telephone companies should not shut down the system. Everyone is using the telephone," Zahid said.

"Why is the Taliban doing this?" I asked, hoping he would say more than the obvious reason that they were fighting the government.

Zahid had heard that the Taliban were extorting money from the telephone companies to finance their war. If the situation continued indefinitely, it would severely hurt his radio station and the community. The call-in shows gave people the chance to voice their complaints on all sorts of issues, Zahid said. "Without telephones, we are not able to hear about their problems. It is a huge problem for us."

"Is there anyone who liked less phone service?" I asked, somewhat jokingly.

Zahid nodded and called one of his part-time employees into the office.

"It is good this stopped," said the employee, Ahmad Jan Khadem, who had an athletic build, a trimmed beard, and a sincere, thoughtful manner. He was a student with a young family, and he harbored strong Taliban sympathies. "People are spending a lot of money on telephones." Life was more peaceful without the phones at night, and students were studying instead of talking to their girlfriends. The cut in phone service was punishment [by the Taliban] for recent telephone rate increases. "Now they will analyze the situation about how much [money] they are losing. And the government will realize that [it is] weak now. [It] can't do anything about it," he said.

"I am a student and it is good for me," he said of limited phone service, because it saved him money and he spent more time studying. "I've experienced this before," he said of the Taliban exerting its control. "During the Taliban, they said, 'Don't grow poppies,' so [farmers] stopped. The Taliban are powerful. The Taliban are religious people. Afghanistan likes religion."

Even if people didn't like the Taliban, they kept their promises, Khadem said, unlike the government, which "doesn't keep its promises. Taliban are not like that." The government was humiliated when it announced that full telephone service would be restored and then was unable to fulfill the promise. "One hundred percent, the Taliban are stronger. If they wish, they can do what they want. In a short time, they are coming back. When the Taliban are back, foreigners will not be allowed here," Khadem said. "Religious rules will be followed by all Afghans."

"Why are you such a devotee of the Taliban?" I asked. "When the Taliban was in power, they brought little if any improvement to life in Afghanistan."

When the Taliban took over in 1996, they "were weak," Khadem explained. Over time, things slowly improved, even though the Taliban were occupied by fighting in the north in their attempt to consolidate the country. "They needed more time, about twenty years to set up," but were interrupted when the United States and its allies invaded in 2001, scattering the Taliban. If foreigners leave, it will give the Taliban a second chance. "If the Taliban comes, then all foreigners must leave, even you," he said.

"Do you dislike foreigners?" I asked.

"If we were in your country, would you like us to rule?"

Taliban and Telephones

While Khadem was a fan of the Taliban, others were not only annoyed with them—they were angry. Many in the Helmand press corps were convinced that the Taliban were extorting money from the telephone companies, and I wondered if it was true.

The Helmand-area Taliban spokesman was a man named Qari Yousaf Ahmadi, no relation to the governor's spokesman. I contacted him with the help of a couple of Helmand journalists. As I had done in Herat Province, I prepared a list of questions that were asked by my Afghan colleagues, and the conversation was recorded and transcribed.

"While the curtailed phone service may have helped the Taliban, it annoys the vast majority of people in the province," I said. "Isn't that counterproductive for the Taliban?"

"Yes," Ahmadi admitted. "They'll be upset, but they will support it. We knew that people would get upset, but we accepted that to avoid casualties of civilians." The Taliban argument was that this cut in phone service was for people's safety, all but admitting that mobile phones had been used by coalition forces to target Taliban commanders and their units. But the Taliban's public safety spin skillfully underlined Afghan anger at civilian casualties at the hands of the coalition forces.

"Some people are saying that the Taliban did this to get money from these phone networks and buy weapons. Is this right?" I asked.

"No, no. It has never happened like this so far," Ahmadi said. "Our mujahideen have enough weapons, like RPGs and AK-47s, so there is no need for other weapons that we have to buy."

It was no coincidence that Ahmadi's reference to his Taliban colleagues as mujahideen was similar to that of Sheikh, the Taliban commander in Herat, who also used that moniker for the Taliban interchangeably with the name of Afghanistan's freedom fighters.

"President Karzai and Governor Mangal say that the Taliban are weak and are finished in Helmand Province," I said.

As I expected, Ahmadi disagreed. "They are just repeating their previous words. As you and all media know, there is always action by the Taliban in this province, especially in [the districts of] Marja, Nad Ali, Kajaki, and Grishk. These are the places where every day we have one, two, or three reports of events by the Taliban."

"What do you think about the [Karzai] peace commission?" I asked. "Do you think the Taliban will join it?"

"No, never, never," Ahmadi said. "From the beginning, no one has joined them. The ones who are joining them in the name Taliban, actually they are not Taliban. It could be the tactics of the government to show the world that they have brought peace in Afghanistan, that nobody wants to support Taliban anymore, and that day-by-day the Taliban are surrendering to the government. There are no facts behind it. This war will be continued."

I pressed him on this issue. "You said Taliban were not joining the government, but we've heard that Taliban will join the government if the foreigners leave the country."

"Well, it doesn't mean joining," Ahmadi explained. "We always want foreigners out of the country. Whenever the government wants the Taliban to join it, this is the first condition. We don't want foreigners in the country."

"It means you'll join the government if the foreigners leave the country?" I asked.

"Yes, we've said that."

Expectedly, Ahmadi had denied that Taliban were extorting money from the telephone companies. Even if the Taliban were not, it still meant that the drastically curtailed phone service showed who controlled the province. It also clearly demonstrated that the Taliban fully expected to have total control in the province when foreign troops pulled out. But I wanted to know more. I headed for Marja.

The Killing Fields of Marja

The next day I was in the backseat of a dark-green Ford Ranger pickup truck along with my translator, Umar, a clean-shaven Afghan in his late twenties who carried himself with confidence. His English wasn't bad, either. Two members of the Afghan National Police sat up front as we headed south from the governor's highly protected compound in Lashkar Gah. We swerved sharply to the right and rolled across the bridge over the Helmand River and past an amusement park with a Ferris wheel that rose above the dense foliage to our right. Umar smiled and pointed to it, explaining that he and his friends had gone there for Nawroz, the Afghan New Year's Day, just a month earlier. Though the park was designed for kids, he confessed, "We were the kids that day."

We negotiated a gauntlet of butcher shops crowding the road. Freshly skinned carcasses hung from hooks in the open, their white membranes glistening in the morning light, the scent of slaughter in the air. We dodged an approaching convoy of heavily armored British vehicles, tan like the parched earth that surrounded us, each draped with protective netting and wire that made them look like rolling cages.

Moments later the expanse of Helmand Province opened around us, extending into the distant and hazy horizon. Fields of green, waist-high wheat flanked the road, each dotted with pink and white poppy flowers, reminders that until lately, these fields had grown the region's most critical crop. The wheat fields were a cosmetic tribute to the international coalition's anti-poppy campaign. While the green stalks of grain swayed in the wind, the compliance they presented betrayed what lay beyond our vision. This was early spring and the poppy harvest was in full swing, as evidenced by the fields filled with blooming flowers less than five hundred yards away.

The day before I went to Marja, a correspondent for Swiss Television, Ulrich Tilgner, had accompanied a unit of Afghan National Police on a poppy eradication mission. Tilgner told me that when he arrived to film the event, the police were in an intense firefight with Taliban fighters defending the poppy growers. The Taliban were driven sufficiently back to allow a few government tractors to roll into a large field of poppies and uproot the plants. The Taliban blasted away as the tractors raked the field with deep prongs. Tilgner continued to film.

The poppy farmers had advance notice, he said, because they had flooded the field, turning it into a bog of sticky ooze, hoping the tractors would get stuck. It didn't work. The farmer's family stood by helplessly, the women crying, the men stoically staring as an estimated $20,000 or more worth of poppies was mashed into the mud. Bullets flew. Miraculously, no one was hit. The Taliban fought so hard for the poppy farmers because, some suggested, 60 percent or more of the Taliban's money came from its control of the Afghan drug trade.

Eradication efforts had gone miserably awry. According to the United Nations' Afghanistan Opium Survey, published in October 2011, opium production in Afghanistan had actually increased from 2010 to 2011 by 7 percent. More provinces were producing opium than ever before, despite a 50 percent increase in poppy field destruction. In terms of the total weight, opium production was up 52 percent compared to a year earlier. The price of freshly harvested opium had jumped by more than 40 percent, from about $128 to $180 per 2.2 pounds. Opium sales were nearly 10 percent of the Afghan economy, up from just 5 percent in 2010. These increases meant opium was not going away. Potential opium production was estimated to be up by more than 61 percent.

The fields west of Laskhar Gah were fed by canals, dikes, and ditches that diverted water from the Helmand River deep into the desert, providing vital moisture for an estimated 250,000 acres of parched earth. This irrigation system that made the district the heart of poppy country ironically had been built by Americans, both private companies and the United States government. For decades Helmand had been called Little America.

The region had long been a crossroads for ancient cultures and a southern strand of the Silk Road for traders traversing from Europe and the Middle East to India and China. At the dawn of the twentieth century, the Helmand Valley had withered. Afghan engineers made plans to restore some of the ancient canals and to build new ones. During the 1930s they were helped by the Axis powers of Germany and Japan.

But it was not until 1946, just after World War II, when canal construction gained momentum. According to an August 5, 2011, article in the *Washington Post*, Afghanistan's King Mohammad Zahir Shah had hoped to use profits he earned from the European and American presence in south Asia during WWII to launch his country into the twentieth century. The king hired the American engineering firm of Morrison Knudsen to dam the Helmand River for irrigation and electricity and to build a wide system of canals. A variety of towns, including Marja, rose out of the desert, along with schools and health clinics, paved roads, and suburban-styled homes.

Riding a wave of new-world enthusiasm, the battalion of American engineers, agriculturalists, contractors, and consultants bypassed basic soil studies, taking local word that the soil was fine. Had the studies been done, they might have revealed that the soil was shallow and sat just atop an impermeable clay-like layer. The Afghans liked to flood their fields, and lacking proper drainage, the water puddled and dried, leaving a crusty residue that was bad for healthy crops. Some fifteen years later, after the expenditure of millions of US dollars, the grandiose plans languished. Locals grew hostile to the foreigners' plans to ban headscarves and open coed schools. Desperate for success, the Afghan government appealed to the US government in 1960.

Help came in the form of the Bureau of Reclamation and the US Agency for International Development. But over the next twenty years, the foreign community all but vanished, and by 1979, when the Soviet Union entered Afghanistan, the Helmand Valley was much like it had been for the previous thousand years, composed of scattered communities where people survived on subsistence farming.

The new asphalt road on which I was riding to Marja, with its freshly painted white stripe down the center, abruptly ended about five miles outside of Lashkar Gah, turning into hard-packed gravel filled by convoys of lumbering armored vehicles. Every mile or so, an Afghan army or police outpost rose at the roadside, their high walls looking like ziggurats of plastic green sandbags topped by coils of razor wire. Muzzles of machine guns protruded from the dark recesses, and the green, red, and black flags of Afghanistan fluttered. The deeper we drove into the countryside, the more the land took on the look of most of Afghanistan—flat, dun-colored grit that swirled and danced on the wind—broken by occasional irrigated fields that fronted family compounds hidden behind high walls of dried mud bricks.

Our Ford Ranger pickup was one of many thousands that had been purchased by the US government and given to police units throughout Afghanistan. They were the four-door variety, with a roll bar, and often a machine gun mounted on it. We swerved and bounced wildly along the road, driving at a speed this light, top-heavy truck was not meant to travel without a stabilizing load. As we slammed into ruts and potholes, the truck shuttered and shimmied as the oversized knobby tires whined loudly.

I told the driver to slow down, that we were not late for anything. He smiled and explained that the national police always drove this fast. It was for security, he said. If one drove fast enough, the thinking was, it was hard for an insurgent to properly time the detonation of their remote-controlled roadside bombs to demolish the police truck. I reluctantly nodded. As a concession, he agreed that he would drive only "medium-fast."

The other of the two Afghan police officers in front introduced himself as Rafiq (not his real name) and said he was from Marja, our destination. He proudly proclaimed, "Hello," showing off his limited English. I answered him in my equally limited Pashto.

We bounced off the road and swerved into the Marja police headquarters, a compound behind the gray, fabric-lined wire baskets filled with dirt that looked much like all of the other hastily built military posts that dotted the landscape. Inside the concrete-block building that served as the district police headquarters, I found chief Al Haj Ghulam Wali, known as Wali Shakar. He was a large man who wore traditional Afghan clothes rather than a police uniform. He sat near me, listening as a half-dozen elderly men, all similarly dressed, carried on a noisy conversation. They were there to discuss a problem, and they needed Shakar's help or at least his blessing to solve it. After ten minutes, the entourage left and Shakar turned to me. I asked him about the security in Marja.

Shakar shrugged. "For the past year, it's been secure here," which coincided with the US forces' battle for Marja. But maintaining control of the region had not been easy. The Taliban had retreated but continued to fight. A combined force of some one thousand Afghan army and police units were attacking a Taliban stronghold just six miles away that same day, he said. "The Taliban are working there. They have started fighting and attacking police and army outposts. The people there are in favor of the Taliban."

"Why?" I asked.

"The people are compelled to like the Taliban," Shakar said.

"Do you like what the US Marines have done in the region in the past year?" I asked.

He nodded. "They have brought peace. We wish that they would stay for a long time. People are tired of war." If the foreign forces stayed, Afghans would "be able to live and get a good education. People want peace. That's all."

"How have the Taliban managed to stay so strong in Marja District?" I asked.

Again, Shakar shrugged. "All the right people love them and they support the Taliban." These "right people" were clan leaders and guardians of the opium trade, he explained, and the Taliban protected their poppy fields. They hid the Taliban when the government forces tried to arrest them. They planted land mines and bombs near their homes and detonated them when government forces approached. "They are friends [with the Taliban] and that is why they support them."

It was business, Shakar explained. The Taliban protected the poppy growers who were "far from government control," but for a price. The Taliban were the middlemen, buying the raw opium paste and selling it to others who would process it into heroin. But in recent years, Marja poppy growers had realized that profits could increase dramatically by selling their own heroin rather than raw opium. For a bit more work, it meant a huge jump in profits. Hundreds of processing labs appeared across Helmand, according to a February 2010 investigative report on the province's drug trade by Helmand journalists, titled *Helmand Heroin Menace Grows*, published by the Institute for War and Peace Reporting.

According to the report, converting the poppy paste into heroin was a relatively simple process. It required only a heat source and enameled containers for boiling the raw materials. The process began by converting the opium into morphine, which was then mixed with acetic anhydride, which precipitated out the heroin. Since Afghanistan did not produce the acid, it was brought into the country by the same networks that smuggled the heroin out via Iran, Pakistan, and the northern border countries of Turkmenistan, Uzbekistan, and Tajikistan.

Almost everyone in the town of Marja was involved in the drug trade one way or another, the journalists learned. The Taliban jealously guarded their heroin shipments and routes, according to the smugglers, and were well paid for their trouble. The heroin exited Afghanistan via a well-developed network, sometimes west through Iran to Turkey and then north into Europe. According to the Helmand drug trade insiders, no one could move heroin without the Taliban's permission.

Supporting the report by the Helmand journalists, in early March 2012, the US Treasury Department would identify a high-ranking officer of the Iranian Revolutionary Guard Corps's elite Quds Force, General Gholamreza Baghbani, as a drug kingpin. According to the department, Baghbani was stationed in Zahedan, a town near the Iranian-Afghan border, and allowed Afghan smugglers to move their drugs through Iran in exchange for transporting weapons to the Taliban on behalf of Baghbani. In addition, the department would charge that the general also facilitated the import of the acetic anhydride into Afghanistan that was needed to produce heroin.

"The Taliban are strong here," Shakar told me. "They are free to do what they want. The government has killed many Taliban and arrested those who favored the Taliban." But it had had little effect.

"In other regions where the Taliban was active," I said, "men in your position were targets. Are you afraid for your life?"

"I'm not afraid," he said. "I'm working well for the community. People want peace. For a long time, they have had war. But still, some people are involved in the Taliban activities."

One of the elders who had lingered in the police station joined the conversation but refused to give me his name. "When the US came, many people were killed here. The Taliban have many weapons. They are so strong." But the community likes the Americans, he said. "People are happy because [the Americans] are trusted. They should not leave. Fifty years ago," the man recalled, referring to the development project of past decades, "America helped the Afghans here, just for peace. Not for anything else. Marja District people have deep trust in the Americans."

The Marja Market

Umar and I headed for town with our police escorts. We turned onto a wide dirt road that was the main market area of what was left of the town of Marja. We climbed out, stepped across a sewage ditch, and entered an open-air electronics shop owned by Mohammad Qasem. He eyed me suspiciously as he and a couple of friends stood beside his glass counter filled with new and used mobile phones.

"Has the fighting of the past year improved life in Marja?" I asked.

Qasem shrugged. "We want peace. We're tired of war," he said. "Three years ago, people were unhappy with the government. People were treated harshly. So the Taliban came for a while."

"Why were people unhappy with the government?" I asked.

"The government demanded money. They only worked for themselves and their families and friends. The common people were helpless. There was a lack of security, especially. There was a lack of trust," Qasem said. "When the Taliban came here, we were safe."

Once people in Marja began to feel safe with the Taliban, things began to change, he said. "After some time, the Taliban were demanding money and gifts from the people." If people didn't pay, the Taliban said, "We will close your store and we will kill you."

When the US forces arrived in early 2010, the fighting lasted three months. "It was very difficult to come from home and buy something in the bazaar" due to the fighting, Qasem said. "Now there is peace."

But that peace was only in the town of Marja, he cautioned, since the Taliban were still strong outside of town.

"Do people still support the Taliban?" I asked.

"They are compelled" to support the Taliban, Qasem said. "They are afraid" that if they don't, they'll be killed. He was worried about the future, since only the overwhelming firepower of the United States had been able to dislodge the Taliban from Marja. "If America does not want the Taliban to come, they will not. If the US leaves and ceases its activities here, [the Taliban] will come back. When the US leaves Afghanistan, they will rule and we will be compelled to follow them."

Qasem's uncle, Naseer Ahmed, a man in his fifties, wore a gray turban and traditional clothes. "People say they want [to impose] Islamic rules," he said of the Taliban.

"Do the people of Marja want that?" I asked, considering their treatment of women.

"During the Taliban times, women were not killed," Ahmed said, but women's activities outside the home were severely restricted to daily visits to the market, always accompanied by a male family member. "They were just supposed to go to the bazaar."

"Do you like the US military in your town?" I asked Ahmed.

"I'm not happy with them, and I'm not unhappy with them. If they leave, they must help the Afghan people," Ahmed said. "The police should be strong, otherwise the dangerous people will be back."

Ahmed didn't like the bullying behavior of the US forces, however. The Russians were more polite. "Now the US goes on a mission and everybody must stop. The foreigners should be here but must follow the rules of Afghanistan. The US forces are not giving way to us. That is wrong."

Down the road and around the corner, I found Haji Mohammad Ismail, a man in his late thirties, sitting behind the counter in his large retail shop. The entrance was lined with cloth sacks filled with spices and dried beans, and his three boys played among them. I sat with Ismail in the back of his shop on the woven plastic mat that covered his floor and sipped green tea as he talked about the battle for Marja. It had been bloody and destructive. Most of the shops in the market had been damaged or destroyed.

Ismail motioned to the ceiling, which had collapsed when US mortars rained on the market after the Taliban had hidden there. "The US arrived here and was searching for the Taliban. The Taliban started to attack the Americans. There was a fight. Some were wounded and killed here."

Ismail closed his shop for ten days due to the damage and, like the other merchants, had struggled to recover. "Every shop here was damaged. Some shops were burned. My shop had collapsed. We were very sad. We lost many things. I spent all of my money to rebuild the shop. I have nothing left."

The US Army came around later and offered to pay for the damage, but when Ismail told them what it would cost to repair, they disputed the amount, saying it was too much.

"Are you angry about that?" I asked.

"What will I do if I become angry?" Ismail replied. "I am disappointed. I am unhappy."

"What about the other merchants?" I asked.

Most of the shopkeepers were unhappy, Ismail said, but not angry. "They all have their lives. No matter that they lost their shops. We are happy to be alive."

The Americans were swindled by dishonest translators, Ismail complained. The translators would negotiate settlements for repairs, then would only pay the merchant or a contractor a portion of the settlement for the work and would pocket the difference. "We are happy that the Americans are doing all of this work, but half goes to the interpreters and half to the contractors, so the contractors are not satisfied." The US Army should have employed professional engineers to assess the damage, Ismail said, since they knew local costs and could be trusted. "They should have their own engineer to visit the sites. [Translators] should not be able to hide the money. That's not good."

Ismail had yet to receive money for his collapsed roof. He showed me a form that he had been given by a US Army officer, which he had duly filled out in English, even though he didn't speak the language. His repairs were estimated at $420. "The Americans came here and visited my shop. They said, 'We will give you your money for that damage.' Now . . . they say the money is not there."

"Was life better under the Taliban or the Americans?" I asked.

"There were no thieves under the Taliban. I'm not in favor of the Taliban or the Americans. I'm in favor of peace," he said.

"Why was the Taliban so strong in the province?" I asked.

"The rich men give them some money," Ismail said flatly. It was like a Taliban tax, and it was like any government. The Taliban demanded money, he said.

"What will happen when coalition forces leave?" I asked.

Ismail answered metaphorically, saying, "It takes only a couple of hours to destroy a wall, but it takes a long time to rebuild it." But he was optimistic. "Afghan people will be self-sufficient. I have a belief that Afghan people will survive. For tomorrow, no one knows what will happen."

By the time I finished with Ismail, it was early afternoon. Umar, the two policemen, and I stopped in a restaurant on the main street and ordered a platter of kabobs. Rafiq, the policeman who had introduced himself to me earlier, had been listening to my interviews all day and had wanted to jump into each conversation, like a kid sitting at the front of the class, waving his hand to be called upon. He was twenty-six, he said, and was a veteran of many encounters with the Taliban. He was of average height, fit, with sandy hair and gray eyes. He was proud to be a policeman and could think of nothing else he'd rather be doing.

"A year ago we couldn't come here like today," Rafiq said of the restaurant. He had been a policeman when the Taliban had controlled the town. There were only forty or so officers, and it was not enough. Today, there were 450 policemen, and the town needed all of them, he said. "The Taliban were telling me that I had to quit or they would destroy me. If people were seen with me, after a few days, they would be killed."

At the time, Rafiq was working for what was known as the "local police," an auxiliary force to the national police that had been created by coalition forces to help fight the Taliban. He had joined to avenge the death of his best friend. "My friend had been killed by the Taliban. I promised myself that I would fight against the Taliban," he said.

Rafiq took the cell phone out of his pocket, punched a couple of buttons, and then showed me a photo. It was of a bearded dead man, eyes closed and bare-chested. It was the Taliban fighter who had caused him so much trouble. "He had threatened me many times."

"Did you kill him?" I asked.

Rafiq said no, "He was killed by a helicopter gunship." Rafiq identified the body and took the photo for posterity. When he came across Taliban sympathizers, he showed them the photo and said, "If you join the Taliban, you will end up like this."

Rafiq laughed with delight.

Four days earlier, he had been fighting a Taliban unit just three miles outside of Marja. Four of his friends were killed. Most of the countryside was controlled by the Taliban, he said. "The majority of Taliban are there."

"How did the Taliban stay so strong?" I asked.

"Many Pakistanis are helping them. Their poppies are growing now. The government doesn't want poppies. That is why [the Taliban] are helping the people." The Taliban tells the farmers, "We will buy your poppies, and the price will be high. That is why people are helping the Taliban. The Taliban do not want the government to interfere. Every day the Taliban are attacking when they go to eradicate the poppies."

Despite the daily battles, Rafiq didn't fear the Taliban. "The Taliban is not so powerful," he insisted. The real problem is corruption in the government. "When we arrest a Taliban, then the Taliban pay money to get him out," Rafiq said in dismay. "If bribery was gone, we would have peace here. We have to pay to get our bullets."

Rafiq had been with the police for nine years. "Do you ever see any other life for yourself?" I asked.

"I have seen and heard of many innocent people being killed. Many women become widows," he said. "If peace was here, I would work as a businessman."

Rafiq smiled at that thought, as if it were a distant dream, then rose and grabbed the high-caliber machine gun he had put on the floor. We had to be going, he said, before the road back to Lashkar Gah became unsafe. I didn't argue. As we rolled down the hard-packed gravel road, the heat of late afternoon intensified, eased by the air that swirled through the truck cab. In the late afternoon the canals doubled as swimming holes for children, who scampered along the dusty paths separating the fields, their bodies glistening brown and wet in the searing sun, hair clinging to their scalps. That young boys and girls shared the same swimming hole was remarkable, I thought. Perhaps it was a remnant of Little America from decades past. Then again, they were children.

Rafiq casually pointed out the fields and compounds that belonged to the Taliban and poppy-growing families. Most were just a couple hundred yards off the road, some very near the sandbag and dirt towers manned by the Afghan police and army.

With each that he noted, I realized that words like *secure* and *progress* and *peace* could not describe Marja or Helmand Province. Coalition forces would trot foreign journalists out to towns and villages that had been "cleared" of Taliban and were being "held" by a substantial military presence, and local villagers would say what was expected. The moment these forces left, the Taliban would be back—in fact, they had never left.

But time already had run out for some Afghans in other corners of the country, even where the Taliban did not hold sway. For them, it was neither the war nor politics nor poppies that controlled their lives. It was an ancient culture that put young women on the lowest rung of society. As the Western world saturated daily life in Afghanistan, some of these young women had taken matters into their own hands, protesting their lot in life by turning themselves into pillars of fire. To find them, I returned to the western Afghanistan city of Herat.

10

BURNING IN HELL

ZARGHANA'S HEAD WAS SWATHED in dingy gauze, her face swollen and scabbed, glistening with salve. Her forehead beaded with moisture as tears dribbled down her cheeks. Her lips quivered as she struggled to speak. Just a year earlier, Zarghana had been nineteen and happy to marry the boy who lived in the bottom half of the house where she and her parents resided. She did so amid dreams of a life with a loving husband, children, and her parents close at hand. But not long after she moved in with her new husband and his family, Zarghana's life became a living hell. In a fit of rage and desperation, she doused herself with kerosene and set herself on fire.

Now she lay in a hospital bed in Herat, clinging to life with severe burns over 75 percent of her body. Zarghana shared a sunny room with five other burn victims, each a case of self-immolation and most younger than her. One thin young girl, perhaps no older than fifteen, looked on with bright, defiant brown eyes, her face and hands scarred and scabbed, her head bound in gauze. Others lay under thin blankets, their heads topped with the blousy pink caps issued by the hospital. The disgust with their lives was palpable, saturated with an anger they had tried to burn away by holding a match to their kerosene-soaked clothes.

"I did it because of my mother-in-law," Zarghana whispered through puffy, blistered lips. "She was always talking bad about me." Her domineering mother-in-law had been joined in these verbal assaults by her sister-in-law, berating Zarghana endlessly as she cooked and cleaned for her new family. "Both didn't like me from the start." When her husband returned in the evenings, he often joined the haranguing.

Zarghana's parents lived upstairs, having rented the downstairs of their house to the family, who were distant relatives, believing that they needed financial help. Zarghana's new in-laws followed her every move from morning until night and refused to let her go upstairs to visit her mother, Fatima, to escape the torment.

"I would see her once in a while," Fatima said at Zarghana's bedside, "but I said [to her], 'They are good people. They are poor and don't mean anything.'"

Her mother's words provided little comfort as Zarghana endured the abuse day and night. Even the birth of her daughter brought little relief.

"I had no choice," Zarghana said of her self-immolation. "My husband wouldn't listen to me. He said, 'My mother is right.' One evening, when my husband came back, my mother-in-law began complaining about me. I left my four-month-old baby daughter, went into the kitchen, and burned myself. My mother- and sister-in-law just stared. They didn't do anything."

Hearing her daughter's shrieks of pain, Fatima ran downstairs to find Zarghana flailing around the house like a human torch. Fatima grabbed a pillow and pummeled Zarghana, trying to put out the flames, swatting with her hands and arms. After ten minutes, the flames were finally out. Now, little more than a week after the burning, Fatima rolled up her sleeves and showed me her scabbed burns as she sat at Zarghana's bed, blotting her daughter's tears and perspiration with tissue paper.

Zarghana's doctor, Aref Jalali, a tall, clean-shaven Afghan in a white clinical coat, looked on with his arms folded across his chest. As the head of the Herat Burn and Plastic Surgery Center, Jalali had seen hundreds of such cases. He was not optimistic about Zarghana, confiding that "if she survives," she would be in the hospital for many months to recover. "Her condition is not good. There are complications with the burns." Infection was one of the major reasons people with severe burns didn't survive, he said.

"What does the future hold?" I asked Zarghana.

She had nothing to say except, "My husband is not to blame."

"Would you go back to him?" I asked.

She nodded.

"After she survives, I will take her home with me," Fatima said. "Her husband can come live with our family. If he says no, they will get a divorce."

Zarghana was just one of an epidemic of self-immolation by young women that had plagued the Herat region for much more than a decade. Experts struggled to explain the phenomenon, which peaked in 2004, when some 384 cases were reported to authorities. Many of the women arrived in the Herat Regional Hospital from the neighboring provinces in western Afghanistan. After a public awareness campaign by civic groups and aid agencies, the number of cases dropped dramatically, but today about a hundred cases per year continue.

Many Afghans blamed the problem on neighboring Iran, which exerted a strong cultural and economic influence over western Afghanistan. Iranian television and other media showed young Afghan women how women live elsewhere in the world, in freer, more affluent societies, unburdened by cultural values that had changed little from the medieval ages. Others said it was because Afghans heard of similar suicides by Iranian women who killed themselves by turning on their gas ovens and asphyxiating themselves. Since Afghans don't have such easy access to natural gas, they reached for kerosene, which was plentiful and used for cooking and heating.

Jalali said he doubted that Iran was the problem. "Never has any person told me they had seen news of this from Iran" or told him that was why they decided to commit the act. Many of the cases came from rural areas where the victims had little or no education, access to international television news, or understanding of their options under Afghan law and tradition. "When they do this self-immolation . . . it's a last-ditch decision. Ninety-five percent don't know their rights. They have no knowledge. [Some] families are obligated to sell their daughters" or force their daughters into arranged or "exchange" marriages as part of land ownership arrangements. While women are guaranteed extensive rights under the Afghan constitution, these protections frequently are ignored in favor of local custom and tradition. Most cases were like Zarghana's, Jalali said, where "we have a lot of conflict with the woman's [new] family, with the mothers- and sisters-in-law."

Another typical case was that of Negina (not her real name), a very young girl who had been admitted to the burn unit just days earlier. Negina claimed to be fifteen years old but looked no more than twelve. She said she had been married three years earlier, a fact that Jalali said was probably correct. She had been brought to the Herat clinic from a rural village in Badghis, the remote and rugged province north of Herat.

Negina lay in her bed in another room of the burn unit, which she shared with six other victims of self-immolation. The girl in the bed beside her had a face charred black and slipped under her blankets as Jalali, my translator Noorullah, and I walked into the ward. While most of the burn victims were young, an exception was a woman who looked to be in her forties, whose hands and arms were wrapped in bandages, her face partially singed.

Negina agreed to talk about her ordeal but struggled to keep her eyes focused, the effects of the pain-killing drugs coursing through her small body. Questions were repeated, and it took time for her to form her brief answers. Her husband had been thirty years old, and she had objected to the marriage from the beginning. But, she said, "I was a child and small," so she could do little to alter the events that had taken her to the doorstep of death.

"My in-laws didn't give me food, water, or clothes. I worked a lot, but they beat me. They said I didn't do anything." Negina was expected to work for the family day and night. "I decided to burn myself. The family was beating me," she repeated, and "didn't try to help" when she was engulfed in flames.

Negina was driven to the regional hospital in Qala-e-Naw, the capital of Badghis Province, by her husband's family. They were told the hospital could do nothing for her. She was then driven through the night to the burn center at Herat. "I'm surprised she is alive," Jalali said, considering that she had serious burns over 50 percent of her body. She made the trip without the aid of intravenous fluids, which are critical for the burn victim's survival, especially during the first twenty-four hours after the injuries. Negina's burns were "so deep," he said, and were mostly third degree. She would need extensive skin grafts to properly heal, but such extensive surgery was "dangerous for patients," Jalali said, since it added trauma to an already severely damaged body.

Despite the severity of her condition, Negina thought about going home. "If I survive, I have my parents," she said. "If my husband comes, [we] can be at my family's house. I like my husband and he likes me. The problem is with the in-laws." Although her husband was not allowed to visit, he still called, she said.

Jalali said that before resorting to self-immolation, abused women often appeal for help from their local mullah or community elders. If the elders agree with the woman's complaint, the offending husband or family is brought to the council and reprimanded. "They decide how to solve problems between the families," he said. But often a woman's appeal is ignored. "They get no answer from the council," which itself is a message telling the woman to put up and shut up. Jalali said he had a patient who had gone to a local mullah three times, seeking protections from an abusive husband. The mullah grew tired of her and "told her he would buy the fuel so she could burn herself because the fault was all hers."

Jalali had been working in the burn clinic since 2004, had seen nearly a thousand burn cases, and had conducted hundreds of operations. Only about 20 or 25 percent of the self-immolation victims survive. Most of the victims are young, between fifteen and twenty-five years of age, with some being even younger, as Negina was thought to be.

Although the vast majority of cases are self-immolation, three so far in 2011 were women who were doused with fuel and set on fire by someone else. Of the forty-eight cases he'd seen in the past five months, forty-five were women, but three were males. "We now have self-immolation with men," he said.

The burn cases are generally not discussed by families "because of the shame," Jalali said. This makes it difficult to find out the true circumstances behind the event. Many families bring burn victims to the hospital and claim that the injuries were an accident. "Families push women not to say anything, but women will talk after they've been healed and often confess that 'I was a self-immolation. It was not an accident.'" There is little that can be done six months or a year after the fact, he said. "By then the police case is closed. It gets listed as an accident."

Typically a burn victim needs at least two to three months to heal sufficiently to be able to return home. But even so, the victims still need extensive counseling to cope with their wounds, their families, and their marriages. "All of the patients have psychological problems," Jalali said. "They need a lot of support, but we have no permanent [counseling] help." Many of the victims are from rural areas that lack even basic medical services. Pain-killing drugs are a luxury, he said. "[The patients] are from poor families. They try to steal drugs from us."

Keeping the burn victims in the hospital long enough to receive the care they need is also a problem. Those who know they have little or no chance to survive will find a way to escape the hospital, saying, "If I'm going to die, I want to be with my family," Jalali said. In such cases, there is little he can do, he said.

Shelter from the Storm

Suraya Pakzad's office was in a large and sunny house in a quiet corner of Herat, hidden behind a high wall with an unmarked gate. As head of the Voice of Women organization, Pakzad operated a nonprofit women's shelter for young girls and women who had fled abusive husbands and families. While many ran away to save themselves, they did so despite threats of revenge from husbands and families who saw running away as shaming a family, akin to prostitution. The shelter provided long-term protection and legal counseling for the women. "The situation [for women] has improved," Pakzad said. "By law, women have freedom and equality in the constitution. But [treatment of women] is a cultural issue. [The law] is violated by people and the warlords."

One recent case in Herat that drew news media attention involved a teenaged couple that was pulled off the street and jailed on charges of "attempted" sexual relations. The couple had met at an ice cream factory where they both worked. They fell in love but kept their relationship secret. Having decided to get married, they began appearing in public together. But by doing so, they violated a strict social taboo: women were not allowed to appear in public except in the company of their husbands or a close male relative. The couple's families were enraged. The couple was captured by a crowd of angry relatives and dragged out of a car, and the boy was nearly beaten to death before both were taken into custody by police and placed into separate juvenile prisons.

"They were the lucky ones," Pakzad said, since they were rescued before the crowd killed them. The subsequent news media attention created a bubble of protection for them, she explained, despite the fact that their lives had been threatened. Others are not so fortunate. "Thousands of other women are in jail each year," for similar or lesser offenses. Typically when the boys are arrested, their families work hard for their release. But all too often, the young girls are left in jail, abandoned by families who believe that the girl has shamed them. "The girls have no one waiting for them when they get out. They have no hope for the future, so they come to the shelter."

Pakzad and her staff then bring the families together with their daughters to convince them to take the girls back. "The lucky ones get a chance to go home or to find a husband." While these two choices are not ideal, they are better than begging on the street. "The huge majority of them are not educated, and the only jobs they can find are being a cook or cleaner."

The young couple that landed in jail was dubbed "Romeo and Juliet" by the community, Pakzad said. While most people were sympathetic, the couple faced death threats from their own families, who said that when their six-month sentences were over, they would be killed if they tried to return home. "The uncle said he will kill her if her father is not willing to do it. She is being punished for something she did not do."

The police said they were holding the girl on a charge of running away. But, Pakzad explained, "there is no specific article in the law that says running away is a crime." Officially, Juliet was accused of "attempting to have sexual relations with the boy." When the couple was arrested, the girl was taken directly to a hospital to determine her virginity. The doctors confirmed that she was a virgin. Although the boy, Romeo, was in jail recovering from his wounds, there were no grounds to keep him either, since they had not had sexual relations and "[Juliet] confirmed that she had agreed to run away with the boy."

When other young Afghan couples are stopped under such circumstance, Pakzad said, they often escape prosecution by saying they were going to the courthouse to get married. In such a limited situation it is not a crime for an unmarried couple to be in public together. The legal age for marriage in Afghanistan is sixteen for girls and eighteen for boys (though despite the law many young girls are forced into marriages at very young ages).

Pakzad hoped for a good ending to the Romeo and Juliet story. "The boy is ready to marry her. The father is supporting her, and he can be a witness [for the marriage]. They can marry, and then they can leave Herat and have a life." Leaving the community would be necessary since "even the community was against her. They expect that girls should listen to the community too, in addition to her parents. They were beating the boy because he was from another community," she said.

The social pressure on women is enormous. "We have a number of girls here because they didn't want to marry the husbands selected for them. They had someone else on their minds," Pakzad said. "She contacts the boy and they run away."

Some women flee to the shelter, saying that their husbands from arranged marriages are treating them badly. Pakzad was aghast that Afghan society permitted older men to marry very young girls. "How can [a man] take a fourteen-year-old and marry her if he is forty?"

Such marital arrangements make women feel trapped and desperate. "One day they find themselves in a difficult situation" and decide to kill themselves, Pakzad said. A small event usually pushes them over the edge, triggers them to do what they've been contemplating for a long time. "The last incident makes them decide to burn themselves. Naturally, they are not in a good way."

These women are "victims of violence, but they don't want to die silently. They [want] to show the pain that is in their heart to others," Pakzad explained. The deaths are warnings and messages to their families and friends, "so that others see they should not be pushed into marriages they don't like. Why do they burn themselves? It is a very powerful statement. If they die silently, it would be very easy for the husband to say [the woman's death] was an accident. But if women burn themselves, everyone knows about it. The husbands are investigated. It will help the other daughters as well," she said, because a father will then be reluctant to force his other daughters into arranged marriages.

Self-immolation cases investigated by the police occasionally result in an abusive husband going to jail, Pakzad said. This punishment is in addition to the public humiliation that the husband and family face from a woman burning herself.

Pakzad said she counsels families of burn victims to look closely at their lives. "We ask them, 'Why does this happen?' and talk to them about the causes." Even if the burn victims recover, they had little to look forward to. "It is not accepted by Islam. If they recover, they will suffer all of their lives."

Most cases at the shelter do not involve self-immolation. "We have had cases with women who have four and five children and they run away from an abusive situation." The custom in these situations is for children to stay with the father, no matter the age, but under some circumstances, children can stay with their mothers until the age of seven and then move in with their fathers. Cases are resolved by bringing the husband to the negotiating table, Pakzad said. Instead of getting a divorce, local community leaders and clerics draft a legal agreement that is signed by the husband, in which he promises not to abuse his wife and to feed and clothe her and his family properly. If a man has a second or third wife, each has to be treated and loved equally, as dictated by the Koran. "If a husband makes such an agreement, he signs it," Pakzad said. If it is violated, "the man will go to jail." Under such arrangements, women are not left destitute but "can go back home and she will have a place to stay and enough to eat."

Such situations become more difficult, however, if a married woman runs away with another man, Pakzad said. "She will go to jail. For a married woman, the punishment is always stronger" than for the man. Women who survive such predicaments are sometimes allowed to stay with uncles or grandparents, "just to give her a room, and food, and so she will stay alive. A single woman can't live alone. They won't be safe. They will be attacked."

When I asked to interview several of the women at the shelter, Pakzad's eyes brightened. She readily agreed, saying that few foreigners had ever asked or taken the time.

Samira's Story

Samira (not her real name) glided into Pakzad's office wearing a black chador with a gray floral pattern and sat meekly at the table. She was one of six children, with three sisters and two brothers, from a very poor family. The winter of 2008 was particularly cold and bitter, and people died due to extreme temperatures and exposure. Her father struggled to provide enough food for the family, so he decided to sell one of his daughters into marriage. At the age of nine, Samira was sold for $1,000. The marriage sale was not a shock, because she had been promised as a bride to her first cousin when she had been just one year old. But the pending marriage was canceled when the cousin whom she was supposed to marry rejected the arrangement. Samira was forced to marry her cousin's brother. "It was not love," she said.

As she prepared to move in with her new family, she recalled putting her clothes in her bag along with a handmade doll she'd crafted from the remains of an older sister's wedding dress. "She was very happy to be at Auntie's house," explained Pakzad, as she translated Samira's story. "She thought her life would be better." But Samira soon found that her life had taken a dramatic turn for the worse.

"We bought you to clean up the house," her new in-laws barked upon her arrival. "You think you are his wife? We bought you for this," Samira recalled them saying. Her new husband then told her, "I will get another wife soon."

Even at the age of nine, Pakzad said, "They also expected her to act like a woman and wife," which meant having sexual relations with the man. "She was always being punished by the family [because] she did some of the work but not all. She was still a child." Samira's mother-in-law beat her to make her work faster, Pakzad said. "The husband started to beat her as well."

Samira ran away twice but was forced to return to her husband's family home each time. The third time, she convinced her mother to go with her to the authorities, and Samira ended up in Pakzad's women's shelter. Her in-laws told the police that they'd bought her for an agreed amount and therefore owned her and could make her do what they wanted. In effect, she was a slave. Samira and her family objected, of course. Realizing that Samira was now a problem for them, the family agreed to sell Samira back to her father but demanded $5,000 to return her—five times what they had paid.

Samira's family could not afford that, so an outsider familiar with the situation offered to pay the family $1,500 to secure her freedom, 50 percent more than the original bride price. But her in-laws refused, insisting on $5,000. Samira's father offered to take a job to pay off the debt but was now more worried than ever since he had three other daughters to care for. "I know that I should not have married off a daughter at that age," he told Pakzad, though he said he believed that he had no choice. "Poverty is one of the reasons for these forced marriages," Pakzad said.

One viable option for Samira was what was known as an informal divorce, Pakzad said. Common practice was that after a couple had been estranged for three years, they could seek a divorce through a mutual agreement. A committee of community elders and officials witnessed the agreement, which was informal yet legal. It meant that Samira would be living in the shelter for up to three years during the required waiting period.

Samira still feared for her safety. She had told her story to me just days before the Eid holidays that followed the holy month of Ramadan. She was invited home by her mother for the holiday celebrations, but Samira decided against it. "She is afraid that her husband will come and take her someplace," Pakzad said.

Laiqha's Lament

Laiqha was about fifteen years old and had arrived at the women's shelter just a week before we talked. She had been married three years earlier, at the age of twelve, to a man who was forty years old and who had two other wives. "For a few months, it was OK," Laiqha said, "but then he started to beat me as well, just like he did with the other wives." The abuse didn't stop, even after she became pregnant. "I thought he would change his behavior, but he didn't." Her husband was a drug addict, she said. After her son was born, she told him not to smoke in the house since it was not healthy for the baby. The man replied by hitting her. "My face was bruised and swollen."

She repeatedly complained to authorities about her husband's behavior but could not convince them to do anything. Finally she went to the local office of the Department of Women's Affairs and showed them her bruises, "to prove that she was beaten," Pakzad explained.

Her husband was jailed for three months, Laiqha said, during which time she lived with her parents. A divorce was granted, but it required her to leave her child with her former husband. Glad to be out of the marriage, she tried to find a new course for her life but was soon told that her father had already arranged another marriage for her. "It was with another old man," Laiqha said, but at least, her father told her, this one was rich. Laiqha wanted nothing to do with the man or the marriage and told her father, "Even if he is a good man, I don't want to marry again." When her father insisted that she marry again, she fled to the shelter.

Laiqha would probably return to her father's house, Pakzad said, since he had agreed that Laiqha did not need to marry anyone anytime soon.

Zarha's Story

"God does not want me to die," said Zarha, with joy and wonder.

A loquacious woman of eighteen, she sat wrapped in a black chador, often adjusting the cloth on her head as she told how she escaped four years of a brutal marriage to a Taliban fighter. Her husband had been ten years her elder when she was married into a poor family in rugged mountains east of Herat. After just a year living with her husband's family, she had given up hope. "He was fighting with her and beating her," Pakzad said as she relayed Zarha's story. She tried to kill herself twice, once by an overdose of drugs.

The family was poor, she said, and her husband was unable to find work. "Finally, he joined the Taliban. They were giving him some money. I don't know how they got that money, but when he came home, he would have 10,000 Afghanis [$200]. When my husband was not there, I had to be the slave of the family. They had the right to beat me. I had to wash, cook, and clean. I had to take care of the family," Zahra became pregnant but lost the baby after just four months, attributing it to the fact that she was seldom able to rest.

Besides household chores, Zahra did heavy physical work normally left to men. "It was not women's work. I didn't know what the problem was" that caused her to be treated so badly, she said. "I never did anything wrong." Once she was beaten unconscious. As with other women caught in such abusive situations, the family refused to let Zahra leave the house. "They were afraid I would talk to the neighbors. If I was seen talking with neighbors, my father-in-law would beat me. The situation was not tolerable."

Finally, she overheard her in-laws plotting to sell her to another family in the neighboring province of Badghis. They also agreed that if they couldn't get a decent price, they would kill her. Hearing this, Zahra fled.

I felt there was much more to the story, and I was right. I told Zahra that it made no sense for the family to kill her or sell her when she did so much work for them.

Zahra explained that four years earlier, just after she was engaged to her husband, she was invited to attend a wedding in a neighboring village with her mother and married sister. She bought wedding presents at the market and headed home, walking down a lonely rural road with her packages. She was stopped by two boys on a motorcycle who forced her to a nearby abandoned house where they tried to rape her. She fought them off, she said, and they took her packages.

She returned to her father's house, where she lived at the time, and reported the attack to the police. The boys were arrested and charged with attempted rape. Despite being the victim of the attack, Zahra's version of events was challenged, and she fell prey to the widely held belief that women brought rape upon themselves and that she had been solicitous. "I wasn't able to prove that I had been shopping by myself," Zahra said, since the packages were gone. She was accused of violating the custom of being accompanied at all times by a male relative while in public.

Zahra's brother was among the most critical and doubtful of her story, Zahra said. He was convinced that he had to kill her to salvage the family's honor. Pretending to be concerned about her welfare, he convinced Zahra to accompany him into the countryside, then tried to stab her to death. Slashed and bleeding, she fell unconscious. Thinking that Zahra was dead and that he had completed his "honor" killing, he threw her into an abandoned well. "He wanted to clear up her bad name for the family," explained Pakzad, who was translating for her.

But Zahra wasn't dead.

The next morning, she awoke at the bottom of the well, barely alive and too weak to climb out of it. Resigned to a dismal fate, she sat slumped in the bottom of the well until she heard the faint tinkling of bells tied to goats and sheep. Shepherd boys were near. She began to shout. Soon a shepherd boy leaned over the well and stared down at her, shocked at what he saw. "He thought I might be a ghost. But I said, 'I am like you. I am a human being.'"

The boy ran away but returned with a rope and helped her climb out. She went to the hospital, where her wounds were treated, then to the police to report the attempt on her life. Her brother was jailed in Herat.

By this time, Zahra's life was wildly off track. Her status in the community could not have been worse, despite her claims of innocence. "The rumors grew that I . . . had gone willingly with the boys [accused of raping me]." Despite the events and the doubts that had darkened her reputation, her husband reluctantly agreed to marry her but did so without a wedding celebration. Her married life was one of servitude for her husband's family.

What had once been doubts about Zahra's story became hardened facts in the minds of her husband's family and the community. When she overheard her husband's family talking about getting rid of her, she acted quickly. She fled, but in disguise. Zahra knew she would be caught on the street immediately if she wore her black chador. Instead, she dressed like a man, putting on a *shalwar-chemise* and covering her head with a cap and turban.

When her husband and in-laws discovered that Zahra was missing the next morning, they went straight to the police. As she stood at the taxi-van stop on the dirt road leading out of the village, a police vehicle roared past with her husband and father-in-law inside. "They didn't recognize me." Without speaking a word, she climbed into the waiting taxi-van that took her to the town of Obe, sixty miles east of Herat. There Zahra turned herself in to the governor's office, saying that she had escaped from an abusive husband and family. The officials were stunned. "The difficult part for me was to tell them I was a woman at the district offices. They were all laughing," she said, about the fact that she had initially fooled them into thinking she was a young man.

While the ruse allowed her to escape, there was little about her life that was funny. She spent four nights in protective custody at the district headquarters in Obe and then was transferred to the women's shelter in Herat, where she'd been living for the past five months. Her father-in-law had requested her release, saying that her life would be good if she returned. Zahra had scoffed at the man's promise. "I am not a child to believe what they say. I would prefer to be executed than to live in that house. Death only lasts a few moments. If I returned to that house, I would die a thousand deaths," she said.

Zahra had no clear notion of her future. She planned to stay as long as necessary at the women's shelter. "Now there is no way for me to go anywhere." She paused and looked out the windows of the shelter's office. "I'm tired of hearing the words of men. None of them were good to me. I don't want to marry again." She was getting a divorce with the help of the shelter's lawyers. In a society where women are unable to live alone, she conceded that eventually she would need to take another husband, but there would be conditions. "I would need someone who loves me and respects me. I need a place to stay that is safe and sound."

There were many private, painful, and personal wars being fought in Afghanistan, as I learned in Herat. The country remained at war, however, just as it had been for thirty years, which led me to think that the wars of the past were long gone. But they were not. From Herat, I went to northern Afghanistan and found that the remainders of those wars could still be found in shallow graves.

11

BONES IN THE DESERT

A N ORANGE SUN ROSE over the town of Shiberghan, the capital of Jawzjan Province in northern Afghanistan. It was early morning in May 2011 and the warm air stirred. I stood atop a dune at the edge of the remote and forbidding desert of Dasht-e-Leili as grains of sand tumbled against my shoes.

Bodies had been buried in shallow mass graves not far from here a decade earlier, and the discovery of those skeletal remains became one of the dark chapters of America's war in Afghanistan. The bones belonged to some of the thousands of Taliban fighters who had fought and died in northern Afghanistan during the late 1990s. Many came from Pakistan, having poured out of that country's fanatical Muslim madrassas hoping to impose the Taliban's rigid version of Islam on the northern Afghan provinces. For a short time they succeeded.

Northern Afghanistan was littered with mass graves, but few were as notorious as this one. The fighters buried here had been part of the wholesale surrender of Taliban troops in late 2001, just weeks after the US-led assault knocked the Taliban to the ground. A revitalized Northern Alliance army led by Uzbek warlord General Abdul Rashid Dostum and backed by US Special Forces and deadly accurate US air power had quickly turned the war.

Dostum was one of Afghanistan's most notorious commanders. He was trained by and fought with the Russian army against the mujahideen during the Soviet occupation. He was known to love his vodka as much as the prized horses he used in the Afghan national sport of *buzkashi*. After the Soviets left in 1989, Dostum became a major player in the Afghan civil war and the battle over Kabul during the early 1990s.

The Afghan civil war was one of the bloodiest, darkest eras of Afghan history. Ethnic militias had divided Kabul and turned on one another, grappling for control of a capital city that they methodically turned into a wasteland. The atrocities committed during this time were horrendous, the details of which were only whispered. Stories told of checkpoints where a person might die because of the way he pronounced a word. Of nails pounded into the heads of captives. Of hot oil poured onto beheaded prisoners, whose bodies pranced like headless chickens. Afghanistan foundered on the shores of human cruelty.

After the Taliban rolled into Kabul in late September 1996 and ended the civil war, the warlords from northern Afghanistan formed the Northern Alliance to keep the Taliban out of their territory. The Northern Alliance included commanders Marshal Fahim, Ismail Khan, Ahmad Shah Massoud, and Dostum, and for a while they were successful. But ultimately the Northern Alliance was defeated, and Dostum fled Afghanistan in 1998. He returned in late 2001 to lead the campaign that crushed the Taliban.

At the end of November 2001 when the Taliban knew they could not outrun the US-backed Northern Alliance, surrender was arranged not far from Kunduz, the capital of Kunduz Province. What actually happened over a series of sunny, wintery days on the windswept desert is murky. But what is known is that thousands of prisoners ultimately died, many in mass executions that pointed to war crimes that few Afghans or American officials have been willing to discuss. The circumstances suggested that the United States knew what was happening but did nothing to stop it or to punish the perpetrators.

The Taliban Surrender

One of those familiar with the events during those days was Saleh, the Taliban sympathizer I had met earlier while talking to Afghans about Taliban justice. As an assistant to the Taliban governor of Balkh Province at the time, Saleh had been part of the Taliban surrender at Kunduz in November 2001. He described for me the chaotic events that had drawn me to the mass graves at the outskirts of Shiberghan, where I had wandered the dunes.

The Taliban had been assured by General Dostum that "if you surrender your weapons, you will be safe. I will take each of you to your homes," Saleh said. The ethnic Pashtun commanders of the Taliban knew that without weapons, they were defenseless against the Northern Alliance and would be quickly killed, since many fighters in the north had died at the hands of the Taliban. At first the Taliban refused to give up their weapons, Saleh said. But the Northern Alliance commanders insisted, saying, "We guarantee that none of you will be killed." The discussion was somewhat moot, Saleh said, because "before the Taliban collapsed, some had already given up their weapons." The terms of surrender were finally agreed and included a promise that the Taliban commanders would be spared punishment or execution.

During the days that followed, thousands of Taliban fighters were loaded into trucks and driven about sixty miles west to Mazar-e-Sharif, where they were imprisoned at the notorious Qala-e-Jangi, or "war castle," a massive and ancient mud-brick fortress about five miles outside the city. "It was a big convoy of Taliban [prisoners]," Saleh recalled. Among them were Arabs, Chechens, and even some Sudanese Muslim fighters. When the convoys reached the eastern edge of Mazar-e-Sharif, the Taliban fighters "were lined up and gave up their weapons one-by-one, [then] their hands were tied by Dostum's forces." The prisoners were separated and "put into steel containers and taken to Shiberghan. At [the town of] Balkh, the prisoners were asking for water." But according to reports, some of the containers were riddled with bullets, killing some of the captives. "Most died on the way [of asphyxiation]," Saleh said. Many of those who survived were then killed at the mass grave sites in Dasht-e-Leili. The use of the steel shipping containers as execution chambers was not new to Afghanistan; it was a practice that had grown out of the civil war. During the blistering summers, prisoners were locked in the containers and left to die.

The Taliban surrender at Kunduz went on for days, with few if any of the prisoners knowing their fate or that of their fellow fighters. "They didn't know what was happening to them," said Saleh, who was among those who surrendered on the second day. To avoid the ignominy of surrender and the likelihood of execution, some Taliban commanders bribed the Northern Alliance commanders to ensure their escape. Some Taliban commanders used this later to claim that they in fact had not surrendered but had escaped. When Saleh reached the Qala-e-Jangi fortress, he said, the Taliban prisoners were already being transferred to the prison in Shiberghan, where they were later killed.

Saleh said he witnessed some of the brutal and deteriorating conditions that preceded the Taliban prisoner revolt and takeover of the fortress. "When you don't receive water or food, it is obvious that [the prisoners] will rise up," he said of the many hundreds of men crammed into the mud-walled war castle. The takeover was easy. Armed guards escorted prisoners in groups of twos and threes to the toilet. "When they freed their hands, they jumped on soldiers and took their weapons. When two or three took the weapons, they went to the other prisoners and freed them. They started to riot. Some were killed by Dostum's soldiers."

Afghan and US forces counterattacked and dropped bombs on the war castle. In all, about six hundred, or approximately half of the estimated twelve hundred prisoners in Qala-e-Jangi, were killed, he estimated. Some managed to escape in the confusion that followed the recapture of the fortress, only to be hunted down and killed by Dostum's fighters mounted on horseback.

Saleh spent two days in Qala-e-Jangi before being transferred to Nasangi, another makeshift prison in Mazar-e-Sharif. Saleh was among nearly two thousand prisoners there, he said. They were given one toilet break, half a liter of water, and one small loaf of bread each day. "The soldiers were beating the prisoners. Anyone in that situation is not happy." No one from the international community was allowed to see the prisoners or talk to them. The prisoners were sorted into groups. Some were selected to be sent to Guantanamo for interrogation, while the Taliban from Helmand, Kandahar, and Uruzgan Provinces in southern Afghanistan were sent to Shiberghan. After several days in the Shiberghan prison, the Taliban prisoners were taken to the edge of the Dasht-e-Leili desert. "That was the place for killing. They were taken to Dasht-e-Leili and killed," Saleh said, as General Dostum's revenge.

With help on the outside from family and friends, Saleh said he paid a hefty bribe to the deputy police chief and was set free. But freedom did not remove the sting of defeat. "I was very angry that [the Taliban] would face this fate [at the hands of General Dostum]. We were naive to think this would not happen." Saleh fled to Iran and stayed for four years.

The Taliban prisoners' fate at Shiberghan was first exposed by *Newsweek* magazine reporters in an August 25, 2002, story titled "The Death Convoy of Afghanistan." Witnesses and survivors described as many as one hunded men or more stuffed into the containers, with many dying of suffocation and dehydration. By the time they arrived in Shiberghan, only ten or twenty were alive.

The graves outside of Shiberghan at the edge of Dasht-e-Leili were discovered in early 2002 by members of the Boston-based Physicians for Human Rights group, when human bones and pieces of clothing began appearing from the shallow graves near the town's landfill. The remains were exposed by scavenging dogs and gusting winds. In 2008, when forensic scientists revisited the site, it had been disturbed, raising complaints that the bodies had been moved, reportedly under orders from General Dostum. A detailed investigation of the site has never been completed. Human rights activists cite resistance not only from the Afghan government but also from the Pentagon and US officials who may prefer not to potentially denigrate former heroes in the war against the Taliban and possibly expose a US role at Shiberghan.

An Undiscovered Grave

Three months after my visit to the mass graves at Dasht-e-Leili, I was again with Saleh, scuffing along the crusted moonscape about ten miles east of Mazar-e-Sharif, headed to yet another mass Taliban grave. We had zigzagged and bounced in a four-wheel-drive vehicle over the shallow ditches that crisscrossed the land to mark property boundaries. The sun was blistering. Camels meandered in the distance, plodding with their graceful gait, pausing to chomp on the thorny green plants that defiantly dotted that landscape.

"They had long turbans and were bound together," Saleh said, gesturing to a mound nearby where part of a black turban had been unearthed. Beside it was a jawbone, the teeth firmly intact. "They were forced to kneel on the ground, then shot, ten at a time." Unlike the well-publicized graves at Shiberghan, this one was previously unknown and undocumented. Yet it was on the outskirts of Mazar-e-Sharif and not far from a village of mud-plastered houses obscured by leafy green trees. It was a Taliban village, Saleh said. His village.

Saleh had told me of this mass grave months earlier and it had intrigued me ever since. Saleh gestured to the north, saying that there were more mass graves like this one scattered across the land like garden plots of the dead, stretching all the way to Tajikistan. The Taliban prisoners in this particular grave came from the early battles between the Northern Alliance and the Taliban, he said. Flush from victory in Kabul in October 1996, the Taliban steadily pushed northward. Six months later in the spring of 1997, the Taliban were at the gates of Mazar-e-Sharif. If Mazar fell, all of northern Afghanistan would become Taliban country. The Taliban knew they could not defeat the Northern Alliance head-on. But there was another way.

The Northern Alliance included strongman Ismail Khan, who controlled the west; General Dostum, who controlled the Uzbek provinces of Faryab and Jawzjan; and Atta Mohammad Noor and Marshal Fahim, who commanded Balkh Province and sections of the north. In the alliance were two powerful Uzbek brothers fighting under the command of General Dostum: General Abdul Malik Pahlawan and his older brother, Rasul. When Rasul was assassinated by a bodyguard, Malik blamed Dostum for instigating the death.

The alliance cracked when Malik made a deal with the Taliban that would let them enter Mazar-e-Sharif, which would lead to their control of the north and force General Dostum out of the country, thus avenging the death of Malik's brother. The Taliban agreed, promising to respect Malik's rule over Mazar-e-Sharif but only if Malik would turn over Ismail Khan to them. Malik kept his part of the bargain, captured Khan, and handed him over.

Malik's agreement was that the Taliban could occupy Mazar-e-Sharif but had to respect the "way of life" in the north. This meant that women could go to school and people could continue with most other aspects of life in the more liberal and progressive north. Instead, the Taliban blatantly defied their promise, fanned throughout the city, shuttered girls' schools, and forced women off the streets. They went from house to house, collecting weapons. They marched into the markets, demanding cash from merchants. Merchants and residents responded by grabbing their guns and starting to shoot. By the next day, at least three hundred people were dead. The killing continued for days. Seeking revenge for the Taliban's betrayal, Malik's forces attacked the Taliban, pushing them out of Mazar-e-Sharif. But this also allowed General Dostum to return in October of that year, and he exacted his own revenge by defeating Malik in November and forcing Malik to flee to Iran. Ismail Khan, meanwhile, escaped from the Taliban.

The Taliban fighters buried in the ground where we were standing had died during that time, Saleh said. They had been taken to this spot and shot in the dead of night, their bodies left to rot. When villagers collected their camels the next morning, they came across the carnage. Some Taliban fighters had miraculously survived and were taken to the nearby village where Saleh now lived and were treated.

Wrong Elements

General Abdul Malik lived on a graveled lane in a quiet corner of Mazar-e-Sharif. When we met in mid-August 2011, four chairs had been arranged in the shade on the grassy lawn that fronted his multistory house. It was late afternoon, and the heat of the day lingered in the listless air. I wanted to talk about his days battling the Taliban, the dirty deals, the Taliban collapse, the mass graves, and the bones in the desert. But I didn't. Enough was known of Afghanistan's past, and Malik's version of events was one of many.

Before we could get to discussing justice in Afghanistan for past crimes, we needed to talk about how Afghanistan could first find peace. I had already realized that the many cases of injustice were not just being swept under the carpet in Afghanistan; they were being ignored. Afghans were prepared to roll up their carpets and leave. Their house was on fire.

Malik walked slowly from his front steps to our circle of chairs. He wore a flowing green robe and settled into a chair and smiled.

"What do you think of the past ten years, and where do you think Afghanistan is headed?" I asked.

"What the international community has done is not right," he answered. "They've spent a huge amount of money. All of it was a mistake." When the foreign forces arrived, they thought that "whoever had a Land Cruiser or money was good to work with." This showed little or no understanding of the history or regional dynamics, and as a result, the coalition selected "the wrong elements" to run the country when the Taliban fell. "It made the rich richer and the powerful more so."

Afghans were disgusted when the United States "brought a person who owned a restaurant and made him the president because he speaks good English," Malik said of President Karzai. Instead of building a country, Karzai and the power elite took control of the land, the banks, and the drugs. "Afghanistan is in the hands of a small mafia. They will not let the international community connect with the Afghan people." If the international community wanted to help Afghanistan, the top two hundred most powerful people in Afghanistan would have to be removed and the past two fraudulent elections would need to be negated, Malik said. "Then Afghanistan can be comfortable."

When the coalition first arrived in Afghanistan, he said, "We thought they'd make each province like their own country. But we were wrong. They brought some thieves. They did it for themselves." In the past ten years, "Nothing has been done for the people. [Those in power] have tricked the Afghan people. They were deceived. The Taliban were terrorists [but] are now being negotiated with. This is a mystery to people." In fact, "no Afghan has any interest in the Taliban," he said. But when the United States decided it wanted to make a peace deal with the Taliban so it could exit Afghanistan easily, the Taliban were given renewed power and credibility. "They think that the Taliban are now the true way," Malik said.

Nearly fifteen years earlier, Malik had negotiated a peace deal with the Taliban but on a much smaller scale. "Do you think the American and Afghan governments' efforts to talk with the Taliban will result in peace?" I asked.

"It will have no result. I am in favor of peace, [but negotiation] is only a waste of time. I know the Taliban. I had an agreement with the Taliban in 1997. It didn't have any result. We [must] accept that the Taliban is our ideological opposite."

The international presence in Afghanistan had been an abject failure, Malik said. Security was worse in 2011 than it had been at the height of the occupation by the former Soviet Union in 1988 and 1989. Schools were better under the Soviets, and so was the economy. "The Afghan people think like this," he said, which was why the Taliban were getting stronger. "Mistrust of the government has been increasing."

Afghanistan would have been much better off, Malik said, if each of the forty countries that sent forces as part of the coalition had simply taken one thousand young Afghans to their countries for an education.

"We would have forty thousand professional youths. Instead, the West is leaving, but what remains here? If we had educated people, we would have hope."

Afghans were angry that little had improved. "Everyone is lying to the Afghan people, from the president on down to the soldiers. The [international community] should directly contact the Afghan people, especially with education and job creation," and should not work through the existing governmental structures, he said.

"Schools and clinics have been built," I said, "even in remote areas, and roads throughout the country have been paved and improved."

That was fine, Malik said, but Afghanistan still was unable to stand on its own two feet without massive aid. "What has been done? We have oil and gas in the north. Do we have gas in our homes? Do we have refineries? These are questions people are asking." The best and brightest Afghans were leaving for education and economic opportunities. "They do whatever they can to feed their families," he said.

What Malik described was true. A couple of my Afghan friends had earned advanced degrees under the United States' Fulbright educational grants. When they returned to help rebuild the country, they could not find jobs that matched their skills. "Do you, like many other Afghans, say that Iran and Pakistan are the source of Afghanistan's problems?" I asked.

Iran and Pakistan had successfully destabilized Afghanistan, despite the billions of dollars spent and the presence of nearly 140,000 foreign troops from the world's best armies, Malik said. But in the process, Afghans were the ones who suffered. Iran and Pakistan had influence over the Afghan government because Karzai let them have it. These counties "are in contact with the high level of government officials. They are always listening to them," Malik said, noting that Karzai had admitted to accepting large amounts of cash from Iran for dubious reasons. The Afghan people could never benefit in the same way, he said. "The [Pakistan] ISI and Iran will not pay any money to an [average] Afghan."

Until recently, Malik believed that Afghanistan had a strong future. "I was hopeful. I was never weak. But today I am very worried for my sons and daughters. I was born in this country. I fought against the Soviets. I fought against the Taliban. I have witnessed the tragedies of this land," he said.

When coalition forces leave Afghanistan, things will worsen, he predicted. "The international community can't stay forever. [But] the police, the Afghan National Army, the security forces cannot solve our problems. Afghanistan will be one of the most dangerous countries in the world. The drama will not end. Another page [in Afghan history] will open."

"What will be written on that page?" I asked.

"Within one month of the international forces leaving, the Taliban will be in control," Malik said. "I will be either killed or I will escape."

"Would you stay and fight, as in the past?" I asked.

"We will not surrender to the Taliban. We will fight with the Taliban," Malik said. "We might be killed, but there is no other way."

Graves, Jobs, and Human Rights

Investigating Afghan human rights violations and what are broadly called war crimes was the duty of the Afghanistan Independent Human Rights Commission. For the past ten years, the commission, an official agency of the Afghan government, had compiled ten thousand cases of civil and human rights abuses that had taken place over the previous thirty years. A compilation of these cases was to have been released publicly in June 2010. Instead, it was kept secret. If the files were made public, it was feared, they would spark another civil war, possibly worse than the first. The files would only be released "when the time is right," I was told by Nader Naderi, the commission director at the time. When that time might be was anyone's guess. Even though no names were used in the report, Afghans knew who had committed what atrocities, where, and when. Memories of the atrocities were still raw.

Pressure mounted throughout 2011 for the release of the report, but in late December 2011, when most of the international community was gone for the Christmas and New Year holiday, Karzai fired Naderi and his closest associate, Ahmad Fahim Hakim, both of whom it was said had become too cozy with the international human rights community. Karzai's office explained Naderi and Hakim's unexpected departure by saying that the two men's terms had expired, so the president replaced them. In effect, Karzai's move ensured the report would never see the light of day, sparing many high-ranking members of his cabinet from embarrassment.

But the United States also had an interest in keeping the report under wraps. US officials had long feared that the report's details of Taliban atrocities in the late 1990s and the vicious response that they had provoked might derail efforts to get the Taliban to the peace table. "Now is not the right time" for the report's release, said a US official who was quoted in the *New York Times*. The past was Afghanistan's problem. The United States wanted a deal with the Taliban so it could go home.

But the volume of human rights atrocities that had accumulated over the prior thirty years was more than just an Afghan problem. Without some acknowledgment and discussion of the crimes of the past, Afghans had little hope of bringing the perpetrators to justice. Without justice for the victims and survivors of these crimes, there was little way Afghans could move forward with a sense of having resolved their differences.

South Africa had dispelled pent-up racial animosity from apartheid by setting up truth and reconciliation commissions where perpetrators and victims were able to confront each other and confess. Rwanda had done something similar following a dozen years of trials at the International Criminal Tribunal for Rwanda. Tribunals had been set up for war crimes committed in the former Yugoslavia and in Sierra Leone. The International Criminal Court (ICC) in The Hague, Netherlands, had issued indictments and was conducting trials for war criminals from Uganda and the Democratic Republic of the

Congo. A UN-sponsored court had been set up in Cambodia, where the Khmer Rouge had been on trial. But in Afghanistan, nothing had been done to resolve the war crimes of the past, ensuring that when international troops left Afghanistan, civil war would likely return. Old scores remained to be settled.

Qazi Same headed the regional office of the Afghanistan Independent Human Rights Commission in Mazar-e-Sharif. An affable man with a quick smile, Same's calm demeanor belied his delicate, if not dangerous, job. "If you look at the three periods of history, there are lots of mass graves," he said. "During the communists, there were not many. But when the mujahideen and Taliban were fighting for power, there were lots."

To illustrate how tenaciously Afghans could cling to past crimes, he told a gruesome joke. One day an Afghan came across a friend busily cutting off the leg of a dead enemy fighter. The Afghan asked his friend why he was doing that, since the man was already dead. The friend said, "Because someone already cut the head off." In this dark way, Same illustrated the need for war crimes justice.

The rights commission's mandate was to document cases, Same said, not put the culprits on trial. "Maintaining justice is up to the government. We have filed the cases." When the commission learned of an unreported war crime, such as a mass grave site, it was surveyed and documented, then reported to the local police so that it was not disturbed by those wanting to destroy incriminating evidence. The commission then interviewed witnesses and survivors.

It was virtually impossible to identify those responsible for the mass graves, Same said, because most of the commanders were still alive, and many held high positions in government. "People don't have the [power] to point fingers at certain commanders. The only thing we can do is specify during which regime [the killing] took place."

The most difficult cases to document took place during the Afghan civil war era, he said.

"Why is that?" I asked.

"It starts at the [Karzai] presidential palace. The commanders are there. It is too difficult because they own the government," Same said. This made his job and that of human rights activists difficult and dangerous. While there may be pressure from victims and the international community for justice to be rendered, there was resistance from and fear of those who controlled the government. Understandably, few people were willing to step forward and make accusations. "The worries people have are true," he said.

As a government official, Same's clout while investigating war crimes had diminished dangerously. Past and present militia commanders jealously guarded their power and only reluctantly ceded control to central government agencies such as his. "With warlords in government, the government is weak, it is true. The government can't maintain security."

Escalating attacks across the north crippled the work of the commission, which once aggressively followed up on attacks and assaults committed by the Taliban, the Afghan forces, and the international community. But as the security situation deteriorated, so did the commission's safety. "Before the election [in September 2010], we were able to go into every district and province to investigate human rights violations. When people saw our vehicles, they were afraid." But no longer. "When the Taliban kill children and accuse them of being spies, or kill people in a bank, what are they going to do when they see our vehicles?" Same asked.

For investigators and witnesses alike, danger lurked inside and outside of government. "There is no security from the government. If forces don't maintain security for people, [justice] means nothing for the people," Same said. Revenge could come from any corner. The commission had all but given up its work in the field.

"Do you think the Afghan commanders will ever be brought to justice?" I asked.

"We have hope that the situation will not remain like this," Same said. "The situation might change. There might be a day when these people are brought to justice. If the international community continues to support the Afghan National Army and the Afghan National Police, then there will be changes."

If international forces withdrew, however, Same had little hope for the future. "Without the international community, the Taliban will attack. People will defend themselves. Civil war will take place. But if the withdrawal was on schedule, and the Afghan national forces improved, then they can keep security."

The problem in Afghanistan was that development had taken a backseat to military objectives, Same explained. "In the past ten years there has been little infrastructure built in Afghanistan. But millions of dollars have been spent on the military." Irrigation projects were not built so farmers could grow crops, and power plants and refineries were not built to take advantage of northern Afghanistan's natural gas and oil deposits.

"When people are busy and have jobs, there will be no insurgency," Same said.

Mass Graves and Science

There was nothing ambivalent in either Same's or Malik's predictions. Without a sustained international military presence, civil war would erupt as surely as the sun rises and sets. It would be a fight to the death. The cycle of attack and counterattack would resume. Would the international community have to step back in, perhaps just months after it left?

On a quiet Kabul day in spring 2011, I met with Stefan Schmitt, who headed the International Forensic Program for the Boston-based group Physicians for Human Rights. This same organization had done much of the investigation of the mass graves at Dasht-e-Leili and Schmitt was intimately aware of those details. But he didn't want to talk about that site anymore, Schmitt said, since there was so much more to discuss if Afghanistan was to ever lift itself from the ashes of war and escape the endless cycle of ethnic bloodshed. He was convinced that a commitment by the international community might help avert what seemed to be Afghanistan's inevitable slide back into civil war.

Schmitt was keenly aware of the problems in Afghanistan, having lived there in the past and then eventually attending the Florida State University, where he received an advanced degree in criminology and criminal justice and specialized in forensic anthropology and crime scene analysis. Schmitt had worked for the International Criminal Tribunals for Rwanda and the former Yugoslavia and as a forensic consultant to the UN in countries such as Iraq, Afghanistan, and Liberia. He had also worked on human rights abuse cases in Guatemala, Honduras, El Salvador, Colombia, Algeria, Russia, and Kyrgyzstan.

"I don't like the term *warlord*," Schmitt said, correcting me often as I used the term frequently. He said it complicated matters since "those who are the warlords are in government. These were thugs from day one. They raped and pillaged. They'd taken entire neighborhoods [in Kabul] for themselves." During the Afghan civil war and Taliban period of the 1990s, territory often changed hands. As a result, "we don't have a clear perpetrator and victim," since groups were aggressors and victims at various times.

To sort through it, Schmitt suggested that Afghans and the international community begin a dialogue about war crimes and crimes against humanity. "By not talking about it, it's only going to get worse."

But there were problems to overcome. "How are we going to determine the truth? Who are we going to believe?" Little progress on these fronts had been made in Afghanistan because so far that situation had been "the powerful over the truth." His experience in other countries had shown that "this is not easy. You're going to have a lot of people fighting you," he said.

Afghan war crimes were extensive. The Afghanistan Independent Human Rights Commission had more than one hundred mass graves on record, and the death toll over the past twenty to thirty years could easily be 1.5 million people. "That's a possibility," Schmitt said. "There's a real need to address this."

The Afghan legal system was a major stumbling block. As in most countries, he said, "the courts are not interested in the truth. The courts are interested in whether a law was violated or not." This was the heart of the matter in Afghanistan. In 2007, a coalition of former warlords and others in parliament approved the National Stability and Reconciliation Law, which prevented the prosecution of those responsible for large-scale human rights abuses in the decades before December 2001. The law stated that anyone who engaged in armed conflict before that date could "enjoy all their legal rights and shall not be prosecuted."

Bowing to international pressure, President Karzai refused to sign the law, leaving it in legal limbo. Then in early 2010, the law was quietly published as part of Afghanistan legal code, though no one knows exactly why or how, or if the publication was legitimate. Regardless, most assumed that the law was in effect.

Courts were an arm of the state, Schmitt said, and as such, "the Afghan judicial system is not going to be able to conduct fair trials." He suggested that the natural body to investigate Afghan war crimes was the International Criminal Court, the world's first permanent court in The Hague, Netherlands, formed for the purpose of conducting trials for war crimes and crimes against humanity, including genocide. The United States is not a member of the court, ironically, with US administrations having argued that since America is the world's superpower, the court could become the tool of people interested in undermining and damaging American hegemony.

The impetus for justice should come from the Afghan communities most affected, Schmitt said. This was where forensic science fit in. Analysis of mass graves and massacre sites provided people with factual evidence. "You want to empower victims . . . by handing them a truth, or something as close as you can get . . . so they can begin to find their justice." It could take many years to prosecute individuals for war crimes. "We think they're going to fix this in a short period? You're not going to get over a war like this in a matter of decades."

Chances that the ICC would get involved in Afghanistan were slim, however. "Justice is an international responsibility," Schmitt said, but "we pretend we're not responsible." Rather than getting more involved, the world was leaving Afghanistan. "People in the US are just tired of [Afghanistan]. They want to withdraw at any cost." That cost could be higher than most want to admit, he said. "Afghanistan is the biggest challenge the world has. If we fail here, the war [against terror and injustice] is lost. It would be foolhardy to withdraw. I think it would be a big mistake."

While most Afghans were convinced that the return of the Taliban and another civil war was inevitable following the departure of international forces, others were not so sure. These Afghans had been actively fighting the Taliban at home on a daily basis, often with great success. Theirs was a very localized and often personal battle with the Taliban. One place they had been finding success was in Kapisa Province, just north of Kabul. I went to talk with them.

A woman leaves the voting station on election day, 2010, Kabul.

A seventeen-year-old boy shows his finger, inked from voting on election day.

A Kabul carpenter.

Pharmacist Gulam Hussein.

Destruction inside Darulaman Palace, Kabul.

A market in a village northeast of Kabul.

A boy in a pottery shop in Istalif, a village north of Kabul.

Community leader Abdul Manan signs papers at the Omar Farooq Mosque, Kabul.

Abdul Ghani, video shop owner, Jalalabad.

A cauliflower seller near Jalalabad.

Abdul Salam Zahid, the owner of Bost Radio, Lashkar Gah, Helmand Province.

Shopkeeper Mohammad Qasem, left, with friend Mohammad Nabi, Marja, Helmand Province.

Shopkeeper Haji Mohammad Ismail, Marja, Helmand Province.

Haji Mohammed Ismail's sons.

My translator, Umar, left, and police escort.

The author in a poppy field, Balkh Province, 2004.

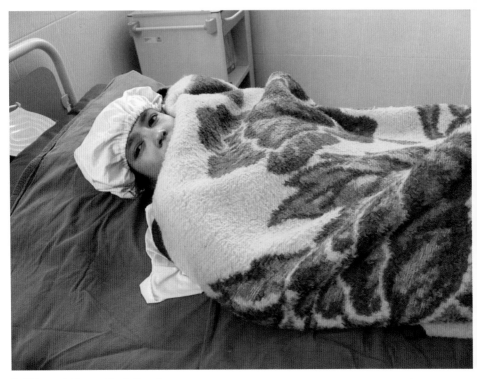

Self-immolation patient, Herat.

A *buzkashi* game, Kabul.

Human remains at a mass grave site near Mazar-e-Sharif.

Women at Blue Mosque, Mazar-e-Sharif.

A view across the Bamiyan valley to the site where two fifteen-hundred-year-old Buddha statues, destroyed by the Taliban in 2001, once stood.

Afghan archaeologist Zemaryalai Tarzi at the Bamiyan excavation site.

Children living in caves, Bamiyan.

Hazara women at the
Band-e-Amir lakes.

Excavation, Mes Aynak site.

Buddha statue remains, Mes Aynak site.

A busy market in northern Afghanistan.

A pomegranate seller, Samangan Province.

12

REJECTING THE TALIBAN

MAZARAI WAS FRUSTRATED. After two years as the deputy commander of a thirty-member unit of the local police in the village of Landakhel, he was leaving. "When we catch prisoners, we hand them over the government," he said, but, "When the Taliban arrests us, they hang us from a tree. If I stay here, I'll be killed by the Taliban. Many of us have no choice."

The village of Landakhel was in Tagab District in Kapisa Province, just northeast of Kabul. Like Wardak Province to Kabul's west, Kapisa was largely under the control of the Taliban. Kapisa's southern boundary was the highway between Kabul and Jalalabad, and it was from the rugged mountains of Kapisa that the Taliban scrambled down the rocky canyons that flanked the highway and routinely blasted the fuel tankers en route to Kabul.

Kapisa was nominally under the control of the French forces, which in 2011 and early 2012 would be attacked not only by Taliban fighters but by renegade soldiers in the Afghan army units that the French had been advising and training. Kapisa had not been kind to French soldiers. In early July 2011, a small French unit posted to Tagab District had been attacked by a suicide bomber as it assisted Afghan forces at a security checkpoint set up to protect a local council meeting. Five French soldiers and two Afghan civilians were killed, and

185

four French soldiers and two Afghan civilians were wounded. The Taliban claimed responsibility.

The attack came just a day after former French president Nicolas Sarkozy arrived in Afghanistan to say that France was pulling out about a thousand of its four thousand soldiers by the end of 2012. July 2011 was one of the deadliest months ever for French soldiers, the worst having been in August 2008, when ten French soldiers were killed in a mountain ambush just twenty-five miles from Kabul that involved some one hundred Taliban. The battle lasted more than twelve hours and involved NATO airstrikes.

Later, in December 2011, another two French soldiers, both members of the French Foreign Legion, would be shot and killed by an Afghan army soldier who was part of a joint Afghan-French army post in Tagab District. The Taliban would again claim responsibility for the attack and say there were more such Taliban infiltrators in the Afghan army and police waiting to strike.

The strike that the Taliban predicted in late December would come on January 20, 2012, when another Afghan soldier killed four French soldiers who were part of that same French-Afghan force in Kapisa. In all, fifteen French soldiers were wounded in that attack, eight of them seriously. Nearly eighty French soldiers have been killed in Afghanistan since late 2001.

Despite the widespread presence of the Taliban in the province, their grip was tenuous because of fighters such as Mazarai, who told me in August 2011 that he had joined the local police force shortly after the unit was created a couple of years earlier. These armed local police units were part of a controversial program pushed by US general David Petraeus, the former commander of the Afghan theater, to supplement the Afghan National Police. They were called the Afghan Local Police and were known colloquially as the *arbaki*. The units took able-bodied young men who were otherwise unemployed, then trained and equipped them to keep the peace. If nothing else, it kept them from being hired by the Taliban to fight the government and coalition.

While the *arbaki* were supported by the coalition's Provincial Reconstruction Teams, their true command and control was vague at best. Because of this, the local police program had varying degrees of success. In cities such as Mazar-e-Sharif, local police units were criticized for being little more than an auxiliary guard for the provincial governor. Others complained that the units were composed of criminals—the men who couldn't get jobs with either the police or army, which took almost anyone—and should not be armed. Rather than keep the peace, some said, these local police units added rogue elements to an already explosive situation.

In Landakhel, the local police had worked well. "They wanted security in their village," Mazarai said of his friends and neighbors. Police and government officials were being attacked, and bombs were buried alongside the roadways. "The Taliban were coming and destroying things. They were shooting police and kidnapping people. They did whatever they could to disrupt life there."

The Taliban commander was from a nearby village, Mazarai said, and went by the name of Mahibullah. Although the Taliban numbered only about twenty or thirty fighters, the force could swell to two hundred with an influx of additional men from surrounding districts. To counter the Taliban threat, Mazarai and his friends joined the local *arbaki*. "[We] were fighting them every night and could push them back. They wanted to fight the government and take control of Tagab District. I don't like them because they were doing all those bad things. The people decided to stand against the Taliban. They had no choice. We started with 11 and are now 120."

Mazarai bragged that he and his fellow local police had decimated the Taliban in his district. "The numbers of Taliban are less in Kapisa." But his brag was tempered with disappointment. "A lot of people here worked with the government, and we supported the government, but the government does not support us," he said.

Mazarai complained that management and support of the local police had switched from the NATO's Provincial Reconstruction Teams to the Afghan Ministry of the Interior. Because of this, the unit was not being paid, he said, suggesting that under Afghan control, the money went missing. "It was good," he said of the NATO direct support. "But since the [Afghan] government has taken over, we haven't been paid for months. We have to buy bread with our own money. We don't have any support from the government. We haven't even gotten bullets. That is why we are quitting. I am going to Iran."

Without the financial support from the top, command and control was virtually lost, Mazarai said. "They don't listen to their commanders," he said of men in his unit. "They will go rob some shops to get money. Where else will we get money?" Another problem was the quality of their weapons. "We have old AK-47s. The Taliban has new weapons. So the Taliban is increasing because they know they can fight these people," he said of the national police and army. The Taliban were carrying RPGs and mortars, he said.

Curious as to how the coalition was handling the local police, I contacted the international coalition and was told that the *arbaki*, contrary to Mazarai's claims, were not abandoning the fight against the Taliban in Kapisa. The coalition spokesman expressed surprise at what Mazarai had said. The coalition had "no information" about problems with pay, desertions due to the lack of pay, or old weapons. Control of the local police and their pay had been handed from NATO teams to the Afghan security forces just a month earlier. Prior to that, pay for the local police had been prompt, I was told.

I wondered if Mazarai had been intimidated by the Taliban or if he had just grown tired of the fight. Or had he seen the writing on the wall? "If you and your friends leave, does that put the village at risk?" I asked.

The unit might be reduced by about half, Mazarai said, but the remaining fighters were highly motivated. "About fifty people will be left. The rest will quit." The remaining local policemen will be "those who are personal enemies with the Taliban. They will go with the Afghan National Police. Me, I don't have any personal enemies."

As Mazarai detailed his frustrations, he revealed how Taliban fighters had terrorized families and communities. When any of his fellow *arbaki* were captured and hung, he said, "The Taliban doesn't let the families come get the body." This violated the Islamic practice that a dead body be buried within twenty-four hours. "We have to go fight for it. It [has] happened two times. That's what they do."

Once, "when [a local policeman] was hanged by the Taliban, we got the body down. But the mullahs from the villages wouldn't go to say the prayers because they were afraid of the Taliban. They sent a letter to the mullah not to do the prayers." Mullahs who contradicted the Taliban's orders "were beaten by the Taliban after the funeral. The mullahs were trying to hide from the Taliban. There were lots of cases like this." Mazarai and his friends turned to mullahs from outside the area to conduct the burial ceremonies. In the end, "they were buried with the prayers of a funeral," he said.

"If the local police force was reduced by half, was the door opened for the Taliban?" I asked.

"Of course," Mazarai said. "[Taliban] will come because they know the Afghan Local Police are decreasing." This did not bode well for anyone who supported the government. "It is dangerous for the Afghan Local Police to live there," Mazarai said of his village. "The people linked with the government will be killed by the Taliban."

Mazarai hoped to find work as a laborer in Iran. "If you have a passport and documents, they treat you well." His wife and family would also leave the district and would live in Kabul while he found work. "I cannot leave them [in the village]. It is too dangerous," he said.

"What is the future of Afghanistan?" I asked.

"Only God knows about the future."

The *Arbaki* and the Taliban

In mid-August 2011, not long after I spoke with Mazarai, the Taliban conducted a brazen and deadly attack on the provincial governor's office in Charikar, the quiet capital of Parwan Province, adjacent to Kapisa Province and immediately north of Kabul. Governor

Abdul Basir Salangi reportedly was grilling his police chief and top aides about a rumored attack on his office just as suicide bombers detonated a carload of explosives that demolished the gate of his compound and broke windows more than a block away. Rocket-propelled grenades were fired as five suicide attackers swarmed into the compound, beginning a three-hour gun battle. At one point Salangi, a former mujahideen commander, picked up the rifle of a fallen guard and shot an attacker, an action he gladly recounted for local television. In the end, twenty-two people were killed, six of whom were police officers and the rest of whom were government staff and civilians. At least thirty-four were wounded, ten of them police officers.

The attack left the province shaken. It was part of the growing insurgency in what had been subdued provinces such as Parwan, which was within sight of America's sprawling Bagram Airfield. The attack on the Parwan governor's office came just eight days after the Taliban had downed a Chinook helicopter in the Wardak Province, immediately west of Kabul, killing thirty US Special Forces members. The crash included some SEAL Team Six members, the commando group that had killed Osama bin Laden. These attacks undercut US command's claims that the Taliban were growing weaker, and they came as military officials were implementing the first drawdowns of US surge troops deployed to Afghanistan more than a year earlier. Parwan was due to transition from NATO to Afghan control in the following months.

With the help of Afghan colleagues in Charikar, I contacted a local Taliban commander who went by the name of Shahin Sapai and who operated in both Parwan and Kapisa Provinces. The Taliban were increasingly active in these provinces, I said, despite the fact that many people were joining the *arbakis*. I asked Sapai why.

"The Taliban are active because people support them. This government is a corrupt and non-Islamic government," Sapai said. "So from the Islamic point of view, the people don't like this government, and this is the reason that . . . people are mujahideen. People like the Islamic Emirate of Afghanistan [because] the foreigners attacked our country. These *arbakis* are criminals. They've left their religion and [therefore] they don't have a place in society. They demand money from people and are beating elders. All people here are our supporters, and only a few [non-Taliban] do anything for money."

"Why does the Taliban attack the fuel tankers on the Kabul-Jalalabad highway," I asked, "when civilians are injured and their travel is disrupted by these attacks?"

"On the Kabul-Jalalabad highway there are some money lovers who support foreign forces by delivering fuel and other materials. Those materials are used against Islam. Our mujahideen are taken to Bagram and Guantanamo prisons, so we have to do this. It only stops the traffic for two hours, or a maximum of one day. The important thing is that we neutralize the plans and operations of foreign forces. It creates a lot of problems for them."

"How are the Taliban able to fight both foreign and Afghan forces?" I asked.

"We have the support of God. With the help of God, we will fight all these *kafirs* and their friends. In the beginning of Islam, the number of mujahideen was also few, but they could defeat their enemies."

"Are the Taliban supported by Iran and Pakistan?" I asked.

"Whenever there is cruelty against a Muslim, other Muslims can support and help them, wherever they are. Yes, we do have the support and help of Muslim countries like Iran, Pakistan, and other Islamic countries," Sapai said.

"Would you ever make peace with the Afghan government?" I asked.

"We will never talk with the government. We do what our God and Koran say. If these *kafirs* leave the country, then we won't have any problem with people. But now this country is colonized by America, and this government does what America wants. We will succeed, and we will bring Sharia law to this country," Sapai said.

"What will happen when foreign forces leave Afghanistan?" I asked.

"When they leave, we will clean this soil of their traitorous [Afghan] friends. Actually, these foreigners are [already] defeated from this country, just like the Russians. We will have our Islamic emirate in Afghanistan again. The only thing we are afraid of is their airplanes. Otherwise, we would have complete control of Afghanistan by now," he said.

Sapai's comments echoed those of Sheikh, the Taliban commander with whom I had spoken in Herat, and Ahmadi, the Taliban spokesman in Helmand Province. It was a coordinated and consistent message from the Taliban to rally Afghans to their resurgent cause. Afghanistan was an occupied country, and the Taliban portrayed themselves as the liberators, capitalizing on the frustration and disappointment that most Afghans felt with foreigners. Sapai offered an ominous warning to the *arbakis* and anyone else they considered friends of the government: the Taliban would get these people, and Afghanistan would be cleansed of them.

With the help of a local Afghan journalist, I met with six Kapisa residents who described the realities of life with the Taliban in their villages throughout the Kapisa and what they saw ahead for themselves and their country.

Sharpoor Safi

Safi was in his late twenties and taught the Pashto language at the high school in his village. His distaste for the Taliban dated from the late 1990s, when the Taliban controlled Afghanistan. "Before, when there was the Taliban, they'd make a lot of trouble," he said. The Taliban were just as they always had been. They had entered his school, essentially holding the students and faculty hostage, using them as human shields as they fought with Afghan police and army. The Taliban had grabbed Safi's nephew, given him a weapon, and told him to use it against the Afghan army and police. When Safi confronted the Taliban about it, demanding that they leave his nephew alone, he was accused of working for the government.

Safi was disgusted with the Taliban's lack of morality. To the Taliban, he said, "killing and beheading was OK. Just like an animal, [it was] neither good nor bad." If anyone in his village resisted the Taliban, it meant death. "A lot of them were beaten. If they argued with them, they'd get killed." More than once, Safi had fled his village for his own safety.

He was convinced that the Taliban could not survive without foreign help, in particular from Pakistan. "A while ago, I was given a letter by the Taliban and told to read it to my class. It told the students to fight against the government and the foreigners," he said. Safi believed the letter had been written by Pakistanis, explaining that "it was printed on a computer" and was part of the Taliban's information campaign. He refused to read it to his class, he said.

"Why do you resist the Taliban so strongly?" I asked.

"They don't let hospitals use female doctors. How can people tolerate that?" he asked. He knew of instances where the Taliban had refused to let a woman get medical treatment. "They were threatening doctors who treated women."

The Taliban had been kept at bay by the *arbaki*, who numbered about fifty or sixty fighters in his village. Safi was despondent about the departure of foreign forces from Afghanistan. "If foreigners leave, I don't know what the future will be."

Jawed Rahimullah

Rahimullah was twenty-one and from Alasai District in Kapisa, which he said was controlled by the Taliban. Though his family had vacated his village and moved to Kabul, Rahimullah remained behind to complete his twelfth year of school so he could graduate and attend a university in Kabul, where he wanted to study English, he said. The Taliban disrupted schools and intimidated students, especially young men. "If they see you without a beard, they stop you. They stop cars and take [music] tapes. If someone works for the government or the police, they injure them and their family, such as an uncle or cousin. Sometimes the Taliban comes in the afternoon, stops people in the bazaar, and asks them what they do. The schools for girls are closed by the Taliban."

"Why does the Taliban do those things?" I asked.

"If the girls study, then girls can get jobs with the government," he said, which was considered evil by the Taliban, who said women belong only at home.

The Taliban were getting money, weapons, and fighters from Pakistan, Rahimullah said. "There are some foreign people with the Taliban. We see them." He said he was baffled by US policy toward Pakistan, which was playing a double game by taking US military aid as it claimed to be fighting terrorism, yet at the same time supported the Taliban and other antigovernment forces. He hoped coalition forces would not leave Afghanistan. "If the international community stays, it will be good. If the foreign countries don't leave, it is possible to remove the Taliban," he said. But if foreigners left, the Taliban "will soon have control of the province."

Mohammad Saber

Saber was about twenty-five years old and from Nijrab District in Kapisa. He had fought the Taliban as a young teenager, in the late 1990s. With the arrival of the US forces in 2001, he became a farmer and grew wheat and corn. The Taliban were in his community but didn't control it. "They can't stay there. They just pass through," to conduct attacks in other parts of the province, Saber said.

"How do you know they are Taliban?" I asked.

"They all had beards," he said. While the Taliban fighters didn't stay in the area, they deeply affected life in his village. "The schools are not working properly because of the Taliban. They stop people and accuse them of working for the government. They disturb me a lot. If I see them, I go the other way."

"Do you send your children to school?" I asked.

"They go to school because we take them. If there is fighting, we don't take them," Saber said. All too often, there was fighting, usually two or three times each week. The Taliban regularly attacked police and army convoys and stopped vehicles at checkpoints, forcing men in the village to help them. "They're doing some bad things," he said. "Even my family has guns. I couldn't live without a weapon."

"What happens when international forces withdraw?" I asked.

"We won't let the foreigners leave the country," he said. "They've made enemies for us. They can't leave us here." It was a serious dilemma for many Afghans. The war against the Taliban had forced most Afghans to choose between the pro- or antigovernment groups. Withdrawal of international forces was a virtual death sentence for those who had sided with the government and international community against the Taliban.

"What about the Afghan forces?" I asked. "Won't they provide protection?"

He doubted it. The Afghan National Army only came to his village if there was a major battle to be fought. His village was best protected by the local police. "The *arbaki* is better because they are local and are fighting the Taliban very well."

Nek Mohammad

Nek Mohammad was twenty-seven years old. He lived in Nijrab District in Kapisa Province. Roughly translated into English, the name of his village was Big Valley. He had been a math teacher for ten years. The Taliban occupied the neighboring village and, said Nek Mohammad, "they're threatening people at night." As in Helmand and other provinces, the Taliban had threatened telephone companies, forcing them to cut telephone service at night. "After the evening prayers, if they don't turn off [service], they'll shoot the [towers] with rockets. People are scared," Nek Mohammad said.

"Have you or your neighbors complained to the telephone companies?" I asked.

"Yes, we've complained. But they're not able to do anything," he said. "They've spent a lot of money on towers."

"Have the Taliban destroyed any towers?" I asked.

"No," he said. "They have only threatened them."

Nek Mohammad was disgusted with the government. "The government should take control of these people and provide good security for us. In our area, no one likes the Taliban. They are doing a lot of bad things. When they fight, they just shoot civilians."

The withdrawal of foreign forces was a big problem for Afghanistan, he said. "The Afghan army and police will take control," he said, "but they will have problems." He doubted that peace with the Taliban was possible, even though some of his neighbors "believe that if foreign troops leave, then the Taliban won't fight anymore."

Nek Mohammad considered the Taliban to be criminals. "These people who come in the name of the Taliban, I hate them. They're not real Taliban. They are just using the name. They have traveled from Pakistan. If I catch any of them, I will kill them." His dislike of the Taliban stemmed from the late 1990s, when they controlled all of Afghanistan. "People will never forget that, even until doomsday."

Abdul Razaq

Razaq was thirty and also from Nijrab District. He farmed, growing and harvesting walnuts. The Taliban traveled the district, threatening people, and "the people don't want the Taliban there," he said, and so far had resisted them. But the Taliban were relentless. "Day by day, people see strangers" they suspect of being Taliban from elsewhere. "They have had bad experiences," he said of his home villagers. "[Taliban] are stopping cars and government people."

More than a decade ago, Razaq had been arrested and jailed by the Taliban, accused of being from the Panjshir Valley north of Kapisa Province, the home of the Taliban's fiercest resistance. He fully expected the Taliban to take over the country when foreign forces left. "Their only purpose is to destroy our community. They destroy our security. They even kill scholars. That's against Islam. If they come," Razaq vowed, "we will stand together and fight them."

Atta Mohammad

Mohammad was forty and from Tagab District. His village was under the protection of the local *arbaki*, but the Taliban were a constant threat. The worst problem was being caught in the middle of the frequent gun battles between the Taliban and the Afghan forces. "Shooting by the Afghan and foreign troops has a lot of danger, mostly from big weapons. They don't care about civilians," he said.

While he disliked the Taliban, Mohammad had little love for the Afghan government, which he said was corrupt. "I don't like the government. My hope is to have a government [that is] not a slave of other countries. We need good government." He was angry that the international community was preparing to vacate Afghanistan, however. Their job was unfinished. "If you build a building, you have to finish it," he said, referring to Afghanistan. "You just can't build the walls and leave. If they leave it half done, then everything will be destroyed."

Afghanistan would survive only "if the army and police are well trained. Then it will be OK. We don't have any money, [so] we still need help from foreign countries. Inshallah, we have good hope for the future." Though Afghanistan needed more foreign assistance, Mohammad quipped, "I hate foreigners. My hope is that they try their best to stop this war and to put pressure on Pakistan and Iran. Afghans should forget their ethnicity. I wish they would stop discriminating [against each other] and live in peace and unity."

Born in War, Die in War

At the end of one particularly long day in Mazar-e-Sharif, I sat down with Enayat Najafizada, the young Afghan journalist who worked with me as a fixer and translator. We rested on cushions and drank black tea on the top floor of what had become a de facto news-media building, which contained numerous radio stations and bureaus of the national television networks. Beyond the glass windows, the famous Blue Mosque glimmered in the setting sun.

Najafizada's earliest memories of the Taliban were of their attacks on Mazar-e-Sharif in 1997 and the city's eventual collapse. "This was my life as a young Afghan," he said. "I was born in war and I will die in war. This is a tragedy." He paused to sip his tea and continued. "Every human has the right to a life in peace. But Afghanistan is a playground for superpowers. We Afghans are the most unlucky people in the world. We can't overcome all the turmoil and chaos in our country," he said.

Najafizada remembered the Taliban bursting into his house, rousting his uncle from his bed, and dragging him into the night. It began an extended period of travel and turmoil for Najafizada and his family, who fled to Kabul and later to Pakistan. "We decided to go to Pakistan because the girls were not allowed to go to school [in Kabul]."

The family settled in Peshawar and wove carpets to survive. From Peshawar, they moved to Quetta, where "we started our education from zero." After three years there, in the fall of 2001, he learned of the death of the Panjshiri commander Ahmad Shah Massoud at the hands of Taliban assassins. It happened just two days before the 9/11 attack on the Twin Towers.

The family then moved to Iran, where he continued his studies and lived until his grandfather's death. "I was always with my grandfather. My grandfather loved me very much. When he died in Iran, I was with him. It affected me."

Najafizada returned to Kabul in 2003 with his father and uncle and attended a private school, where he mastered English. He excelled at his studies and skipped several grades, receiving his diploma in 2005. He moved back to his hometown of Mazar-e-Sharif, where he attended classes at Balkh University by day and translated for the German army at night. An older brother worked for the BBC, and through this connection, he was selected for a journalism training program in Berlin for three months. It was an uncomfortable time, he recalled, because, being an Afghan, he was viewed with suspicion. "They were always thinking that I was a suicide attacker." Najafizada returned to Afghanistan and began contributing stories to major Western news media outlets.

During the next six years, Najafizada developed an extensive array of contacts, including the Taliban, police, and military and government officials, as well as religious and civil society leaders. It gave him a deep understanding of the dilemma faced by his country, which made him invaluable to foreign journalists, such as me, and others who worked for publications such as the *New York Times*, the *Washington Post*, and *Der Spiegel* magazine.

"This [Afghan war] will continue for a few years more," he predicted, since "the level of interference from other countries is very high. Every day the situation is worse." Security had deteriorated steadily due to escalating attacks by the Taliban and other antigovernment groups. After ten years of war and occupation, Afghans were war weary and cynical, he said.

Early in the war, that was not the case, Najafizada said. When foreign forces arrived, "Every Afghan was hopeful that Afghanistan would be like a European country in ten years. But it was just a dream." In 2006, skepticism began to take hold. "The Taliban began to reappear in the villages. We heard of attacks by the Taliban, [but] we never thought they would be attacking the government. No one believed that the Taliban would again be as they are now. ISAF was here. We were feeling fine."

The Taliban continued to grow and in 2007 reemerged in their heartland of Kandahar and Helmand Provinces. "The Taliban began to fight the government in the south." In 2008 and 2009 the fighting intensified, and by 2009, the Taliban surfaced in the northern provinces of Kunduz, Baghlan, and Takhar. By 2010, "the Taliban was poised to attack the government in Mazar-e-Sharif," something that had been unthinkable just a couple of years earlier. "In the past two years, the Taliban have appeared in every province," Najafizada said.

"How has this happened?" I asked.

With the stunning collapse of the Taliban in 2001, Afghanistan was left with no government and no formal organization to replace it, Najafizada explained. The American forces were more concerned with chasing the Taliban remnants and capturing Osama bin Laden than creating a new and democratic government. Taking the easy way out, the United States turned to the Northern Alliance and the existing warlords who had controlled—and nearly destroyed—the country prior to the ascendency of the Taliban. These former mujahideen commanders, all of whom had participated in the Afghan civil war, were once again in power.

The former Taliban leadership faded back into society but continued to exert enormous influence in Afghanistan, while the Pashtun ethnic group, the country's largest, was effectively excluded from power. Although Karzai was president and a Pashtun, his two top vice presidents were a Tajik and a Hazara, and many of the key cabinet posts were occupied by non-Pashtuns. The ethnic Pashtuns who did fill out the cabinet were moderates, many of whom had studied and obtained higher-education degrees abroad. But an even more telling indication of the alienation of the ethnic Pashtuns was that the officer corps and the rank-and-file soldiers of the Afghan army were largely Tajiks, Uzbeks, or pro-government Pashtuns from the Kabul region. This meant that in eastern and southern Afghan regions, where fighting was the heaviest, the war pitted ethnic Tajiks and Uzbeks of the Afghan National Army fighting alongside coalition forces against the mostly ethnic Pashtun Taliban of Afghanistan's south and east.

"The Taliban were never given a chance to be part of the government," Najafizada explained. "Yet, they also want power and money and to live in peace. But the Taliban were extremists. The mujahideen were not extremists, and because they witnessed the Taliban government . . . the mujahideen did not want to be like that."

Pashtuns dominated southern and eastern Afghanistan and were scattered across the north, but they were never treated equally by the government, Najafizada continued. "They got angry," he said of the Pashtuns. Meanwhile, "the Taliban were not sleeping. They were waiting for an opportunity. They saw that there was unemployment. There was no security." So the Taliban told sympathetic elements in Pakistan that, "This is the time you should help us."

The exclusion of the Taliban from any meaningful role in government generated resentment among Pashtuns and led to the resurgence of the Taliban. It could well be the future demise of the Afghan government.

"One of the big mistakes by the Bush [administration] was that they didn't want a [power-]sharing government in Afghanistan," Najafizada said. "[Bush] wanted to control the country with the mujahideen warlords. He made a big mistake because the Afghan people suffered a lot from [mujahideen] during the civil war. But they accepted [the return of the mujahideen commanders], because they remembered the harsh Taliban government. If we had a [leader] who was not linked to any of these groups, we are sure it would be different now," Najafizada surmised. "Karzai was not a good choice."

It had been a choice for the Afghan people between the lesser of two evils. The Taliban government had been bloody and brutal—but, then, so had the Afghan civil war when the former mujahideen commanders had fought over the country; an estimated tens of thousands of Afghans had died. Most Afghans had accepted the return to power of the mujahideen warlords only as a transitional phase. But the transition did not happen. The old power structure became a permanent part of the new and supposedly democratic government.

When Karzai and the former mujahideen leaders were reelected for another five years in 2009, Afghans felt helpless, Najafizada said. They became convinced that the United States and its European allies had ulterior motives for being in Afghanistan. Defeating the Taliban was not the objective but was instead an excuse to stay. "If there are 140,000 forces here, what is the purpose?" Najafizada asked. "Why can't they do something [against the Taliban]?"

Why, indeed? I wondered, but I didn't have an answer. Later, as I thought about Najafizada's question, I agonized over the growing strength of the Taliban. My frustration only increased when US officials began to say that al-Qaeda, which was a bit player in Afghanistan, and not the Taliban, was in fact the enemy. This amounted to a sweeping concession of Afghanistan to the Taliban and a reneging on American promises, both spoken and implied, and negated a decade of war, not to mention the loss of thousands of American soldiers.

Still, there was one place in Afghanistan where the Taliban had no control, yet it had left an ugly scar nonetheless. It was the province of Bamiyan, home of the Hazara people who lived high in the Hindu Kush mountains. I went there to learn more about what the Taliban had done there and how the Hazara had maintained their autonomy.

13

THE CAVES OF BAMIYAN

SAID MIRZA HUSSEIN PRESSED the bicycle tube against the knee of his grease-stained overalls and roughed the rubber around the small hole as he talked about the Taliban. "When the Taliban came, I lived in a cave between the big one and the small one," he said, referring to two Buddha statues that once towered over the central Afghanistan valley of Bamiyan.

In March 2001, after condemning the fifteen-hundred-year-old Buddhas as idols of the infidels and an abomination against Islam, the Taliban set about destroying these UNESCO World Heritage landmarks. "First they tried with tanks and rockets," Hussein said. "Then they put explosives in the feet." None of these methods was getting the job done, so the Taliban rounded up Bamiyan villagers to help or be killed.

Now the proprietor of a small bicycle repair shop in the town of Bamiyan, Hussein had lived for fifteen years in one of the hundreds of caves carved into the cliff of the soft rock that rose more than two hundred feet above the green patchwork of potato and wheat fields that covered the Bamiyan valley. These same caves had once housed Buddhist monks and pilgrims who came from as far away as China to meditate and practice their religion from the first century to about the eighth century AD. They plastered and painted the cave walls with religious designs and images of Buddha. Today, some fifteen centuries later, these caves provide free housing for Bamiyan's poorest families, just as they did in 2001 when Taliban fighters took over their town.

"When the Taliban came, I moved from the caves into the village," Hussein explained, hoping that the move would allow him to blend in and be more protected. Hussein was an ethnic Hazara, people said to have descended from Genghis Khan's Mongolian invaders who captured the Bamiyan valley in 1221 after swarming across Asia and the mountains of Afghanistan. Khan's soldiers killed anyone who stood in their way and left their genetic imprint—a distinctly oriental cast to the faces of future generations of Hazara.

As Hussein wandered the town one day in 2001 looking for an odd job and a bit of cash to feed his family of six, several members of the Taliban, who were largely ethnic Pashtuns, grabbed him, tied his hands and feet, and tossed him in jail.

"I didn't have any hope of being released," Hussein recalled, glancing up from his tube repair. "They would kill all who they arrested," he said, adding that he was beaten and burned with scalding water. "The crime was being Hazara. They accused me of being a *kafir*."

The Hazara were Shia Muslims, not Sunni Muslims like the Taliban and most other Afghans. The split between Shia and Sunni Muslims dates from the death of the Prophet Muhammad, when a debate arose over who should lead the Muslims. Shia Muslims believed that leadership should have passed directly to Muhammad's cousin and son-in-law, Ali. Sunnis, on the other hand, sided with the Prophet's companions who argued that the new leader should be elected from among those most capable of the job. The Sunnis prevailed, but the Shia Muslims don't recognize the authority of elected Muslim leaders and instead follow a line of imams who they believe have been appointed by the Prophet Muhammad or God.

Hussein said he was imprisoned by the Taliban for about a month, just as the destruction of the Buddhas was getting under way. At night, he was locked up and tortured. During the day, he was taken to the base of the largest ancient Buddha statue, where generators had been brought to power large electric drills. Hussein was forced to grind holes into the massive feet and legs of the stone figure, into which explosives were inserted and then detonated. The ancient statue crumbled into boulders, rocks, and pebbles that tumbled across the valley floor.

The destruction started at the bottom, as each day workers made their way up the sides of the Buddha using the ancient labyrinth of stairs that had been carved in the rock and hidden from view. At the top, Hussein was strapped into a makeshift harness and lowered from above the Buddha's head, dangling by ropes as he drilled hole after hole.

Hussein shuddered at the memory and looked up from his work. He and the others had no choice but to help in the destruction. "Those who refused were shot." Even so, some refused. "They were ready to die. I would see my dead friends every day." The drilling went on for seventeen of the twenty-five days it took to destroy the larger Buddha, which was called Salsal, roughly meaning "the light that shines through the universe." In all, Hussein drilled some one hundred holes, averaging about seven or eight each day.

Destruction of the smaller Buddha sometimes referred to as Shamama, or Queen Mother, was much more efficient, Hussein said, since the engineers learned their lessons from the demolition of the larger Buddha. The holes were drilled, the explosives were packed in, and then sandbags were piled in front, about halfway up the statue. The sandbags created a barrier, redirecting the blast back in on itself. "It destroyed the whole thing," he said.

Hussein finished patching the bicycle tube and methodically worked it back inside the bicycle tire. He glanced at the distant cliffs, barely visible over the tops of the small complex of shops that were converted shipping containers. The memories flooded back. "I felt very sad. [The Buddhas] belonged to all Afghan people. If it was not good for Islam, then why did Muhammad not destroy them? They were here before him."

Hussein was convinced that the destruction of the Buddhas was not ordered by the Taliban but by outsiders. Those who supervised the work were not the Taliban; they were people Hussein had never seen before who spoke Arabic. It was a language he didn't understand but did recognize from the local mosque when the Koran was read aloud. The supervisors treated the Taliban like servants, he said, and wore long robes. Some reports suggest that Osama bin Laden may have been personally involved in the Buddhas' destruction.

"They were here to destroy the Buddhas. They were foreigners. [The Taliban] were ordered to do this," Hussein said. "They were saying [the Buddhas] were the gods of the Hazaras. They were saying that we were worshipping these Buddhas. I heard that a thousand times, that we should be killed because [we] are worshipping these gods. Their aim was to destroy the country, all of these places. They were trying to destroy things, that is all."

Hussein lifted the bicycle upright and held it as his son pumped air into the tire. The tire was as good as new. Someone from a nearby shop appeared and told Hussein that since the bicycle was fixed, he'd take it to his friend, the owner. Hussein said no, explaining that he would only release the bicycle to the rightful owner.

Hussein spoke of the destruction of the Buddhas as if it had happened yesterday. In fact, it had been ten years earlier and at a time when the power of the Taliban had peaked, just months before 9/11. Now the Taliban were resurgent as international forces were beginning to withdraw. The people of Bamiyan were acutely aware of the changing dynamics. "I feel sad if they are leaving," Hussein said of the international troops. "They made the Taliban go away. If they are leaving, it could be the same as in the past."

"Do you think that the Taliban will return?" I asked.

"One hundred percent. They [will] come back in different ways and destroy things," Hussein said, just as they had ripped the heart out of Bamiyan by blasting away the Buddhas. "When the Buddhas were destroyed, the lives of Bamiyan people were destroyed, because they could not make money anymore from tourists. Even now [tourists] are not coming."

The Taliban were already at the doors of Bamiyan, he said. It was unsafe to drive from Bamiyan to Kabul, because the road passed through Gorband District in neighboring Parwan Province, a dangerous stretch where the Taliban occasionally set up deadly roadblocks. Hussein noted that the head of the provincial council, Mohammad Jawad Zahak, had been captured on the road by Taliban and beheaded just weeks earlier, according to some reports. "He was well known and was doing a good job here. That is why they killed him."

"It is dangerous now," Hussein said. "When I look at the current situation, I don't have hope for a better future for Afghans. I am worried about my security. I have been interviewed by many reporters." He had not refrained from criticizing the Taliban, and because of that, "I could get killed. I'm not going to give any more interviews."

Uncovering the Past

The clink of pickaxes and the scrape of shovels filled the air as two dozen men combed through tons of dirt and gravel not far from the shadowy depressions where the two ancient Buddhas once stood. Hands on his hips, Professor Zemaryalai Tarzi stared at a piece of pottery half buried in the dirt. Sporting a light fabric fedora, a multipocketed vest, and cargo pants, he had the look of an aging Indiana Jones. Tarzi had arrived just moments earlier, having rushed from his office in town to this archaeological excavation. A couple of French archaeological students stood nearby, grinning like children on Christmas morning. He called for his camera. This was something significant, and Tarzi's excitement was obvious. To the uninformed eye, it was little more than a large piece of broken pottery. Tarzi lifted the camera to his eye and took several photos, then smiled.

It was part of a large ceramic sculpture of the Buddha, unrelated to the larger Buddhas, he said later, but further evidence of the importance of the ancient Buddhist monastery below our feet that he was methodically uncovering. He called it the Royal Monastery. Already a stupa (a moundlike structure usually in an open area that typically contains Buddhist relics and is used as a place of worship) and other rooms had been unearthed as the workers carefully removed the centuries of dirt and gravel that had covered them. Tarzi was even more excited about what he called the East Monastery, an equally significant find buried under gravel just several hundred yards away. This would all be a museum, he said with a sweep of his thick arm.

Later in the quiet of his office, Tarzi sipped black tea and explained that the smaller Buddha had been built sometime during the third and fifth centuries, or 200 to 400 AD. The second and larger Buddha probably was built during the next two hundred years. "Some people think the Buddhas were rebuilt" more than once. It was an interesting remark, since there had been talk that the smaller Buddha could be reconstructed sometime in the next ten years by either the Japanese or German governments. Already metal-pipe scaffolding filled the hollow space where the small Buddha once stood, which made such a project seem possible.

Fragments of the wood that once had been integral parts of the Buddha sculptures had been carbon dated, Tarzi said, and were from three separate eras—the third and fourth centuries, the fourth and fifth centuries, and fifth and sixth centuries. This showed that the wood had been replaced over the centuries and was evidence that the Buddhas had been rebuilt periodically. Tarzi speculated that the Buddhas were rebuilt first in the fourth century around 380 AD and then again in sixth century, or about 550 AD.

How long the site had existed was hard to determine, but one clue was the ancient Greek coins found there that dated from the second century BC, which was about two hundred years after the Greek conqueror Alexander the Great had swept across the region. Indian coins from the third century AD were also found, as were bronze coins that were thought to be common currency from the third to the ninth centuries.

The Taliban-fueled attack on the Buddhas in the spring of 2001 was not the first time such destruction had happened. When Islam arrived in Afghanistan in the ninth century, the Afghan commander Ya'qub bin Laith as-Saffar (840–879), from what is now Lashkar Gah, the capital of Helmand Province, was reputed to have destroyed Bamiyan and spirited all the gold he could find off to Baghdad, including golden Buddha statues. Though the splendor of Bamiyan had been ravaged, the carved stone Buddhas remained.

Perhaps the darkest days of Bamiyan's long and colorful history came in 1221, when the Mongolian hordes of Genghis Khan arrived in the valley. The castle of King Jalaluddin was in the heart of the Bamiyan valley, and he managed to hold out for months. Genghis Khan's army "suffered a lot here in Bamiyan," Tarzi said. "The defenders were stronger here than in Balkh [to the north]. His grandchild was killed here, so [Genghis Khan] ordered everyone killed, even children in women's wombs," Tarzi said.

But there was also a backstory. According to legend, Jalaluddin's daughter fled the castle in a fit of indignant rage, because her widowed father had married a young princess from Ghazni. Thinking that she would gain favor with the attacking Mongols, Jalaluddin's daughter revealed how the hordes could breach the castle's defenses and force the king to surrender. It worked. The king and other inhabitants of the castle were killed and the castle was destroyed. Khan's commander then called for Jalaluddin's daughter, who rushed to the man's tent, expecting a reward. Instead, she was dispatched by a sword, along with every other living thing in the valley. In memory of that, the castle was called Shahr-e-Gholghola, or "city of screams."

"The thing about Bamiyan is that it gets back on its feet," Tarzi said. "The people are still here." Replete with history, the focus in Bamiyan during the past half-century has been the Buddhas and the large complex of Buddhist shrines and temples that have drawn Buddhist pilgrims to this pristine valley for more than eight hundred years.

"What were Bamiyan and the Buddhas like back then?" I asked.

Tarzi's eyes lit up. It was a question that had occupied him for all of his professional life. What little was known about that time came from the sparse references in the writings of a Chinese traveler and pilgrim called Xuanzang, who passed through Bamiyan around 632 AD and described Bamiyan as a thriving center of Buddhism with more than ten monasteries and a thousand monks. It was the giant Buddhas, however, that caught Xuanzang's eye. They were decorated with gold and jewels, he wrote. "The golden decoration of the big Buddha was so bright that people could see it for miles," Tarzi said. The giant Buddhas had ruby eyes that glittered and sparkled in the night, as if on fire.

"Why was Bamiyan the site for the huge statues of the Buddha?" I asked.

The common explanation was that the Buddhas were an attraction on Silk Road, Tarzi said, but added, "It's not correct." At more than eight thousand feet in elevation, Bamiyan was high in the central mountains of Afghanistan, which made for an arduous trip by donkey, horse, or camel. For a merchant with a caravan, going to Bamiyan was a difficult detour, since easier routes were further to the north through provinces such as Jawzjan and the capital of Shiberghan, which was mentioned in Marco Polo's writings.

More likely, Tarzi suggested, Bamiyan was a destination in the ancient world, a Buddhist retreat with a world reputation. Then, as now, it was a quiet and calm place, ideal for reflection and meditation—essentials of the Buddhist practice. The caves that pocked the cliff had been easily carved into the soft aggregate rock. The work had been done by the monks and pilgrims, he said, attracted by the clean air, pristine environment, and solitude. In short, it was a perfect place to leave behind the distractions of the world and to seek enlightenment.

As the reputation of Bamiyan spread throughout south Asia over the centuries, more and wealthier people arrived, Tarzi believed. Attractions such as the giant Buddha statues were needed. Royalty and wealthy merchants may have been tapped to pay for the bigger and better meditation centers. "Maybe they paid for the temples." At its peak, Bamiyan had hundreds of such meditation caves and today some nine hundred have been catalogued.

A thriving commercial and agricultural system was needed to support the population of such a sizeable center. "How much money and time was needed to build, plaster, and paint these caves and temples?" Tarzi asked. "It had to be a big kingdom and it needed a big economy. There had to be a big city here, and it needed a big army, schools, and such. It took a big budget to pay for this. The king would [pay] the locals to do the work." Properly funded and managed, Tarzi explained, Bamiyan could sustain a large population. It was still one of the few self-sustaining economies in Afghanistan due to its fertile soil and agricultural base. Bamiyan may also have been a thriving commercial center, he suggested, with carpet-weaving, wool-growing, and related crafts. "I think there was an iron industry for weapons and for horseshoes. Bamiyan had an income from these activities. This is what allowed them to build these big Buddhas. It was both a strategic place and a place for relaxing. It was a religious place."

The Chinese traveler Xuanzang also wrote of a third, even larger, reclining statue of the Buddha thought to be some three hundred meters long. Finding this had become Tarzi's latest quest. "It is my job," he said. "I will work on it. Where is it? I don't know. Where I have looked, it has not been there." Xuanzang mentioned that the reclining Buddha was less than one thousand meters from the larger, western Buddha, and somewhere between it and what Tarzi said was the eastern monastery. As we talked, Tarzi drew a diagram showing how he had measured the distance and had concentrated his search within the prescribed semicircle that fronted the cliffs. Already he had unearthed a fifteen-meter-long sleeping Buddha, but he had quickly covered it again until it could be properly preserved before being made public.

Tarzi speculated that the giant reclining Buddha could also have been carved into the base of the cliff between the two standing Buddhas. If so, it remained buried under tons of gravel and debris just like the remains of the monasteries he had uncovered. The other possibility was that the giant reclining Buddha was gone, having disappeared into the annals of history. "If it was made of mud, it would be gone now," he said with chagrin. The ultimate discovery of the reclining Buddha might be a prize that someone else would claim, he conceded.

Back at the excavation site, there was an air of excitement and a sense that by unearthing more of Bamiyan's past, the destruction of the giant Buddhas might be avenged. It was a notion shared by workers such as Sharafuddin, forty-five, who had been working at the site with Tarzi for eight years. Once a potato, onion, and wheat farmer, Sharafuddin had traded his hoe for a pick and shovel. "It's good money," he said with a smile, then spoke bitterly of the Taliban for demolishing the Buddhas. "I was sad that they destroyed our history." If the Taliban had not been stopped, "they would have destroyed all of Afghanistan."

Sharafuddin felt he was rebuilding his country by working at the site. "It is good here. They are discovering things under the ground. It is good for the country." He pointed proudly to the excavated spot now covered with mounded bricks just twenty feet away. "I found that stupa two years ago. Last year I found two pots that were very big, and there were bones inside. They would put important people in those pots and kept them there. It was interesting. They were very old bones," he said.

"How do you work with a pick and shovel without damaging valuable artifacts?" I asked.

He shrugged. "I am careful. When they find something valuable, they clear the area around it."

"Do you think they'll find the giant reclining Buddha?" I asked.

Sharafuddin shrugged and grinned. "Maybe. It's possible."

As we spoke, his friend Ahmad Sakhi joined the conversation. Sakhi had been working at the site for six years "to [earn] some money," he said, and like his friend, he had formerly eked out a living as a farmer. Sakhi pointed to the ceramic piece that Tarzi had photographed earlier, and said he had found that. "It's interesting and exciting," he said of the work. "It is good to get some results and to finish what we are doing for Tarzi."

"What do you think of today's find?" I asked.

"It could be the clothes of a sculpture," he said, since the long, rounded piece had ripples that seemed to be the flowing folds of a robe, much like the ones had were part of the Buddha sculpture.

Like others in Bamiyan, Sakhi was angry at the Taliban for having destroyed the historic Buddhas. "I felt sad," he said, but added that, "it was not the Taliban" who had demolished the Buddhas. "It was Pakistan." It was done "so people would not come here," destroying the livelihood of Bamiyan residents. "All of our insecurity is because of Pakistan."

"Do you think the Taliban might return?" I asked.

"If people have unity, then the Taliban cannot come back," he said. "We have an army and police, so they can't come back."

"Some people say the Afghan forces aren't up to the task," I said.

Sakhi sighed. "If the army and police work with a clean soul, they cannot come back."

He had expressed a notion I heard often, that corruption was at the heart of Afghanistan's problems. Even the poorest Afghans agreed that if one had a pure heart and good intentions, then God or Allah made all things possible. I waited for Sakhi to continue.

He looked into the distance. "I can't think of the future," he said finally. "It is up to God."

Life in the Caves

The next day I returned to the archaeological site, walking eastward along trails that angled up to a complex of caves at the base of towering cliffs where hundreds of Bamiyan's poorest people lived. At the top of a particularly tricky path, my translator Noorullah and I rounded a rocky outcropping and found ourselves facing several caves. Each had been improved with stacked and mortared mud bricks filling the cave openings around framed doors. A rugged-looking woman sat on a rug in front of one, along with a couple of small children who looked up as we approached. She nodded hello and said she would gladly talk to us about life in these ancient caves.

Her name was Mariam. She was forty years old and had lived in the caves for nine years. She and her husband formerly lived in town, but when they ran out of money and work, they were forced to move into a cave. Her husband was off working at the time, she said.

"Doing what?" I asked.

Mariam shrugged and said he had a wheelbarrow that he used to find work.

At the base of the cliffs was an irrigation ditch that watered the nearby fields. "Is that where you get your water?" I asked.

No, Mariam laughed, saying that water was dirty and only for irrigation. She brought water from wells in town, using the family donkey that carried the full plastic containers up to the caves. She cooked using wood collected from the nearby hills, since she could not afford to buy natural gas. "It is hard to live here. We want the government to give us a house." That was unlikely, she explained, because, "Unless you know someone in the government, you have to live here."

"What does the future hold for you?" I asked.

"I don't have any hope," Mariam said. "But I want to go from here," because it was a difficult and dangerous place to live. One of her grandchildren had been visiting recently and had slipped and tumbled down the rocky slope. "Someone found her and took her to hospital. She can't walk now."

"Are you worried about the Taliban coming back?" I asked.

If the Taliban returned, Mariam said that she and her family would do as they'd done before, which was flee. "We just left everything we had and went to the mountains," she said. "They burned buildings and killed a lot of people. Whoever they found, they would kill."

"The coalition forces are planning to withdraw," I said. "Does that worry you?"

"If they leave, the Taliban would come back," she said. "They will kill people."

Mariam considered herself lucky compared to Zainab, the twenty-eight-year-old mother of four girls who lived in the adjacent cave. Zainab had recently been abandoned by her husband because he had borrowed money from his family and friends but couldn't pay it back. He could not find work, so he had disappeared.

"It's difficult," Zainab said of life in the cave. If she and her children had any other options, "we wouldn't live here." Like her neighbor, Mariam, she burned bits of wood and dried leaves for cooking and hauled water from wells using the donkey. "We have no choice."

Zainab had recently joined a seamstress and dress-making class and was earning 1,000 Afghanis per month, or about $20, as a trainee. It was barely enough to survive. Once she graduated, she hoped to find a job in town. And she hoped for her husband to return.

"Do you feel any connection with the monks and pilgrims who lived in these same caves some fifteen hundred years ago?" I asked.

Zainab said no, "It doesn't make much of a difference to me." History was not her concern, and living in a cave was not her choice, just a fact of life. "It's a normal thing for us." She had more to worry about than history and struggled to survive each day.

Some cave residents had been able to leave and find housing in town, I learned later. One such person was Nekbakht, a cheerful thirty-year-old mother of a ten-year-old boy, who until recently had spent the past five years living in a cave. She'd gotten a cleaning job in a local guesthouse that catered to a growing number of international tourists who were finding their way to Bamiyan.

Since she had had few alternatives, Nekbakht said the cave was not so bad. "It was good, but it was dark," she said, since the caves lacked electricity. Light came from a fire, but the fire filled the cave with smoke. Like the others, she had used water from wells in town that was hauled to the caves by donkey. Her husband worked as a day laborer now, and with her salary from the guesthouse, they rented a house in town for $20 per month.

The government was distributing food and providing people with free land so that no one needed to live in the caves, but as Mariam had mentioned, getting some land depended on who you knew in the government. "I heard that the head of the provincial council gave land to his relatives who were in the caves," Nekbakht said. Although she didn't know anyone who had gotten free land, she still held out hope, saying, "If they gave it to me, it would be nice." Of the prospect of being forced to return to the caves, she confided, "I am a little bit sad, because it was not a good life. The big problem was the dust and dirt. And it was dark."

"Did you know that you once lived in one of the world's most famous cultural sites?" I asked.

"It may be important," Nekbakht said of the Buddhas, "but I don't know. It may have some meaning, but I don't know what it is."

Life had turned around when she heard of the cleaning job at the hotel, she said. Now her son had returned to school and was in the fifth grade. This gave her hope for his future. "Does the departure of foreign forces worry you?" I asked.

"I heard they were leaving and it made me sad," she said. "They were good for everything."

Tourism and the Taliban

A long landing strip of hard-packed gravel stretched from east to west on the broad reaches of land at the south side of the Bamiyan valley. It was fronted by a military base manned by New Zealand forces. In the past decade, dozens of modern buildings had been built, many of which housed Afghan government officials, the police, and the Afghan army. It was on the second floor of one where I found Habiba Sarabi, the governor of Bamiyan Province.

Like most Afghans, she agonized over the future of her province but was hopeful that tourism held some promise for the Bamiyan valley. "The landscape of Bamiyan has great natural potential," she said. Besides the archaeology, there are the lakes of Band-e-Amir, whose rich blue color is caused by mineral deposits in the water. "Tourists will bring economic stability and sustainable income for the people of Bamiyan," Sarabi said. "The natural environment is unique and beautiful, but the people are very poor."

I had visited the lakes just the day before and could only agree on the beauty and potential that tourism had for the area. But the Bamiyan valley was without electricity. The few lights that glowed throughout the valley at night were powered by generators. "When almost all of Afghanistan has regular power, why doesn't Bamiyan?" I asked.

"Perhaps the minister of energy does not like for Bamiyan to have power," Sarabi said, with a tone of resentment tinged with ethnic animosities that roiled just below the surface of all Afghan society. The minister of water and energy was Ismail Khan, an ethnic Tajik who was the former strongman of Herat and who controlled much of western Afghanistan. During 2004, my first year in Afghanistan, Khan and his forces had clashed repeatedly with government troops who were moving into the region to exert control. On numerous occasions these conflicts flared into full-scale warfare, with Khan and government forces trading cannon volleys in the city. In one particularly grisly event, Khan's son was killed, and many feared that it would ignite a war in the west. Instead, Khan was put in charge of Afghanistan's water and power.

Since Bamiyan was high in the mountains, Sarabi said, the region had streams running through or near most of the provincial villages and towns, and some micro-hydro-power dams were being built. The lights went on in remote communities where one would never have expected it. "The amount of power is not sufficient for heating, only lights," Sarabi said. But it was a start.

I wondered why Bamiyan might be discriminated against, as she had suggested, since it was the homeland of the ethnic Hazaras, who were about 20 percent of the Afghan population. The Hazaras had some powerful people in government, and among them was Abdul Karim Khalili, the second vice president under President Karzai. Khalili was the head of the powerful Hezb-e-Wahdat Islami Afghanistan (Islamic Unity Party of Afghanistan). Another was Haji Mohammad Mohaqiq, the mujahideen commander who led the Hazara against the Soviets in the 1980s and again during the Afghan civil war in the 1990s. Mohaqiq was one of the few militia leaders who never left Afghanistan and who was never captured by the Taliban. He was elected to parliament in 2010. "Between these two men, it should have been possible to get power to Bamiyan," I said.

Sarabi shrugged. The ongoing war with the Taliban had drained the resources of the government. "People are ignoring Bamiyan," she said. Another complication was that Bamiyan is a World Heritage Site, one of fewer than a thousand properties deemed by the World Heritage Committee to have worldwide cultural and natural significance. Stringing power lines around the valley would diminish the views. Likewise, putting power lines underground could damage the wealth of cultural materials below the surface. Bamiyan's heritage was both a blessing and a curse, she said.

"Why wasn't security a problem in Bamiyan?" I asked.

"People in Bamiyan are not extremists," Sarabi said. "They don't allow extremists. They suffered a lot under the Taliban. They want to keep security here. They want to take advantage of peace." Except for the recent killing of the provincial council president, Zahak, who had been traveling outside the province at the time of his capture, Bamiyan escaped the violence that plagued the rest of the country. "They support the police," Sarabi said of the community, and "the government cooperates with the people."

The capture and killing of Zahak had been an accident, she said. "The community was very upset" and had turned out in droves for his funeral. He had been stopped at a Taliban roadblock, and when the armed men realized who they had, they killed him, she said, making a political statement against the Hazara that had rekindled ethnic animosity of the past.

"That does not bode well for the future," I said.

Sarabi agreed. "We hope [the future] can become better. If not, it will be a shame. More than forty countries came here to bring security to Afghanistan. But NATO cannot stay forever." Before the international forces would leave, they needed "to build capacity for the military and the police." It was the only way for Afghanistan to have a secure future, she said.

"Can the Afghan forces take charge and stay in charge?" I asked.

"As politicians, we have to be optimistic," Sarabi said. "We have to work hard and bring hope to the people."

"Do you think negotiations with the Taliban can end the war in Afghanistan?" I asked.

"If they cannot accept the constitution," she said of the Taliban, "it is a concern for me as a woman and as a Hazara." The Taliban needs to respect human rights, she stressed. "Otherwise, it will be a tragedy. We are watching. We'll see. It's a puzzle for everyone," Sarabi said, as to why the United States wanted to talk to the Taliban, given its history.

Bamiyan and its Buddha statues were the most famous of Afghanistan's trove of historical sites, but Bamiyan was not the only archaeological place that had faced demolition. There was another site not far from Kabul that was about to be wiped off the map as Afghanistan moved into the future. It was where Afghanistan's past, present, and future collided.

14

OF COPPER AND CULTURE

THE FLANKS OF MES AYNAK MOUNTAIN, like the surrounding slopes some twenty-five miles southeast of Kabul, were scarred by angular trenches, as if mauled by a voracious predator. The slashes had been made thirty years earlier by Russian machines that had sampled the ore body below the surface, proving that this site was one of the richest copper deposits in the world.

Nearby, archaeologists supervised Afghan crews probing the powdery, dry earth in search of ancient Buddhist artifacts. They worked with focused intensity, knowing that they had less than three years to extract, catalogue, and house what remained of these nearly two-thousand-year-old antiquities. By 2014, the China Metallurgical Group Corporation planned to dig into the slopes here at Mes Aynak, turning everything within one square mile into an open-pit copper mine.

The copper mine promised to be a boon to the Afghan economy, possibly replacing opium and heroin as its major export. The Chinese won the right to exploit this rich ore deposit in 2007 with a bid of some $3.5 billion. Of that amount, about $800 million was to be paid to the Afghan government, a large amount by any standard, but huge for Afghanistan. Although the Chinese were expected to earn $40 billion or more in profits over the twenty-to-thirty-year life of the mine, it could also mean about $500 million a year in royalty payments for the Afghan government. The mine could also pump another $1 billion per year into the Afghan economy through wages and other economic spinoffs. To get the bid, the Chinese had promised a lot. They had agreed to build a copper smelter on-site and a $500 million generating station for the smelter that would also pour electricity in the country's notoriously unreliable power grid. To fuel the power station would require coal. The Chinese were to mine that as well and build a rail line across Afghanistan from Uzbekistan and to Pakistan as part of the deal. The copper mine was expected to employ up to five thousand people, and the Chinese agreed to build houses, schools, and hospitals for them. Language would not be a problem, since dozens of Afghans were being sent to China to study Chinese language and engineering.

At Mes Aynak, Afghanistan's past collided with its present and future. The site was one of the largest and most valuable copper deposits in the world, yet the mineral sat below one of the most valuable of Afghanistan's archaeological treasures, rivaling that of Bamiyan and other locales.

In mid-September 2011, I went to Mes Aynak with Khair Mohammad Khairzada, the acting director of the Afghan Institute of Archaeology. We had spoken earlier about the project and how he was resigned to the fact that a major piece of Afghanistan's history was about to be sacrificed. Khairzada shrugged it off as being for the good of the country. "Afghanistan wants to raise its economy," he said, and "this site needs to be excavated" before mining could begin. "The economy is important, and so is history. We cannot destroy our culture and heritage. It belongs to the people of Afghanistan," he said. This was why teams of Afghan and international archaeologists were charting the various temples, collecting what they could, and cataloguing it for future public display. "The copper is important," Khairzada said, because the mineral wealth of Afghanistan is critical to the nation. "We have a lot of mines in Afghanistan, but few people have helped us mine these things. The young people are jobless," he said, noting that thousands of jobs were expected to be generated. "The economy of Afghanistan will go up."

Rescue of the antiquities began in 2009, and the pace was expected to intensify in the coming months as archaeologists attempted to meet the 2014 deadline. "We want to finish our job as soon as possible. Our work will take two to three years more," Khairzada said, but he cautioned, "It is not enough time. There is a lot of archaeology at the site. The site is very huge. The sites that are most in danger are more urgent." The focus of activity at the moment was a ruin at the peak of Mes Aynak mountain. "They will destroy the mountain. This is the first part."

Mes Aynak was in the northern part of the troubled Logar Province, where several devastating attacks had hit military and civilian facilities. The worst had been in late June 2011 when a car bomb was detonated at a hospital in a neighboring district, killing an estimated twenty-seven people and injuring fifty-three. Hospital officials said more may have been killed, since people took away the bodies of relatives shortly after the blast. People had been gathering at the clinic for weekly treatment, many of them women, children, and the elderly. The medical facility was demolished, and patients, doctors, and nurses were buried under rubble.

The Taliban refused to accept responsibility for the bombing, claiming they did not target civilians. But most Afghans blamed the Taliban. It was the worst attack against a medical facility since the fall of the Taliban in 2001. Because of this and other Taliban attacks, "you need security at the site," Khairzada said, so that it can be excavated properly.

Several days later, I traveled to Mes Aynak with another American journalist and my translator, Noorullah, as part of a convoy of Afghan archaeologists, including Khairzada, who regularly visited the site. We turned off the main road south of Kabul and wound our way through a village, then rolled down a wide gravel road that stretched into the distant hills. We stopped at a sprawling checkpoint manned by about a hundred Afghan National Police and stepped out of our car. After a cursory pat-down, our car was checked for explosives and cleared. We were waved on. At intervals of about a hundred yards, individual

Afghan soldiers guarded the road until we arrived at the gate of the Chinese camp at the base of what was to become the Mes Aynak mine.

The road around the camp had been washed out by rains a couple of months earlier, so we were unable to use it as was routine for such visits. Moments later we stopped at the camp gate and waited until a Chinese escort could be found to ride with us through the camp, since I was a foreign journalist and not part of the Afghan archaeological team. The young soldier who joined us seemed miffed that he had been assigned such a tedious task but smiled nonetheless. The camp was constructed primarily of prefabricated structures and several concrete-block buildings and was surrounded by a high chain-link fence and several seemingly unmanned guard towers. We drove up the road as it climbed through the camp, and after passing through gates on the camp's other side, we caught our first glimpses of the ancient Buddhist sites.

Our first stop was at the Tepe Kafiriat site, where the monks who had built the monasteries "did it very well," Khairzada explained as we scaled the slope that led to the ruins. Despite nearly two millennia of pounding sun and howling winds, the remains of the site were exquisite. The monastery once had been covered by ornately decorated domes, and the halls and rooms contained gilded and painted depictions of the Buddha. The stone walkways around the main stupa were intact, as were the hallways that led to the living quarters, meditation rooms, and kitchens.

A survey of the site had been done in 2004, just a few years after the Taliban regime fell, Khairzada said, and it was then that archaeologists realized the immense value of the site. But little was done at the time to protect it. "Because of the [security danger], we could not come," and this had opened the door to extensive looting. Cultural preservation alone had not been enough to prompt the protection of Mes Aynak. Security for the site had come only after the minerals were leased. Excavation began in 2009 because "the security is good now. It is much more safe."

"The most urgent work is here," he said, gesturing to the ruins. "We found three golden [objects] and wood, stone, and clay statues."

These objects were being preserved and eventually would be on display at the Afghan National Museum. The sense of frustration and urgency of the project was clear as we toured Tepe Kafiriat. "The [Mes Aynak] site is very large and we only have twenty-four archaeologists." But help was on the way, he said. An international team of specialists had just arrived in Kabul to assist in the work.

The visiting experts were assembled under the auspices of the French Archaeological Delegation in Afghanistan. Days earlier, I had met with the group's deputy director, Nicolas Engel. His enthusiasm about Mes Aynak was tempered with a heavy dose of Afghan reality. "Mes Aynak is 80 percent destroyed already. It was looted. The idea is to rescue as much as possible from the site. It has great potential. It is a shame [that] it will be destroyed," he said.

The international team of archaeologists would include two from China, Engel said. "We are more and more [working] as partners," he said. The goal was to "find another place to put everything. It is possible to rebuild the monastery somewhere else. If you work properly, you can save it." Because of the urgency of the excavation, the project had received several million dollars in international funds. The choice between preserving its past versus development of its resources was a dilemma also faced by other countries, Engel explained. "Every country has to make a decision between progress and its heritage."

According to a brief analysis of the site, which Engel shared with me, the Buddhist monastery and temple at Mes Aynak dated from the first century and together formed a religious and mining center well beyond the sixth and seventh centuries and perhaps even into the tenth century. It boasted a grand stupa that rose some 50 feet high and measured 260 feet by 130 feet. The site now had been a mining center for nearly two thousand years.

"The monastery was a place for prayer," Khairzada said of the site. "Only monks lived here." The irony that Mes Aynak had been a place of prayer and meditation as well as mining for nearly a thousand years and today was in the neighborhood of radical Islamists was not lost on Khairzada. "Muslims go to Mecca. People [back then] would come here. We have a similar stupa in Kabul," he said. The sites were Buddhist centers and were occupied certainly from the second century through the seventh century. "We are trying to take some parts of these stupas because it has a very nice design." That the site was not Islamic should not matter to Afghanistan, he said. "It is part of our heritage. We are trying to keep as much as we can. We will map it all and take photos."

As we meandered the monastery ruins, Khairzada pointed out the protective measures that had been taken, such as wooden roofs over a number of Buddha statues. One was of a seated Buddha, preserved despite the fact that its head and shoulders had been removed and presumably stolen. The stone masonry of the exposed stupa had been assembled with fine detail, built of small pieces of black slate carefully fitted together. Ornate friezes were still evident, and some of the rock used revealed the rich copper content, having oxidized and turned bright turquoise.

Khairzada threw back a piece of hanging canvas to reveal a large and dusty room filled with the remains of large clay statues of the Buddha, each of which had been probably fifteen to twenty feet tall. One at our feet was a life-size reclining Buddha with touches of what had been blue coloring. "We have a sleeping Buddha here that was looted," Khairzada said, pointing to the missing head and shoulders. All the other sculptures were also missing the torso, arms, shoulders, and head, and only the feet, knees, and thighs remained. Looters had removed the portions of the statues that were most easily recognized and therefore highly prized by black-market collectors.

"We also found a wooden statue here. It was amazing; it was from [the Afghan province of] Nuristan. They were Buddhist. There were a lot of wooden statues there. They used wood to support the clay." The clay and wood had survived the centuries despite being vulnerable to the elements. Archaeologists were making plaster molds of what remained, making it possible for these partial statues to be reproduced.

Even in their looted condition the statues were impressive. "Each statue had smaller ones around it," Khairzada said. "They were offering gifts to the Buddha." As we paused amidst this tomb of ancient art, I was dismayed to think that it soon would be gone.

We next climbed to the site at the top of Mes Aynak mountain, a windy peak that commanded a dramatic view of the area. About halfway up, the mountainside was scattered with blackened porous rock resembling cooled lava. The rock was what remained of the ancient copper smelting activities of some fifteen hundred years earlier. Archaeologists were still piecing together the puzzle of the site, but most agreed that the copper had once made the region a thriving kingdom on the Silk Road. The mining and smelting—quite possibly done by the monks themselves—probably supported the monasteries.

The path zigzagged up the slope to a complex of large rooms, some containing large four-and five-foot-high clay pots suitable for storing water and grain. "We have a hundred workers here," Khairzada said of the entire Mes Aynak site, after we reached the mountain summit. "We are trying to get more. This is where the urgent work is. It was like a citadel. For security, they chose this high point," he surmised. "We have found many copper coins, pottery shards, grinding stones, and glass."

An Afghan archaeologist at the site, Aziz Luddin Wafa, guided me through the maze of rooms, which had long been exposed to the wind and blistering sun. Stone benches and sitting areas lined the walls. "This looks like a fire room," he said of one. "When we came here, we saw broken pottery. We think this was a sitting room," he said of another. "We've found lots of structures. Inside the rooms were pottery and wooden objects. Most were destroyed."

The excavations had revealed two different periods of architecture, Wafa said. The complex was covered with domed ceilings and all of the rooms were connected. Today the rooms were filled with dirt and debris, and only the walls remained. "The people who lived here were guarding this place," Wafa said of this mountaintop stone fortress. "The laborers lived down further."

We made our way back down the slope and crossed an expanse of dusty, parched soil, stopping at another largely unexcavated monastery that was the source of some extraordinary objects. We rounded the remains of a well-preserved stupa, ornately decorated with pieces of rose-colored stone that Khairzada said was not native to the region. In one nearby corner of the site, a half-dozen workers, supervised by a couple of Afghan archaeologists, sifted through the soft, powdery soil and were extracting many small sculpted objects. One was a skillfully formed clay head of a female, the hair still painted black. In another corner, two archaeologists worked in the shade of a tarp and used small trowels to scrape the dirt away from a three-foot-high clay figure. It appeared to be a bare-chested warrior dressed in a short tunic. This was a valuable find since it was largely intact and indicated that much more might be found at the site.

Watching the work was Mullah Mira Jan, a lean man with a long grey beard and a turban who managed the workers from the local village. "We're happy for the work" he said, looking on as about thirty of his fellow villagers dug in the soil in various corners. He was happy that the artifacts were being preserved, since "lots of smugglers were here." The site had been largely ignored until after the Taliban fell, he said, but in 2004, shortly after the government conducted its initial survey of the site, serious looting began. "These places were only discovered when the Taliban left. Now we have the government, and the [artifacts] will be safe and secure," he said.

Locals also wanted to safeguard the artifacts. Mira Jan said they were leery of the copper mine and were unhappy that it would demolish the archaeological site. "The people don't want it destroyed," since it was considered part of their heritage. A more pressing problem was that an entire village had been moved off the mine site and the landowners were still waiting for compensation. "They've taken people's land, but they haven't been given anything," he said. Government promises had not been fulfilled.

Even though Mira Jan felt security had improved now that the archaeological recovery work had begun, he warned that it might not stay that way if the displaced villagers were not paid. "If they compensate people, then the security will be the best in all of Afghanistan," he said with a smile.

"And if they do not, then what?" I asked.

Mira Jan didn't answer.

The village workers at the site earned from $160 to $300 per month, Mira Jan said, but the pay had been slow in coming. He agreed that the mine would boost the local and national economy. "It will improve the economy," he said of the mine, and, "Yes, people will benefit. People will get money for their work." But, he cautioned, "The government will get the most money."

To the minds of some people, the copper mine had put Afghanistan into an impossible situation. Mining was a viable escape from the bloodletting of the present, but Afghanistan had to sacrifice its past in order to have a future. This dilemma and the deadline for the excavation had generated resentment with at least one of the Afghan archaeologists. "The terrorists are destroying our country," said an exasperated Abdul Qadir Temori. "Now the Chinese are destroying it with money. It hurts an archaeologist when artifacts are destroyed."

"There are compelling reasons for the work at Mes Aynak," I said.

Temori shrugged. "History will be the judge."

Mountains of Iron

The Afghan governmental agency that supervises the country's mineral wealth, estimated to be $1 trillion worth of untapped minerals, is the Ministry of Mines, housed in one of the better government buildings in Kabul. Just a few days after I visited Mes Aynak, I sat down with Nasir Ahmad Durrani, the deputy minister of the agency, in his office.

"Afghanistan has been dependent mostly on agriculture," Durrani said. "Afghanistan sees its future in mining[, which] will provide the maximum part of the Afghan budget." The Mes Aynak copper mine was a milestone, he said, since it was the "first mine awarded to an investor. It will play a vital role in our economy."

Meanwhile, Durrani said, his department fully supported the archaeological excavation of the Mes Aynak site. Some $14 million has been dedicated to the excavation from various sources so that "these artifacts are preserved safely. We give importance to our history.

We don't want to mine copper and throw away our history," he said. Nearly twenty international experts were being brought to Afghanistan to help with the excavation, along with the Afghans already at the site. Durrani expected that up to nine hundred Afghan laborers would be hired to complete the excavation on time. One million dollars had been donated for a museum near the mine site, he said. "Everything will be documented to international standards. It is not only our history, but the heritage of the world. We respect it."

"Archaeology is only one thing to affect the schedule" at the Mes Aynak mine, Durrani said. Another was the land ownership problem that Mullah Mira Jan had raised. A third was the many land mines scattered around the area. Some seven or eight square miles needed to be cleared of land mines, and this was being done as quickly as possible. Despite these problems, he said, "We believe we will meet the 2014 deadline. We are committed to starting then."

"Why is security rarely mentioned as a factor in the future of the mine?" I asked, since much of Logar Province was under heavy Taliban influence and was reputed to have been infiltrated by the radical Haqqani network. "The 2014 start of mining at Mes Aynak also coincides with the withdrawal of US and international forces," I said.

Durrani dismissed security concerns with a wave. "The withdrawal is subject to conditions," he said, and one was that the situation in Afghanistan had to be calm enough to allow a phased transition to Afghan control. "The International Security Assistance Force was here for what?" Durrani asked. "To bring security to the country. It is vital that objective be achieved."

"But can it?" I asked.

"By 2014, our national police and army will be able to handle the security," Durrani said. Some seventeen hundred police had been assigned to protect the Mes Aynak mining site, he said. "I'm sure we can control security."

Equally as important to the copper in Afghanistan were the country's massive iron ore deposits, the largest of which was known as the Hajigak project. Afghanistan's iron belt straddled the central provinces of Bamiyan, Parwan, and Wardak and was reputed to contain about two billion tons of ore with an estimated value of $350 billion. The Afghan government claimed that Hajigak was Asia's largest deposit of untouched mineral wealth. While the Mes Aynak mine had drawn the most attention, development of the country's iron ore at Hajigak would generate many more jobs, up to twenty-five thousand, Durrani said, and would pump more money into the Afghan economy. Every mining job was assumed to impact the welfare of ten people. The government expected to earn $300 to $350 million per year from the iron mines and more than $1 billion a year for the economy.

After bids were received in early September 2011, the Afghan government divided the Hajigak deposit into four separate blocks. In late November, the government would announce that it had awarded three of four blocks to a group of seven companies backed by the government of India. The fourth block went to Canada's Kilo Goldmines Ltd. The Indian group was led by the state-owned Steel Authority of India Ltd., making India one of Afghanistan's largest foreign investors besides China. The Indian companies reportedly planned to put $11 billion in the Hajigak project and to build a steel mill and power plant in the country. The project would provide a new and strategic role for India in Afghanistan, a role that some experts feared would only aggravate and alienate Afghanistan's neighbor, Pakistan.

Pakistan is a critical player in Afghanistan's affairs, I said to Durrani when we talked in September 2011, and would certainly play a role in the future. But Pakistan has been shut out of Afghan mining development in favor of India. It does not bode well for the future, I said, because Pakistan was universally said to be the primary backer of the Taliban. One can only imagine what steps Pakistan might take to disrupt India's development of Afghan mineral wealth.

Durrani was confident that Pakistan would not block mining in Afghanistan and would eventually stop interfering with its affairs. "They will quit these things," he said. "Pakistan depends on American aid. They will have no choice but to help the United States. There's a lot of problems in Pakistan. They have to look to their future."

An Eye on Mining

One of the groups monitoring the development of Afghan copper and iron ore is Integrity Watch Afghanistan. As the name implies, the group tracks corruption in the country and had produced a report on the problem, titled *Afghan Perceptions and Experiences of Corruption: A National Survey 2010.* "Corruption is rampant and has become more entrenched in all areas of life in Afghanistan," the report said. Afghans paid twice as much in bribes to government officials in 2009 than they paid in 2006, the report said, and bribes amounted to a $1 billion drain on the Afghan economy. "One adult in seven experienced direct bribery in Afghanistan in 2009, while 28 percent of Afghan households paid a bribe to obtain at least one public service."

Corruption has enormous implications on the promise that mining holds for the Afghan economy. The award of the Mes Aynak contract to a Chinese company was done amidst allegations that a bribe of some $30 million had been paid to Mohammad Ibrahim Adel, the former minister of mines. The bribe was initially reported in mid-November 2009 by the *Washington Post* in an article that cited an unnamed US official with access to military intelligence reports. The source said that there was "a high degree of certainty" of a payment of roughly $30 million to Adel and that it took place in Dubai around December 2007 when the China Metallurgical Group Corporation (MCC) was awarded the Mes Aynak contract. Adel denied the allegation and left government service not long after, dropping out of public sight.

Javed Noorani, a researcher with Integrity Watch Afghanistan, wrote a July 2010 report titled *Hajigak: Jewel of Afghan Mines,* in which he revealed some of the problems surrounding the development of Afghan iron ore:

The government is grappling with corruption, a growing insurgency, and the lack of infrastructure. It is unable to finance developmental projects from internal funding sources. The region immediately around Afghanistan is also in flux: China, India, Iran and Pakistan all share borders with Afghanistan and are involved in resource disputes. They are in competition for influence, and they all believe that Afghanistan is strategic and cannot be left to the control of one actor. All four countries are watchful and scrutinize carefully the moves of the others in the region.

There were internal threats as well, Noorani wrote in the report. "Ore exploitation in Hajigak may unleash serious environmental risks. It may threaten already limited but precious water supplies. It will produce gases that will pollute the air, soil, and the glaciers nearby in the Hindu Kush range," the report said. Furthermore:

> There is going to be a heightened level of contention in Hajigak among political parties, which will be struggling to keep the allegiance of the local people. There is a serious concern that new networks of actors will emerge to exploit the natural resources of the country. Experience elsewhere shows that this concern is real. Warlords will certainly be tempted to become active in Hajigak and in the sector, and this will be a sure trigger for violent conflicts over resources.

When I met with Noorani not long after my visit to the Ministry of Mines, he was more upbeat about the mining sector's impact on the country than his report had indicated. If handled properly, he said, the employment that the mines could provide might help bring peace to the country. "In time, security will improve," he said, because when young people are working, "They won't pick up weapons. It will really help the stability of the country."

He cautioned, however, that "there's a massive amount of corruption" at the Ministry of Mines, and his organization had evidence of delayed, underreported, and unreported minerals that were already being mined by Afghan entities. This meant that fees, taxes, and royalties were not being paid to the government, and the profits of Afghanistan's mineral wealth only benefitted the Afghan mining companies and their owners. Afghan minerals were being plundered.

The royalty rate to be paid to Afghanistan from Mes Aynak was also a problem, Noorani said. Payments were based on the market price of copper, he explained, which fluctuated but was capped at 19.5 percent. "It's a very good rate for Afghanistan. As the price of copper rises, we get more money. But it freezes at 19.5 percent. It's a major problem with the Aynak contract."

In December 2011, the Afghan government announced still more mining projects would be awarded. In the far northeastern province of Badakhshan, a vast gold deposit was offered for public bids. In Ghazni Province to the south of Kabul, the Zarkashan copper-gold project was announced for bids as well. A third bid offering was for the Balkhab copper project, which straddled the Sar-e-Pol and Balkh Provinces in northern Afghanistan. And a fourth project up for development was the Shaida copper deposit in Adraskan District in the western province of Herat. As of this writing, the development awards have not been made.

The pending development of Afghanistan's vast mineral resources raises serious questions. Much of the country's mineral wealth is in territory controlled by Taliban or other antigovernment groups. If Afghanistan has any hope of benefitting from the development of its minerals, there has to be peace and security. What little security does exist is largely due to the presence of US and coalition forces, and with a severe drawdown by the end of 2014, foreign military influence will be minimal. The security of Afghanistan will be in the hands of the Afghan National Police and Army, which have shown themselves unable to do much without active international assistance. Without security, there is little hope that mining will ever become the salvation of Afghanistan that many think it could be. Even if one assumes that Afghan forces could succeed, the plague of corruption would siphon away untold millions, perhaps billions, of dollars.

More baffling is that of all nations, the United States has spent the most money and sacrificed the most lives so that that Afghanistan could be free of the Taliban to find its own way. The war in Afghanistan has cost the United States about $1 trillion in direct costs over a decade, which is equal to what some say is the total value of Afghanistan's mineral wealth. Yet not one US company is involved in the pending mineral development. The United States, despite its sacrifice, would not gain one cent for more than ten years of war.

The war in Afghanistan has never been and should not be for profit, obviously; it has been fought to remove the terrorist threat presented by al-Qaeda and the Taliban. But ten years on, the Taliban is stronger than ever, and China will reap the rewards of ten years of American fighting that has been in part financed by Chinese loans and a mountain of American foreign debt. China, meanwhile, has not even provided one soldier to help with the war in Afghanistan, yet stands to earn billions in profits from Afghan copper.

An even larger question looms as to the role that Iran and Pakistan will play in the Afghan future. Will these two Afghan neighbors, both blamed for perpetuating the previous ten years of war and chaos in the country, suddenly quit their meddling? Will they quietly let China and India exploit Afghanistan's resources? Hardly. Pakistan is deathly afraid of India's rising influence in Afghanistan, and with the awarding of lucrative iron ore contracts to India, that paranoia has undoubtedly made a quantum leap.

With this in mind, I fear for the Afghan future.

15

A WAR GONE WRONG

T HE UNITED STATES ENTERED Afghanistan in October 2001, less than a month after the attacks of 9/11, riding a wave of righteous anger and a groundswell of international support. US Special Forces backed by air power led the reconstituted Northern Alliance of Afghanistan against brigades of scruffy Taliban fighters who wore shoes without socks, carried antiquated weapons, and wrapped themselves in worn wool blankets. As the Afghan Taliban collapsed and faded into the hills, attention turned to the capture of al-Qaeda leader Osama bin Laden. But bin Laden slipped away, leaving America and the international community standing in the midst of an Afghanistan in ruins.

But America wasn't finished. Iraq became the next major theater in the war on terror, even though Iraq and Saddam Hussein were not involved with al-Qaeda or the 9/11 attacks. Rather than stay focused on Afghanistan, the United States invaded Iraq on the false assertion that Hussein harbored weapons of mass destruction. He didn't. But Iraq was different. It had oil.

Hussein's standing army provided a perfect "theater" of war, and on March 20, 2003, it was "shock and awe" time. With speed similar to the invasion of Afghanistan, conventional US ground forces toppled Hussein's regime. America and its "coalition of the willing" again found themselves standing in the midst of a country in chaos, surrounded by a stunned and soon-to-be-hostile Iraqi public, with little idea of what to do next. Hussein was eventually found hiding in a hole in the ground, was put on trial, and hanged at the end of December 2006.

The war in Afghanistan became an afterthought as American military resources were dumped into Iraq. Just eighteen months after the 9/11 attacks, America was fighting wars on two fronts: Afghanistan and Iraq.

The situation was eerily reminiscent of World War II. For the neoconservative policy makers in the White House, led by Vice President Dick Cheney and Defense Secretary Donald Rumsfeld, the 9/11 attacks were their Pearl Harbor. On May 2, 2003, as if stepping onto the set of a World War II movie, President Bush landed on the deck of the USS *Abraham Lincoln* just off the coast of California and stepped down from a naval jet wearing a fighter pilot's outfit. He addressed the assembled sailors while standing in front of a banner that proclaimed, MISSION ACCOMPLISHED.

In fact, the missions in Iraq and Afghanistan were not accomplished. The United States remained in Iraq for eight years, fighting not Hussein's Iraqi army but insurgent fundamentalist Islamic forces from within and outside of Iraq. The Iraq war cost the lives of nearly 5,000 American soldiers, with more than 72,000 wounded. An estimated 103,000 Iraqi civilians were killed and another 1 million were displaced.

In Afghanistan, meanwhile, total fatalities among the international coalition forces were approaching 3,000 by the spring of 2012, with nearly 2,000 of them being American soldiers, according to the website www.icasualties.org/oef. Expectedly, fatalities for US and coalition forces had increased dramatically with the Afghan surge in 2009, when 521 soldiers were killed, about half due to roadside bombs. The year 2010 was the most deadly, with 711 fatalities, again with about half dying from roadside detonations. Fatalities for coalition forces in 2011 fell significantly to 566. Approximately 12,000 Afghan civilian deaths were recorded between 2006 and 2011, and an estimated 3 million Afghans were displaced, most having fled to either Pakistan or Iran.

The financial cost of the war was enormous, and its effect on the American economy was disastrous as the country slipped into the worst recession since the Great Depression of 1939. A study by Brown University titled *Costs of War* (www.costsofwar.org) put the price tag for wars in Iraq and Afghanistan, including military aid to Pakistan, at $3.2 to $4 trillion. This amounted to a quarter of the national debt, which at the time was about $15 trillion. The study, completed by the Eisenhower Research Project at Brown University's Watson Institute for International Studies, debunked the widely reported figure that the cost of the Iraq war was under $1 trillion. That $1 trillion was only the direct costs of the war and did not include the interest payments on the money borrowed to finance the war, some of which came from China, nor did it include the estimated $1 trillion needed to care for wounded veterans through 2050. Because the war had been financed almost entirely by borrowing, $185 billion in interest had already been paid on war spending, and another $1 trillion could accrue in interest through 2020, the study said.

Among other findings, the study stated that the wars in Afghanistan, Iraq, and Pakistan had killed at least 225,000 people, including men and women in uniform, contractors, and civilians. By one estimate, 137,000 civilians had been killed in Iraq and Afghanistan by all parties to these conflicts. The wars had generated more than 7.8 million refugees among Iraqis, Afghans, and Pakistanis.

In the wake of the withdrawal from Iraq and the pending 2014 exit from Afghanistan, fundamental questions about the wars went unanswered. Was the world a safer place after the wars in Iraq and Afghanistan? Was the United States more secure? Was Iraq better off? Had al-Qaeda and the Taliban been defeated in Afghanistan? When international forces left Afghanistan, would the country fare better than Iraq? Or would it descend into civil war?

If anything had been accomplished in Iraq and Afghanistan, it was that the United States and its allies had shown the Muslim world that it would invade any country considered to be a threat, be that threat real or imaginary, and would do so with impunity. The United States could and would make a big mess of these places, scatter its people, and leave thousands dead, including insurgents, soldiers, and civilians. When it appeared that the wars were unwinnable and they began to cost too much, the United States would shrug, claim victory, and go home.

The Afghan Failure

No one is more worried about their future than the Afghans. As of this writing, the Taliban is stronger than it has ever been in the prior ten years. Life is more dangerous than ever before. Afghanistan is among the world's poorest countries, and the Afghan economy is totally dependent on the foreign military and civilian aid programs. If the international community packs up and leaves, Afghans know full well that the Taliban will come back to power and again make their lives miserable. As Afghans fearfully prepare for an uncertain future, they have grown increasingly sullen and hostile. Who can blame them? After ten years of war and the expenditure of billions of dollars, what has changed? More important, what has gone so wrong when at first it had been so right?

The failures in Afghanistan can be attributed to an emphasis on the military solution to the exclusion of most everything else. The nation and its people were put on life support while the militaries of some forty nations waged war against the Taliban, itself a creature of a significant portion of the society. Civil society and government were left to atrophy.

In ten years of war, little or nothing has been done to improve basic aspects of Afghan society. A look at the numbers is shocking. Life expectancy in Afghanistan is less than forty-five years, one of the lowest in the world. One in every four children will not see his or her fifth birthday. For those who survive, expectations are abysmal. Only one in five adults can read and write, which is a vast improvement in ten years but still far from adequate. Unemployment is consistently about 40 percent.

Basic infrastructure is abysmal. Electricity only reaches a third of the Afghan population. Though 70 percent of all Kabul households are connected to the grid, power cuts are routine and brownouts are expected. Those who can afford them rely on polluting and noisy portable generators or on bottled gas, kerosene lanterns, and candles. Afghanistan's power is imported from Iran, Turkmenistan, and Tajikistan and bolstered by a line from Uzbekistan, but it is hampered by antiquated and inadequate transmission lines. Although some $200 million annually is reportedly poured into improving the power supply, the projects languish due to cost overruns and the war.

Some people have suggested that Afghanistan would have been better off if countries like the United States had taken $500 billion of what it spent on the war in Afghanistan and given it directly to the people. Divided among the population, every man, woman, and child in the country could have been handed about $17,000. That is about ten years' worth of income for the average Afghan. This notion points to the fact that while large amounts of international cash enter the country, little of it reaches most Afghans. Much of it comes into the country via nonprofit organizations that pay for high-priced international staff, their housing, their transportation, and their security.

As most Afghans have waited for their lives to improve, they have watched as heavily armed and well-equipped foreign militaries prowl the countryside, rolling down roads in every corner of the country. The presence of foreign armies has not made Afghans feel safe or protected. Rather, they feel the opposite. As the Taliban clumsily and ruthlessly detonates roadside and car bombs and launches suicide attacks, civilians bear the brunt of the bloodshed. Foreigners are viewed as the problem, not the solution, even though the Taliban has planted the bombs and conducted the attacks. It is no wonder that the Taliban is poised for a comeback. The lives of average Afghans have changed little in ten years of war, and international forces have gone from a cause for celebration to a thing to be hated.

What baffles most Afghans is why the US and coalition forces have been unable to defeat the Taliban. Many Afghans insist that the United States could have defeated the Taliban any time it wanted but has intentionally dragged out the war. When I asked Afghans why America would do that, they responded with shrugs.

Afghan Voices

Three knowledgeable Afghans, each a behind-the-scenes player, told me that the Taliban were not the problem behind the Afghan dilemma and never had been.

It was not easy to meet with Sibghatullah Mojaddedi, the president of Afghanistan's upper house of parliament, the Mushrano Jirga, or House of Elders. Among his other duties, he headed the Afghanistan National Independent Peace and Reconciliation Commission. I had wanted to talk with him because it was his younger relative in Herat, Safiullah Mojaddedi, who had been kidnapped by the Taliban and ultimately set free in exchange for the release of Taliban prisoners, a deal that involved the elder Mujaddedi.

After negotiating a gauntlet of security at a government building in a quiet neighborhood of Kabul, I was ushered into a long, carpeted hall where about twenty Afghan elders were seated, each wearing a large turban and sporting a long, graying beard. They nodded gravely as I ambled to the far end, where Sibghatullah Mojaddedi sat in a padded wooden chair and casually motioned for me to sit. Despite his eighty-five years, Mojaddedi was a striking figure, dressed in crisp white cotton clothing and a turban to match, much like his colleagues. His large glasses magnified his eyes, which by any measure had seen a lot.

An ethnic Pashtun, he was the patriarch of one of Afghanistan's eminent and extended religious families. Throughout most of his life, Mojaddedi had been integrally involved in the fate of his country. A moderate Muslim, he had been Afghanistan's president for just two months in 1992 when the country struggled to set up a government in the turbulent days that followed the 1989 withdrawal of the forces from the former Soviet Union. He was quickly succeeded by the late Burhanuddin Rabbani, who two years later presided over the Afghan civil war. Mojaddedi resurfaced in 2003 to head the Loya Jirga, the national council of elders that adopted the modern Afghan constitution. He was later named to head the Afghan upper house of parliament, a position he continued to hold.

"Peace in this country is not possible with the ISI [Pakistan's Inter-Service Intelligence agency] and Pakistan," Mojaddedi said. Ninety percent of Afghanistan's problems are due to Pakistan, he insisted, as terrorist fighters, including Chechens and radicalized Arabs, enter Pakistan and then "cross borders and cause problems for us. The main [barrier to] peace is the ISI. The terrorists are exported from Pakistan." Although the US-funded Pakistan army fought against the Taliban in the border regions with Afghanistan, Mojaddedi complained that "it's not enough. [The United States] needs to put pressure on Pakistan. Attack the ISI [training] camps. If they want peace, that is what they must do." Some ten thousand fighters had been trained in these ISI-sponsored Taliban camps, he contended. "They have training centers in Pakistan, so why don't you fight the terrorists there?" Mojaddedi asked. He had complained repeatedly to US officials about their soft approach to Pakistan, he said, but with no result. "I tell them that they can't recognize their enemies and their friends."

"Pakistan is not the only problem," I said. "The Taliban is growing stronger because Afghans are turning to them out of disgust with the government."

"People support the Taliban because they are afraid of them," Mojaddedi said. "If [people] don't agree with them, they kill them." The dislike of the Karzai government had been caused by Karzai himself, he said, who put his family and friends into important posts. Karzai's people were interested not in a better Afghanistan but only in themselves. The climate of corruption was rooted in war. "The character and morals have been changed due to the war," he said. "It's the main reason for the corruption here." Solving the problem was simple. "The people who are corrupt must be punished, and those who are good must be rewarded," he said. But to do that, "we need a strong government," he continued. Such a government would not exist with Karzai at the helm, he said.

Another Afghan who shared Mojaddedi's frustration with the war against the Taliban was Mawlawi Ataullah Ludin, the deputy of the High Peace Council, which had been created by Karzai in the fall of 2010. The council was headed by former president Rabbani until his assassination in September 2011 by a Taliban emissary who detonated a bomb hidden in his turban. The High Peace Council is a separate entity from the one controlled by Mojaddedi but is also charged with negotiating a peace deal with the Taliban.

Originally from the restive Nangarhar Province in eastern Afghanistan, Mawlawi had contact with some of the most radical antigovernment forces at work in the country. He was an ethnic Pashtun and a former high-ranking commander of Hezb-e-Islami, the militant group led by Gulbuddin Hekmatyar, said to have ties to Pakistan's ISI and other groups such as the Haqqani network. Hekmatyar reportedly trained Afghan and foreign fighters in Pakistan's Northwest Frontier Province and ran schools and hospitals there with support from fundamentalist Islamic groups.

Mawlawi's offices were located in well-appointed rooms in the upper floors of a highly guarded government building in the heart of Kabul. The Afghan people were hungry for peace, Mawlawi said, which was why the High Peace Council had been named. "People like to hear about peace, not war. We are in the thirty-second year of war in Afghanistan. It is not something optimal for the country," he said, because war kept Afghans poor. "Due to the poverty, the regional countries misuse the situation to their advantage. It is a problem for us. People need peace. Any step toward peace is needed." Mawlawi described his role as being "a link to the armed groups, such as the Taliban. We negotiate with all armed groups." It was the only way to bring peace to the country, he said.

"The Taliban has consistently said they will never talk peace," I said. "So why bother?"

"What they say is not their attitude on the ground," Mawlawi said. In early 2012, the Taliban reportedly agreed to open an office for negotiations in Doha, Qatar, on the Arabian Peninsula. But those initial steps toward negotiations were quashed by late March 2012, following the burning of Korans at Bagram Airfield and the killing of sixteen civilians by a US soldier in Kandahar that month.

"Why is Pakistan such a problem for Afghanistan?" I asked.

"War has made other countries [such as Pakistan] get involved in Afghanistan. They have a stake in prolonging the war in Afghanistan. Iran is not happy with NATO in Afghanistan. China is not happy with the presence of international forces in Afghanistan," he said. The sooner that international forces withdraw from Afghanistan, the sooner a peace deal can be struck, he said. "We want to know how long the US will stay in Afghanistan."

"President Obama has announced a withdrawal by July 2014," I said, explaining that the US economy was in bad shape and could not afford an extended military presence in Afghanistan. The American public was tired of the war now that bin Laden had been killed.

There were reasons other than the war on terror that kept the United States in Afghanistan, Mawlawi said. "If [the war] is against terrorism and al-Qaeda, then it should not [have been] prolonged." Yet the war in Afghanistan had lasted ten years with no end in sight. "Pakistan thinks that the United States is in Afghanistan due to [Pakistan's] atomic power, to somehow have control over their atomic power," he said.

While Pakistan publically agreed to fight the Taliban and accepted US money to do so, in reality Pakistan considered the United States "an old enemy," because of its past support of India. "India is predicted to use [Afghanistan] as a staging ground against Pakistan," Mawlawi said. Because of this fear, Pakistan has supported the Taliban insurgency so that Afghanistan remains in turmoil. Pakistan knows that the Afghan government cannot exist or fight the Taliban without the international help, he said. Once the coalition forces leave, then Pakistan would control Afghanistan via the Taliban and prevent India from gaining a foothold in the country.

The United States was not helping itself by the way it was fighting the Taliban, Mawlawi said. "International forces in Afghanistan raid homes at night and arrest innocent people. They produce enemies."

"The problem is more complicated than just night raids," I said, suggesting that large segments of the Afghan population are disgruntled with the government.

Mawlawi agreed. "The law has yet to be enforced. There is injustice," he said. There was discrimination against the ethnic Pashtuns by the ethnic Tajiks, which was why Pashtun communities were turning to the Taliban. The average Afghan "does not see the government as their government. Because of the insecurity, there is injustice. Some people feel they've been marginalized and are ruled by minorities," he said, explaining how the Pashtuns, Afghanistan's large ethnic group, viewed the Tajik-dominated government. "They see that as injustice. This has eroded public confidence in the government and they doubt the government can deliver services."

"Can Afghanistan ever find peace?" I asked.

"Yes, as soon as international forces leave," Mawlawi said. The only viable conclusion to the war in Afghanistan necessarily involves the Taliban. Peace talks with the Taliban need to be "an inclusive process," he said, that will allow the groups fighting the government to become part of the government. The best way for the United States to help is to put pressure on Pakistan to stabilize Afghanistan and elicit "regional guarantees" to leave Afghanistan alone.

Withdrawal of foreign forces should not mean abandonment, however. "We want the United States and the international community to leave but to have a long-term relationship with Afghanistan," Mawlawi said. Afghanistan does not need foreign military presence, only foreign aid. The international community needs to support reconciliation, he said, which is a polite word for negotiation with the Taliban. "If the United States stands behind national reconciliation, it can succeed. Without their support, it cannot succeed. The international community can do that if they are willing to bring people together." Without reconciliation, Mawlawi warned, "the decade of the 1990s"—of civil war and Taliban control—"will be repeated."

None of this was new, he said. "The United States knows all of this but doesn't know the people of Afghanistan. We hope the United States will put more pressure on its strategic partner in Pakistan to bring peace to Afghanistan," he said.

If Pakistan had been the problem all along, I wondered, had the United States and the coalition forces invaded the wrong country and been fighting the wrong people? Both Mojaddedi and Mawlawi had said as much. Yet the United States paid Pakistan billions of dollars to fight the Taliban in Pakistan, where the Taliban and other groups had virtual sanctuary. Pakistan had played a lucrative game with the United States, and the United States rarely complained.

I put the Pakistan question to another Afghan. Saeed Niazi could only shake his head at the baffling reality that had persisted for a decade. A year after I had first met Niazi when he was running for the Afghan parliament, I sat down with him in his office to talk about events of the past year. He had lost the election but continued to be active in community and social affairs as director of his own nonprofit organization, the Civil Society Development Center.

"Ordinary people are disappointed by democracy and the rule of law," Niazi said, lighting a cigarette in his dimly lighted office. "Our government is very weak. They can't define who our enemies are." If one listened to Karzai, he said, the United States were "friends one day and enemies the next." Likewise with the Taliban. "We fight them, but then we can share our government with them." Afghanistan had no one to blame but itself. "We can't blame any [other] country. Afghanistan doesn't care about its own interests" and has come to rely too much on the international community. "The only country that doesn't know this is Afghanistan. The people of Afghanistan are losing their country."

With the killing of bin Laden in Pakistan, Niazi said, the world learned that "terrorism is based in Pakistan, and Pakistan is playing a game . . . against the United States." The relationship between the

United States and Pakistan was idiotic, he said, since the United States supported the Pakistan military while Pakistan's ISI supported the Taliban. "Who is the crazy one here?" he asked. "The one asking for the money or the one giving it?"

The Afghan Disconnect

After more than a decade of war, Afghanistan remains one of the poorest countries in the world. The war has dragged on even though the country never posed a threat to the United States or any of the coalition countries. The Afghan war has run amok, mired in mistakes and madness.

A telltale sign of the abject failure of the coalition's war in Afghanistan surfaced in late 2011 and early 2012 as the Afghan soldiers who were being trained, equipped, and paid by the international community began turning on US and coalition forces. In a classified study of the problem, reported in the *New York Times* on January 20, 2012, the coalition admitted that a wall of ill will and distrust stood between the Afghan and US forces. Authors of the seventy-two-page report, titled *A Crisis of Trust and Cultural Incompatibility*, had spoken with more than six hundred Afghan soldiers and policemen, more than two hundred American soldiers, and some thirty Afghans working for the Americans. One Afghan colonel summed up the situation by saying, "The sense of hatred is growing rapidly." While he admitted that his troops were "thieves, liars, and drug addicts," he described Americans as "rude, arrogant bullies who use foul language."

The Afghan antipathy for the foreign forces was not only a symptom of a serious problem; it was also a deadly reality. The single most deadly incident took place on the military side of the Kabul airport in April 2011, when an Afghan air force colonel drew a weapon in a meeting and began killing his American colleagues. In the end, eight American officers and a contractor died before the colonel turned a gun on himself. Investigators reportedly found the words GOD IS ONE written in blood on the walls. Subsequent investigations suggested that

Afghan aircraft had been used for smuggling, implicating the Afghan colonel.

Anticoalition hatred among Afghan soldiers accounted for the death of more than seventy-five coalition troops between May 2007 and the end of March 2012, and the wounding of 110 other foreign soldiers, according to an Associated Press story. While these "green-on-blue" deaths, so called because of the green designation for Afghan troops and blue for NATO, were a small percentage of total coalition fatalities, they indicated a larger problem: the unraveling of the American mission in Afghanistan.

The majority of the coalition deaths at the hands of Afghan soldiers had occurred in the previous two years, and the situation spiraled out of control after the burning of some Korans in a garbage pit on February 20, 2012, at the Bagram Airfield north of Kabul. A report on the incident in the *New York Times* revealed that the Korans had been among more than sixteen hundred books, many secular works including novels and poetry, from the Bagram prison library that had been culled and slated for disposal because prisoners had jotted suspicious notes in the margins. According to some educated Afghans who saw the notes, the jottings had nothing to do with suspected terrorist communications.

Yet the burning, which was halted after just four of the books were charred, provoked deadly outrage among Afghans. On February 23, two American soldiers were killed in the eastern Nangarhar Province by an Afghan soldier. On February 25, two ranking US military advisers to the Afghan government were killed execution style by shots to the head while in the secure Kabul offices of the Afghan Interior Ministry, prompting the wholesale removal of foreign advisers from Afghan governmental offices. On March 1 another two US soldiers were killed by Afghan soldiers on a US-Afghan base in the southern Kandahar Province. The smoldering chaos ratcheted up when, on March 11, a US soldier apparently massacred seventeen Afghan civilians, including nine children and four women, after he wandered off his base in Kandahar and shot them to death in two separate incidents on the same evening. Just two weeks later, on March 26 at a British post in the Helmand provincial capital of Lashkar Gah, a man in an Afghan army uniform shot two British soldiers. The Taliban claimed that they were aware of the Helmand attack before it took place.

Such seething animosity did not bode well for America's exit strategy from Afghanistan, which was based on leaving behind a well-trained and well-equipped security force to protect the country and fight the Taliban. The push to build up Afghan security forces as rapidly as possible to about 325,000 men before the coalition forces left was an underlying problem.

The Afghan security forces were taking just about anyone and everyone they could find, with little time or money available to conduct background checks or other basic screening. As a result, the Afghan forces were typically illiterate and otherwise unable to find jobs except in the army. Another problem was that the Afghan army was largely composed of men from northern Afghanistan, many of them Tajiks, because few of the Pashtuns in the Afghan south supported the government. The ethnic composition of the Afghan army was critical, because without the coalition forces beside them, the Tajik soldiers would not fight and die alone in the south against the largely Pashtun Taliban.

Undoubtedly the most visible sign of the coalition's failures in Afghanistan was President Karzai, who was petulant, angry, and subject to making impromptu and radical changes in Afghan policy, only to reverse himself later. Karzai routinely threatened to throw the fifty or so private security companies operating in Afghanistan out of the country even though they were vital to protecting coalition supplies and supply routes, as well as critical civilian construction projects such as roads. Karzai blamed corruption in Afghanistan, including the notorious loan scandal that nearly brought down the Kabul Bank, on foreigners. He condemned coalition forces for killing Afghan civilians but rarely mentioned that the Taliban caused 80 percent of the civilian fatalities each year. Perhaps the most outrageous comment came in late 2011 during an interview on Pakistani television, when Karzai said that Afghanistan would side with Pakistan if Pakistan went to war with the United States.

When I turned to my Afghan colleagues and asked them what they were going to do with Karzai, they just laughed. "What are we going to do with Karzai?" they asked incredulously. "He's not our problem, he's your problem. You put him there."

Another example of the US-Karzai disconnect came in early 2012, when Karzai demanded that the United States turn over to Afghan control of its prison at the Bagram Airfield. The prison housed the detainees that US and coalition forces considered to be "high value," including key Taliban operatives. The United States was reluctant to comply, although it later agreed to a handover in late 2012. Karzai's demand had come less than two months after the United Nations reported that detainees in Afghan-run prisons were subjected to "systematic torture," and had been hung by their hands or beaten with cables or had their genitals twisted until they passed out from pain. Explaining the Afghan demand, an Afghan official told a reporter, "We have the right to rule on our own soil."

The comment revealed what many other Afghans felt—they wanted their country back. Most Afghans had lost track of why international forces were in Afghanistan. With almost half of the population under the age of fifteen, most of the young Afghans were less than five years old when the United States had arrived. This generation had grown up listening to the older population express their frustration and anger that so little had changed in ten years.

Exit to Chaos

America's abortive drive in early 2012 to establish talks with the Taliban illustrated an aching desire to end the war. The American exit strategy in Afghanistan had been signaled in late December 2011 when Vice President Joe Biden said in an interview with *Newsweek* magazine that "the Taliban per se is not our enemy." This was a remarkable statement, given that the reason the United States invaded

Afghanistan was because the Taliban had given sanctuary to al-Qaeda leader Osama bin Laden. The apparent logic was that if the *enemy* label could be removed from the Taliban, then the Obama administration could deflect criticism that it was negotiating with terrorists. But more important it begged the question that if the Taliban were not the enemy, then who was America and its allies fighting, and why were they there?

The lack of purpose, understanding, and support among the American public for the war in Afghanistan was dramatically revealed in a *New York Times–CBS News* poll of 986 people taken March 21–25, 2012. The vast majority of those polled, 69 percent, said the United States should not be involved in Afghanistan, and just 23 percent thought it was the right thing to be doing. Only 27 percent of the respondents thought the Afghan war had been a success, while 59 percent said it was a failure. Expectedly, 44 percent said that US forces should be withdrawn sooner than the end of 2014, while 33 percent said the 2014 date was fine. Just 17 percent said the United States should stay in Afghanistan. More than half of those polled, 55 percent, said they had no "clear idea" why America remained in Afghanistan now that Osama bin Laden had been killed. Just 42 percent said they knew the reason. But when those 42 percent were asked why the United States was in Afghanistan, only 1 percent said it was because of the attacks of 9/11. Some 15 percent said it was to fight terrorism, while the other reasons offered were such things as preventing a Taliban takeover, stabilizing the country, helping the Afghan people, and installing democracy. Four percent said oil and gas was why America was there, even though such minor resources had scarcely been developed.

The results of the poll showed that in many respects, American attitudes toward the war in Afghanistan paralleled those of Afghans. Just as most Afghans had little or no idea why foreign armies were still in their country, only 1 percent of Americans said that their country was still in Afghanistan eleven years later because of the 9/11 attacks. Not only had the war devolved into an unmitigated disaster as Afghans and US and US-led soldiers turned on each other, few in either the United States or Afghanistan wanted it to continue.

Talks with the Taliban were seen as a key to the American exit from Afghanistan, even if they took a couple of years to complete. If an agreement could be reached, America could exit Afghanistan in 2014, after a dozen years of war, and claim success. Such talks conceivably could lead to a coalition government with the Taliban that might end the war—a result that would be welcomed by all of the NATO countries who were struggling with their own economic problems and budget deficits.

A peace deal with the Taliban will be difficult, however. The United States can put all kinds of conditions on an agreement, none of which the Taliban needs to accept. After all, they are winning. The coalition has the watches; the Taliban has the time.

The questions surrounding a negotiated settlement are numerous and difficult to answer. For example, the Taliban can demand the complete withdrawal of US and coalition forces and in turn promise what? To be a kinder and gentler Taliban? Even if a peace agreement can be reached with the Taliban, what would it look like? A part-Taliban, part-Tajik, part-Hazara government is hard to envision. Will the Taliban accept just part of the government? If so, which part? Why would they settle for just part of the government when they could have the whole thing?

Most critically, would an agreement with the Taliban last? All of the former Northern Alliance commanders are still around, some in the highest echelons of government, including Karzai's vice presidents, Marshal Fahim and Abdul Khalili. Uzbek commander General Dostum remains a viable leader, as does Ismail Khan, the former strongman in western Herat Province. Ethnic militia commanders populate the parliament, most of whom fought the Taliban bitterly. What would be in place to keep them from breaking away from a Taliban-controlled government and returning to their local bases of power and support? As General Malik told me in Mazar-e-Sharif, if the Taliban returned, he would fight to the death.

Without an agreement with the Taliban to end the war, however, the American-led coalition faces little choice but to continue the war and pour aid into Afghanistan. Such a continued war scenario is what appears to have been agreed to in the strategic partnership agreement signed on May 2, 2012, in Kabul by Presidents Obama and Karzai. While the agreement is void of specifics on troop levels or aid dollar amounts, it provides broad outlines for extensive American involvement in Afghanistan through 2024. Military operations, for example, "will continue under existing frameworks" until replaced by other agreements, as will development aid across the broad spectrum of society. Details of the partnership will be included in future bilateral agreements, which suggests that US and coalition involvement could fluctuate wildly, depending on the situations in the United States, Afghanistan, and abroad.

One possible future scenario discussed quietly in 2012 would keep the United States in Afghanistan until 2024 but confined to several large bases, most likely one at Bagram in the east and just north of Kabul, one in Mazar-e-Sharif in the north, one in Herat Province in the west; and one at Kandahar in the south. From these bases, the US Special Forces theoretically would continue to conduct "antiterrorism" raids against the Taliban and would support Afghan security forces. This would create virtual islands of foreign armies in the midst of what likely could be badly deteriorating, civil-war-like conditions in Afghanistan. The thought that US and other foreign forces would isolate themselves inside highly fortified bases from a civil war that rages beyond the gates is unimaginable.

Despite the vague agreements outlined in the US-Afghan partnership, pressure has steadily increased for a wholesale withdrawal from Afghanistan by 2014. This would leave the country to the Taliban, however. It would be conceding defeat. Abandoning Afghanistan, as the United States did with Iraq, is not the answer. It would be telling the world that US foreign policy and military might is random, brutal, and short-sighted. It would make a mockery of the American lives lost and the billions of dollars spent.

As I contemplated these alternatives, I recalled my conversations with women activists and parliament members who feared for their lives should the Taliban return. I thought about the Taliban system of chopping off fingers and limbs, of hanging men on little more than an accusation. I thought of the bombed-out video-shop owners in Jalalabad and the distraught women in the Herat hospital who wanted to burn themselves to death. I thought of the destruction of Afghanistan's priceless cultural heritage. I thought of Afghan colleagues who knew that if the Taliban came to power, their lives were at risk, since they had worked with international organizations and could be executed as accused spies for the foreigners.

The post-2014 Afghan scenario I envisioned was grim. As the last planeload of US soldiers left the ground in Afghanistan, the Taliban would seize control of the government, or major portions of it. The vast majority of Afghanistan's 325,000 armed forces and police, who had been trained and equipped by the United States at a cost of about $10 billion a year, would flee, taking their weapons and trucks. The former Northern Alliance commanders would retreat to their respective provinces, along with their loyal cadres from the army and police. The Taliban would demand allegiance, would use force to get it, but would face resistance at every turn. The civil war would begin, forcing tens of thousands of Afghans to flee across its borders.

The United States already paid a huge price after abandoning Afghanistan when the former Soviet Union pulled out in 1989. Afghanistan had descended into civil war, which paved the way for the Taliban. The Taliban hosted bin Laden as he plotted 9/11. In 2001, America was forced to return to Afghanistan as the remains of the Twin Towers smoldered. The United States could not afford to make the same mistake again. Leaving Afghanistan in the hands of the Taliban, even in the context of a negotiated deal, was to repeat the mistakes of the past. And, had we fought a war in Afghanistan for ten years only to leave $1 trillion worth of minerals for the Chinese and Indians to exploit? It made no sense.

As I discussed the Afghan future with an Afghan colleague and bemoaned how difficult it was to find peace in Afghanistan, he responded by telling a dark Afghan joke. It concerned patients in the psychiatric wing of a hospital who took turns looking through a keyhole to the outside world. They did this every day, week after week, month after month, and had done so for years. One day a new young psychiatrist arrived, having been trained in the West. After a couple of days of watching the patients, curiosity got the best of the doctor. He walked over to the keyhole and squinted through it for several minutes. He then turned to the patients and said, "There's nothing to see!" The patients laughed and replied, "Well, of course. You only looked for a couple of minutes! We've been looking for years but have found nothing."

It is not easy to find peace in Afghanistan, my colleague was telling me. There are no easy answers and no quick fixes. We can only hope that as the United States and its allies withdraw from this ancient and troubled land, solutions will arise that will give Afghanistan hope for a peaceful future that it so badly needs and deserves.

EPILOGUE

Slouching Toward Calamity

IN THE FALL OF 2012, nearly a year after I left Afghanistan, conditions were deteriorating across the country, much as foreshadowed by the Afghans I had interviewed. With more than two years to go before the 2014 withdrawal, Afghans already were preparing for the worst. Property values in Kabul were plummeting. The ornately decorated "poppy palaces" that had once commanded $10,000 per month rent from foreign aid groups and advisers went begging for tenants. Kabul's bustling used car business, once fueled by legions of well-paid Afghan employees of aid organizations, was slowing to a crawl. Those who could afford it were moving to Dubai. Those who could not were gathering resources and making plans to leave. This did not escape the attention of the Taliban, who friends told me were trying to stop the coming exodus by threatening Afghans who were eyeing the exits.

The most serious sign of the coming chaos was the surge in deadly attacks on US and coalition troops by Afghan security forces. Of the more than thirty American fatalities during August 2012, an astounding one of every three deaths was due to these sorts of attacks—point-blank shootings in which members of the Afghan police or army turned on their American military trainers or fighting partners. The absurdity of the situation was staggering.

The killings that month pushed the total death toll of Americans in the Afghan war over the two thousand mark. While that figure was less than half of the number of American fatalities in the war in Iraq, it was still tragically significant, because so little had been accomplished despite more than a decade of conflict. Operation Enduring Freedom, as the Pentagon called it, continues as of this writing, making it the longest war in American history.

The shootings occurred in all corners of the country. Helmand Province in Afghanistan's bloody south remained among the most deadly locales. In early August, three US Marines said to be Special Forces members were killed shortly after sharing a predawn meal with an Afghan police officer and some of his men during the holy month of Ramadan in Sangin District, a bastion of Taliban resistance. A second attack occurred not far from the first, at a joint US-Afghan installation. It appeared that the shooter was a fifteen-year-old boy whose job was to serve tea; he apparently grabbed a weapon and shot the marines as they exercised on the post's gym equipment. As expected, the spokesman for the southern Taliban, Qari Yousaf Ahmadi—the man with whom I'd spoken about telephone service outages in Helmand—claimed the Taliban were behind both attacks.

The spiraling descent of the coalition cause was even more evident as insurgents attacked previously immune locales. In mountainous Bamiyan Province in central Afghanistan, generally a sanctuary in the war-torn country, five soldiers from New Zealand were killed, three by a roadside bomb and two by militants thought to have infiltrated a village. The attacks demonstrated how deeply the Taliban and antigovernment elements had penetrated the countryside, even in this ethnic Hazara and traditionally pro-Western region.

Afghans were also killing other Afghans. In early August, an Afghan police officer killed ten of his fellow officers in the generally quiet southwestern province of Nimroz, bordering Iran. Another twenty-nine Afghan civilians were killed and fifty-seven wounded when a bomber struck a market in Nimroz's capital city of Zaranj. In northeastern Kunduz Province, a motorcycle-borne bomb exploded in a marketplace, killing another ten Afghans. In neighboring Badakhshan Province, where Afghanistan borders China, a district governor and three police officers were killed in an ambush by Taliban militants.

The goal of defeating terrorism and rendering Afghanistan a secure ally in the heart of south-central Asia was slipping away with each passing day. The escalating attacks and resulting loss of life threatened the premise of the American and NATO withdrawal, which hinged on the 320,000 or so members of the Afghan police and army controlling the country by the end of 2014.

One of the US military's responses to the attacks was to beef up their "guardian angels." These were heavily armed coalition soldiers who stood guard over their buddies whenever Afghans were present, even in settings such as mess halls and makeshift gyms and at organized training sessions. In addition, commanders told soldiers to carry loaded weapons at all times.

These protective measures were understandable, even necessary, but they further poisoned the air with distrust. I was reminded of conversations I'd had with former military personnel who were horrified that I traveled around Afghanistan unarmed. They dehumanized Afghans by referring to them as "hajis" and were amazed that I ate "haji food" and lived in a "haji house." The average US soldier never interacted with Afghans, an activity that was limited to commanders under tightly controlled circumstances. Even employees of large US contractors that served the military were never allowed off their compounds.

In an ancient culture in which trust and mutual respect are paramount, assuming an aggressively defensive posture was considered as an insult. Perceived or real, such insults provoked violent reactions, as the response to the February 2012 Koran burnings at Bagram Airfield had shown. Afghans were deeply offended at this behavior by their American allies, and the understanding gap between the average US soldier and Afghan citizen was an abyss of misinformation and suspicion. Trying to win Afghan hearts and minds like this was impossible.

The coalition's public response to the new wave of violence was also telling. Though attacks by Afghan security forces on Western troops had previously been referred to as "green-on-blue" killings, the coalition began referring to them instead as "insider" attacks. The term *insider* suggested that the attacks were secretly planned and carried out by Taliban fighters planted in the ranks. This notion was seized upon by the propaganda-prone Taliban; in late August, Taliban leader Mullah Omar claimed that his fighters had "cleverly infiltrated" the enemy.

In reality, however, the coalition had no ready explanation for why the attacks were happening. The assailants were killed on the spot, often in a hail of bullets, precluding interrogations. And the US military admitted that most of the attacks were probably not premeditated but the result of battle fatigue or personal animosities.

The broader truth, which the military was loath to consider, was that these attacks were eruptions of years of pent-up frustration and anger. The Taliban were stronger than ever. Karzai's government, bolstered by billions of dollars in foreign aid, remained riddled with corruption and hopelessly disconnected. For the average Afghan, the country was as destitute and dangerous as at any time in its history. After more than a decade of war and occupation by 140,000 foreign soldiers, the prospect of endless fighting loomed. If the foreign forces could not defeat the Taliban and secure the country, the Afghans wanted them out.

But the US military tried to downplay the significance of the insider killings. In an opinion article published by the *Washington Post* on August 24, 2012, General John R. Allen, commander of the US and NATO forces in Afghanistan, argued that the attacks were minor blips in the context of the broader mission. Allen wrote that the real story was the "green and blue"—meaning that every day thousands of Afghans and foreign forces worked and fought side by side without problems. Writing as any commander should, Allen vowed that the attacks would not deter the mission, which was "far from over." Allen went too far, however, when he concluded, "We are, in fact, prevailing." The alarming growth in insider incidents meant they could no longer be dismissed as rogue events in an otherwise successful effort to create a credible Afghan security force. Without dramatic changes, little could be done to stop them. Dramatic changes, however, were not on the coalition agenda.

Instead, just a week later, the US military enacted yet another stopgap measure. It temporarily suspended the training of the Afghan Local Police, whose recruits were responsible for some, but not all, of the insider attacks. The suspended training affected about one thousand recruits, the coalition announced, whose backgrounds would be reviewed again, along with those of the estimated sixteen thousand active members of local police units scattered around Afghanistan. However, the suspension did not affect the ongoing training of the Afghan regular army and police.

US defense secretary Leon Panetta, meanwhile, expressed "concern" about the insider killings to Afghan president Karzai and asked for more scrutiny of recruits for the Afghan police and army. Karzai's government promised to increase the number of spies among the Afghan troops, to monitor the troops' telephone calls, and to ban new recruits from using cell phones while training. The Afghans also agreed to track troops on leave to prevent them from contacting insurgents.

The practicalities of such promises were daunting. Security forces numbered between 300,000 to 350,000 army and police. The Afghans said that another 176 intelligence officers were to be inserted among the troops in addition to the 125 or so already embedded, which meant that about one thousand soldiers had to be monitored by each spy. Assuming each soldier made three telephone calls each day, nearly one million telephone calls had to be monitored daily. Following Afghan soldiers on leave also defied common sense. With just 10 percent of the 350,000 or so soldiers and police on leave at any one time, that equated to 35,000 people who needed to be tracked. Who was going do that and how?

Afghan officials agreed that the reason for the high number of insider attacks was that new recruits were not properly screened. The main problem was that for security forces to reach targeted levels by the 2014 pullout deadline, the government had to find more than ten thousand recruits each month. Screening was nearly impossible.

Most men were from rural areas and lacked even rudimentary records such as birth certificates. Those who joined the ranks of the national army or police did so out of desperation, not dedication, since they lacked education and job opportunities and faced a life of subsistence farming.

Recruitment efforts also could not take into account the danger to the recruits' families. Their neighbors knew who had joined the government forces and who had not. With antigovernment hatred rising, and the Taliban present in nearly every village across the country, families were vulnerable to threats and intimidation, as were the recruits themselves. Another neglected consideration was ethnicity. Recruiting efforts were weakest where antigovernment sentiment was strongest, among the ethnic Pashtun communities that dominate southern Afghanistan. This meant that non-Pashtun recruits from the north and west were used to fill the ranks, adding to the ethnic, cultural, and linguistic tensions.

Further evidence that the Afghan house of cards created by the US-NATO coalition was beginning to crumble surfaced in early August 2012 when the Afghan parliament adopted a vote of no confidence against the longstanding Afghan defense minister, Abdul Rahim Wardak, and the interior minister, Bismillah Khan Mohammadi. Both subsequently resigned. The regional warlords who controlled parliament had forced out the two key Karzai appointees, both closely linked with the coalition's war effort. In doing so, the warlords were flexing their collective muscles as the true power brokers, while telling Karzai how little they liked or trusted these critical departments of his government. They were also taking a shot at the US-led coalition, saying they had little respect for the American-trained security forces. The warlords, it seemed, were already thinking of the future, one in which they would take care of themselves.

Meanwhile, fresh reports of corruption in the Karzai administration undermined what little credibility the government may still have had. In late June 2012, the *Telegraph* newspaper in England reported that lucrative oil contracts had been given to Karzai's cousins, Rashid and Rateb Popal. Described by the newspaper as "notorious," the men reportedly had served nearly nine years in jail in New York in the 1990s on drug charges. The oil contract was awarded to the Popal brothers' company, Watan Oil and Gas, a joint venture formed just months earlier with a Chinese state-owned firm. The twenty-five-year development contract gave the brothers and their Chinese partners rights to an estimated 160 million barrels of untapped oil in three fields in northern Afghanistan.

Whether the company could extract the oil was doubtful. The Popal brothers were Pashtuns from southern Afghanistan, and the oil patch is in the north in an area controlled by General Abdul Rashid Dostum—the Uzbek warlord whose men were said to have been responsible for the deaths of thousands of Taliban prisoners in late 2001. Dostum was accused of trying to block the oil deal and extort money from the Chinese. In addition, the *Telegraph* wrote, the contract was awarded to the Popal brothers despite the fact that another of their companies, Watan Risk Management, was under investigation for using US funds to pay off the Taliban not to attack the supply convoys that Watan had agreed to protect.

Other stories focused on fighting inside the Karzai clan over the vast family fortune amassed over the previous ten years. In early June 2012, James Risen of the *New York Times* wrote of death threats among the Karzais over the sprawling Aino Mena housing development in Kandahar, Afghanistan's second-largest city. The Karzais had built 3,000 out of a possible 14,700 housing units on about ten thousand acres that some Afghan military officials complained was illegally seized from the government. Risen also wrote that Karzai's brother Mahmoud, the same one who was enmeshed in the Kabul Bank scandal, was being investigated by a US federal grand jury. Mahmoud Karzai, a US citizen, was suspected of tax evasion, racketeering, and extortion. As of this writing, he had not been charged.

As government corruption festered and the influence of the Taliban grew, the chances for a successful exodus by coalition forces shriveled. In the midst of the gathering darkness, however, one ray of sunshine seemed to emerge. In mid-August 2012, out of Andar District in Ghazni Province, came widespread reports of an uprising against the Taliban. Although the province generally was under Taliban control, towns and villages in this ethnic Pashtun district armed themselves and rose up against their fellow Pashtuns in the Taliban. The fighting had raged throughout the summer of 2012, as one village after another joined forces to shake off the Taliban yoke. Shuttered schools were reopened and marketplaces flourished as women reemerged from the confines of their mud-walled compounds. To protect themselves, the Andar villagers maintained fleets of fighters who patrolled on motorbikes with aging Soviet-era weapons, striking wherever the Taliban might surface.

While the Andar uprising could be cause for hope, drawing inevitable comparisons to the Sunni Awakening movement that took on al-Qaeda in Iraq, the anti-Taliban sentiment did not spread, even to the surrounding Taliban-controlled districts. It's also significant that the Taliban had not been beaten back by the Afghan security forces or the US-led coalition, even though both had a presence in the area. Instead, the Andar villagers had taken matters into their own hands. Their willingness to do so pointed once again to the coming chaos in Afghanistan, by which local communities would rely on family, clan, and tribal ties, not a centralized force, to secure their lives and property.

A further glimpse into the future of Afghanistan came via two separate events involving the Taliban. The first came in late June 2012 when a video surfaced of a public execution of an Afghan woman. The video showed a woman wearing a burka and seated on the ground, apparently accused of adultery. As she was killed by a single shot to the head, several dozen bearded men looked on and cheered. The killing took place in Parwan, the province just north of Kabul where I'd interviewed a number of local police and residents who were trying to resist the Taliban takeover.

The shooting of the woman, known as Najiba, in front of a Taliban tribunal sparked worldwide outrage and drew protesters into the streets of the provincial capital of Charikar. But Najiba's death was only one of at least eleven such executions of women in the province in 2012, Parwan's director of women's affairs told Kabul-based television station TOLOnews. There had been seventy cases of violence against women in the province so far that year, she said, including eleven executions of women by Taliban gunmen in the province's Shinwari District. The executions made it clear that the Taliban had not changed in the past ten years and that their return to power would likely usher in yet another reign of terror against Afghan women.

This fear was heavily reinforced just two months later when Taliban in Helmand Province beheaded seventeen civilians, two of whom were women. The beheadings took place in the Taliban-controlled area of Musa Qala, just forty-five miles from the provincial capital of Lashkar Gah. Reports of the killings were conflicting. According to one version, the Taliban had executed the men for being aligned with the government, and the women for pleading for their husband's lives. Another account said the victims had participated in a music-and-dancing event that included the two women; the Taliban reportedly burst into the private residence, disrupted the gathering, and begun cutting throats. If the latter account is accurate, the killings were reminiscent of a deadly attack in June just west of Kabul in which Taliban gunmen blasted their way into a popular hotel and patio restaurant on the shores of Lake Qargha, Kabul's water reservoir, claiming the hotel was a house of prostitution—twenty people were killed. Regardless of which version of the Musa Qala story is true, mass executions by the Taliban were once again part of the Afghan reality.

Moving Forward

Is it possible for America and NATO to exit from Afghanistan without leaving the country mired in bloody chaos and war? In fact, it is—but it would require a sustained level of aid and continued military presence from the United States and its allies, and a broad and masterful stroke of diplomacy unprecedented in modern history. Unfortunately, ongoing support from coalition countries is unlikely given the lack of popular support in the United States and Europe for continued war in Afghanistan. And the necessary diplomacy is unlikely given the poor relations between the powers in the Western and Muslim worlds. While a peaceful and prosperous Afghanistan is beneficial to everyone inside and outside of the region, this is a truth that Afghanistan's antagonistic neighbors have refused to accept.

Pakistan, which serves as the prime supporter of the Taliban in Afghanistan and provides safe haven to other vicious groups such as the Haqqani network, has been playing with fire—a fire that it may be unable to control. As the Afghan Taliban have grown in strength and sophistication, so have the Pakistani Taliban, who terrorize Pakistan's populace and contaminate its political system by intimidating or outright murdering moderate voices. Fundamentalists, for example, were blamed for the assassination of former prime minister Benazir Bhutto on December, 27, 2007, just weeks before the election that would likely have returned her to power.

High-profile politicians have not been their only targets. In early October 2012, the Pakistani Taliban gunned down fourteen-year-old Malala Yousafzai as she rode home from school on a bus, because she had become, as the subject of a documentary, an outspoken critic of the Taliban's vicious opposition to the education of young women. Yousafzai was shot in the head and neck and critically wounded. She was eventually flown to London, where she was treated and expected to survive. Two other girls were also wounded in the attack. The Pakistan Taliban were unremorseful; a spokesman was quoted in the *New York Times* as calling Yousafzai's support of women's education an "obscenity." The young girl was labeled a symbol of Western culture, and the Taliban warned that her shooting was "a lesson" to others. The brutal and bleak vision of the Pakistan Taliban was clear.

As fundamentalist jihadi groups have grown in influence in Pakistan, so has the likelihood that they could eventually take control of the country—if they have not done so already. Pakistan was home to al-Qaeda leader Osama bin Laden for years, until he was killed by

US commandos. Yet the primary response from Pakistan was not an explanation as to how bin Laden lived there hidden in plain sight, nor an apology for harboring the man responsible for the attacks of 9/11. Instead, Pakistan complained that its territorial sovereignty had been violated in the killing of bin Laden.

While fundamentalists gaining control of a foreign country might not normally be a major concern to the United States, it is hugely significant in this case, since Pakistan has nuclear weapons. Should Pakistan's arsenal of one hundred or more nuclear warheads fall into the hands of a fundamentalist regime hell-bent on jihad against the West, India would be directly threatened, and all US installations in the region would be at risk. So would the Chinese: a neighboring militant Islamic government could foment jihad among China's twenty million Muslims, particularly the estimated eight to ten million Uighurs who make up nearly half the population of the Xinjiang Autonomous Region. The region has already been second only to Tibet as a source of trouble for Beijing.

In addition, should a radical Islamist regime take control of Pakistan, it would certainly be linked closely to a similar regime in Afghanistan, which the Taliban seem well on their way to recreating. Such a regime would have serious consequences for Afghanistan's western neighbor, Iran. Although Iranians have been manipulating events in western Afghanistan for years by supporting Taliban elements there, the Iranians are Shia Muslims while the Afghan Taliban are Sunnis—as are the Saudis, Iran's uneasy neighbors to the west. A Taliban-controlled Afghanistan would leave Iran flanked by hostile Sunnis. Given the chance, the Afghan Taliban could take advantage of an opportunity to strike at Iran, if for nothing more than revenge for years of manipulation.

The rise of the Afghan Taliban and the spread of Islamic fundamentalism supported by Pakistan and Iran has already affected central Asian countries to the north such as Tajikistan, Uzbekistan, and Turkmenistan. Each country has been forced to fight the growing threat of jihadi groups. The threat would only increase if religiously motivated militants controlled the governments of two large southern neighbors. This would further complicate the roles of the United States and its presumed allies in central Asia.

Thus, the diplomatic mountain that needs to be scaled is to convince the governments of Pakistan, Iran, China, and the central Asian states that it is in their collective interest for Afghanistan to be at peace and not controlled by extremists. A negotiated regional settlement in Afghanistan—one that involves not only these nations but also, by necessity, the Taliban—is America's best exit strategy. It would allow the United State to leave something behind in Afghanistan other than chaos and animosity.

This approach was suggested by former secretary of state Henry Kissinger in an essay published by the *Washington Post* on June 8, 2011. Kissinger argued that if a regionally enforceable agreement on Afghanistan could be negotiated, it would perhaps usher in a new role for the United States in world diplomacy. Taking his point a bit further, this means that rather than only being the world's most feared military force, conducting questionable, costly, and unwinnable wars in the remote corners of the world, US power could serve as a military-diplomatic force that helps quiet some of the world's most troubled regions. A negotiated regional settlement would also eliminate the need for a large, ongoing US and/or NATO presence in Afghanistan. This would be welcome news to the war-weary American voting public, which by a wide margin is opposed to a long-term military commitment in Afghanistan.

As much as I advocate a regional settlement for Afghanistan, however, I fear there is little chance for it. Without pressure from Pakistan, the Taliban have no reason to negotiate. And so far Pakistan has been unwilling to discuss, let alone move toward, peace in Afghanistan. Instead, our supposed ally continues to accept tens of millions of American dollars in military aid while supporting the Taliban. That the United States is still pursuing this self-defeating approach only supports the contention that Americans don't know what they're doing in the region.

The Iranians are also an unlikely ally in the search for peace. The United States has waged a covert war with Iran ever since the country's 1979 Islamic Revolution. While the United States complains loudly about Iran's relentless quest for nuclear weapons, imposing sanctions that British banks and Japanese electronics makers routinely ignore, it ignores the fact that Iran may be critical to a regional solution to Afghanistan, a solution that will require workable diplomatic relations or a viable pressure mechanism. But under present circumstances, asking Iran to help solve the Afghan dilemma is out of the question.

Likewise with China, which cares only about exploiting mineral wealth anywhere it can in the world, from Afghanistan to Africa. Should the Muslim population in the west of China become a problem, China won't hesitate to quell the unrest swiftly and violently.

Since a negotiated settlement is the best option in theory but probably unfeasible in practice, an alternative solution for Afghanistan would be to partition the country into semiautonomous regions along ethnic lines. History has shown that Afghans only unite in the face of a common enemy. For many, that enemy unfortunately has become the United States, its NATO allies, and the sham Afghan government those foreign powers have created. Once these beleaguered foreign forces withdraw, Afghans likely will turn on one another, as happened in the early 1990s. Given the strong ethnic identification among Afghans and their traditional reliance on family, clan, and tribe, partitioning the country along ethnic and linguistic lines could be a viable way forward.

The northern Tajik and Uzbek provinces would be one region stretching from the northeastern province of Badakhshan to the western province of Herat, with perhaps the Uzbek provinces being a subdistrict. The Pashtun region would include most of the provinces bordering Pakistan, extending from the northeastern provinces of Nuristan, Kunar, and Nangarhar to the southwestern provinces of Nimroz and Farah; these eastern and southern provinces would be left to deal with their ethnic kin in the Taliban on their own terms. The third region would include the central mountain provinces, primarily Bamiyan, which would be reshaped to include some of the ethnic Hazara populations in neighboring provinces.

Kabul, meanwhile, would remain the capital of Afghanistan and could be mutually agreed upon as neutral ground. Kabul would remain the seat of a coordinating central government and the nexus of certain commercial institutions such the Afghan Central Bank. Security, courts, education, social norms, and religious doctrines would be largely left to the ruling bodies in each semiautonomous region.

This arrangement would allow the country to maintain its overall identity as a nation and continue to receive foreign aid and assistance. Foreign aid would be parceled out to each region based on its population and willingness to accept what is being offered. This would preclude wasteful aid programs under which foreign governments build schools only to have Islamic militants close them down or destroy them. Security would be up to each region and would be supported by foreign forces only by request. This would allow US and other foreign forces to maintain a presence in the country, but not on the scale required to support a centralized authority in all corners. As for the more limited central government, it would be based on traditions such as the Loya Jirga, the grand council of clan and tribal leaders, not the outside imposition of democratic elections, which has proved to be a farcical exercise in corruption.

Though many Afghans may dislike the concept of partitioning, it remains perhaps the only option if Afghanistan is to avoid a civil war once the foreign community completes its Afghan exodus. US forces were set to drop to pre-surge levels of about sixty-eight thousand troops by the end of October 2012. That number would most likely be reduced by half in 2013, leaving about thirty-four thousand American combat troops in the country. This equals the earlier troop levels in Afghanistan that proved ineffective in thwarting the Taliban while most US forces concentrated on Iraq.

Unfortunately, 2012 was characterized by an absence of any serious public policy discussions about the future of Afghanistan, as the American political scene was dominated by a presidential election that focused on domestic concerns. But after President Obama was reelected, a full two years remained before the withdrawal would be complete. That is sufficient time for the future of Afghanistan to be negotiated. A workable plan for Afghanistan must be at the top of the president's foreign policy agenda in the coming years. Afghanistan's future affects not only that tumultuous region but the future of the United States and the rest of the world as well.

ACKNOWLEDGMENTS

A YEAR IN AFGHANISTAN can be daunting, especially if extensive travel is required, as was the case with this book. Help from trustworthy friends and colleagues is necessary to find the people who need to be found and to get into and out of the places where they live and work. Many put themselves in harm's way to do so, and because of this, they remain at risk. This has not gone unnoticed or unappreciated.

To that end, I'd like to thank Tony Borden and Sam Compton at the Institute for War and Peace Reporting, who agreed to bring me on for another year in Afghanistan, as well as Duncan Furey, who helped me through the difficult and frustrating stages of the program.

I thank Noorullah Dawari for his tireless work tracking down sources and his willingness to bounce around the country at a moment's notice, not to mention his accurate translations and knowing when enough was enough. As of this writing, we're still waiting for approval from the State Department for his special immigrant visa.

In Jalalabad, the doors were opened and pathways smoothed by Hijratullah Ekhtyar, a lawyer, poet, and journalist, who knew where to find good fish dinners by the river.

In the northern city of Mazar-e-Sharif, I owe so much to Enayat Najafizada, whose fearless enthusiasm was infectious if not liberating, and whose insights, contacts, and translations were invaluable.

In the roiling poppy province of Helmand, I need to thank Ahmad Shah Patsoon for his steady assistance, even though we missed that one flight out; Abdul Salam Zahid of Bost Radio for fine lunches and conversation; Zainullah Stanikzai, president of the Helmand Independent Journalists' Association; and all the journalists there in Lashkar Gah, including Qudrat, who got me to sing as the car scraped over speed bumps.

In Herat, work there would have been impossible without the help of Shahpoor Saber and Sadeq Behnam, who showed me, over platters of kabobs and pots of tea, that the view of Afghanistan was pretty good from the sunny hillside patios of the 1001 Nights restaurant.

In Kabul, I thank Noorrahman Rahmani for his patience and willingness to educate this Westerner on the ways of Afghanistan, and Afghan Recovery Report editor Hafizullah Gardesh for his singular and sage advice and for always being there at moments of crisis. I must also thank our head house guard, Ahmad Jan, and trusty driver Qasem, who wheeled me over the Salang Pass and many other roads wide and narrow, paved and not.

Back home, I'd like to thank my agent Michele Rubin for her unwavering enthusiasm, and certainly the people at Chicago Review Press, including editor Lisa Reardon and publisher Cynthia Sherry, who believe in the virtue and value of this work.

Of course I thank my wife, Dina, for whom video chats over the Internet were a poor offering to fill the long absences. Her enduring support has been a pillar of my life.

INDEX